A FABLE FOR OUR TIME

Wanda Nash

"Was all this for your own personal exposure?" she asked:
"No" I said.

Lord, let me sing your song with them;
let me weep your tears with them;
let me blow with your Ruach with them
that the mists of evil blow away,
revealing your will for your wonderful world.

FOREWORD

A new departure for an already much-valued writer, this book draws imaginiatively on Wanda Nash's experience in Africa to challenge her readers into fresh levels of understanding and engagement. Those of us in the European churches have so often forgotten the edge, the difficulty and the wonder of a situation where the gospel speaks directly to appalling levels of violence, of need and of suffering with a sense of surprise and joy.

This is a time when the world gives us little hope, it seems. Yet the events of the last year (New York, Kandahar, Kenin and Bethlehem) press upon us the truth of our interconnections; it is up to us to respond. Despair and denial are relatively easy. It is harder, but more necessary to say words of faith — to greet one another, as believers do in Africa with 'Imana Shimwe,' 'Our God be Praised'. I hope readers will learn this from the gift in these pages of Wanda's reflections and parables.

Archbishop Rowan Williams

A FABLE FOR OUR TIME

CONTENTS

ILLUSTRATIONS

A FABLE FOR OUR TIME

PROLOGUE

'May I ask you a question?' I said to the wise, widely-travelled black Bishop.
'Go on' he replied.

'My intuition tells me that the African soul is full of mysticism. It is my failure that I haven't made contact with it; my physical eyes have been unable to see it. I've met the love of God in church worship, I've shared the exuberance of singing and clapping and dancing. Something inside tells me there's more, but it hasn't been shown me.'

The Bishop nodded. 'In our tradition it was Love. Love for each other; Love of creation; Love of God. The sure knowingness of Love. When foreign influences came into our country we became distracted. Our traditional mysticism was crippled. We have to find our way back onto our own feet.'

*****

While not quite completely despairing, our present world is patched with areas of total despair. Sometimes it is whole countries, or certain areas of them, and sometimes it is a glut of individuals who are in the throes of despair. Can we move from a place of despair, to a place where God can be praised?

Is it something to do with the connections?

Moving from a place of   D E S P A I R

to a place where God can be   P R A I S E D

I went to Africa to try and find out.

*****

A fable is about how things may have been. It does not insist upon being accurate fact in every detail

A FABLE FOR OUR TIME

Chapter One: *In the Beginning*

Once upon a time there was a land filled with milk and honey. It was a country at the very heart of a large continent. It was as if the roaring coasts of the continent had pressed inwards and thrown up a thousand hills as the world shaped itself. In this land the sun shone and the rains rained; and the ground swelled with fertility and variety. Luscious fruits abounded, and the shapes and colours of trees and flowers were too numerous to name. Hills rolled in laughter and rivers danced in response. The land was happy and the people took it for granted that it was all held in common.

This favoured place was different to the nations around it. Since far-off days, this land had been ruled by one king, to whom we will give the name Ita. He and his people knew One god, and under the one king and One god the people grew together in one community. In centuries long gone by, different wandering groups had been drawn into this land of milk and honey. When our story begins they had melded into one people with one common language, one common culture, and one common country. They each and all belonged. They belonged to one another and to the community; the community gave loyalty to the king; and the king gave allegiance to the One god. Connectedness between them was real and unquestioned.

In the kingdom of King Ita the people took up one of three occupations.

In the Beginning

There were the cattle-breeders, whom we will call the Atus, the cultivators we shall know as the Utas, and the pot-makers we shall name the Tuas. All of them depended upon each other for the tools of living: the Atus needed the skills of the those who grew things to eat from the ground so they add to their diet of milk, blood and meat; and they needed the skills of those who made containers in which to carry the milk produced by their cows. The Utas relied on the skills of the cattle-breeders for food, and on the skills of the pot-makers for vessels in which they could store what they grew. And the Tuas needed the skills of the cattle-breeders and the cultivators for everything they ate. The network of interdependence worked well, and everyone was content.

The people lived in extended families; as the families expanded they would build their own houses out of the mud of their own land, held in a framework of the saplings that grew around it. There was no need for theft or lying or deceit, because they held everything in common. All their loyalties were focused on their one king and their One god. Each day as they woke up they knew who they were, why they lived, and where they were going. There was no need to ask questions.

King Ita was a forward-looking monarch. He had a cool mouth and a cool heart; his love of harmony and truth fit him to meet any quarrel that might be brought to him. The wisdom of his cool tongue and heart and eye saw

In the Beginning

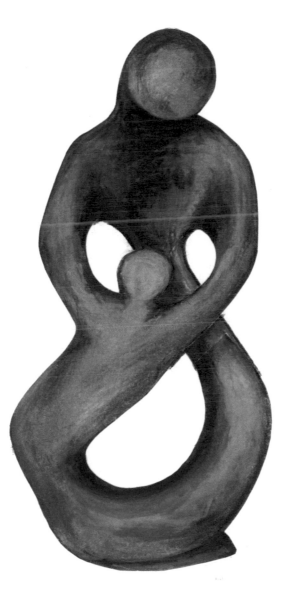

the rights and wrongs of both sides and ways of reconciling them. He was passionate for peace, and to keep it in his land he had headmen in each community and in each region to make sure that order was respected; he had established a system of discipline towards those who made trouble; he had put in place priests, prophets, and medicine men to ease his people's troubles, and advise him on policy. At all times and in all things what motivated the whole land was goodwill in the common good of all.

Then, one day, into the peaceful villages there came people from different, less contented lands. People whose own homes lay very far away, far away across oceans and mountains and seasons. They came from so far away that even their skins had turned a different colour. Everything about them was different: the way they spoke, the way they dressed and the things they ate; the way they ordered people about and expected others to change to be like them; the way they insisted they knew best; they way they competed and contended and commanded. If only these foreigners had sat down under the shady trees and listened. Had they been still and waited and watched and learned; had they then perhaps suggested, invited, or gently persuaded King Ita and all his people - those who undertook the three main occupations - that there were certain beliefs they wished to share ....   But instead they told the Atus and the Utas and the Tuas that their bodies were unsightly and must be covered, that their tried and tested social ways were primitive and inadequate, and that their souls were as dark as their skins.

Many of the natural people did what they were told; they had, after all, lived their lives in harmony with their elders. So they hid their shining, radiant bodies because they had been introduced to shame. They covered up their age-old traditions because they had been introduced to rivalry. They switched their allegiances because they had been introduced to fear: fear about the in-coming God, and what might happen if they didn't worship him.

Something even more corrosive came in with the Uncomprehenders. The men of all the occupations were taught that some of them were 'better', and some of them were 'worse'. That some of them were 'clever', and some of them were 'dull'. That some of them could be given 'trust', while others of them were given beatings. Those who were 'better' and 'clever' and worthy of 'trust' were given preference and privilege and training. The others were downtrod and degraded. They were artificially set against each other, and while their faces smiled with brilliant teeth, their souls raged.

Silently their anger seethed deep below, unseen and unspent, privately swallowed and publicly unacknowledged.

A FABLE FOR OUR TIME

Chapter Two: *The Birth*

In this Land of Our Fable - called LOUFLAND from here on - birth was seldom a difficulty. That is, in the time before the alien influences were inserted by the ones we'll name the Uncomprehenders. The people lived so close to the One god that they prayed 'Thank you for giving us the breath for each time we breathe.' The women lived so close to the land that, watching the animals let go their babies with relative ease, they took it for granted that was the way to do it. Animals never had water on tap, and they seldom needed the skills of a midwife. Likewise, women took their pregnancies as inevitable - it was the way of women - but just in case a pregnancy became unstable, when they knew there was new life in their bodies, they kept the knowledge quiet. Even after periods had been missed, it was usual for a woman to keep her secret to herself. She delayed telling her husband, or her friends, and even her mother, until they noticed the change in the shape of her for themselves. Sometimes, when they didn't undress for their husbands, the actual appearance of the baby was the first moment that the man acknowledged he had fathered a child. After all, this was what happened in nature.

It stood the woman in good stead when times became difficult. It was not uncommon for a woman to deliver herself of her own baby. It was like that for Elia. She had watched the animals as they bit through the umbilical

The Birth

cord, freeing their babies from the placenta. She watched as they licked their newborn clean and dry, returning the nourishment to themselves. If there was no razor blade handy, or no cloths within reach when her own baby appeared, she knew what to do. Just as other women had done before her, she knew how to manage without company, or water, or food. She lay with her baby snuggled at her breast, quietly resting until the next day. Then she gathered her strength and walked to her neighbour's plot for a drink.

The new baby would remain close to Elia's body all through the next year. Slung by a single broad strip of cotton material to his mother's back, with the ends tied securely across her chest above her breasts, the baby's legs straddled her back and so a foot protruded under each of her elbows. He would seldom cry, because suckling was always available. And his excreta posed no problem. Without nappies, it was caught in the cloth which Elia took down to the spring in the valley to wash, and which was dried out on the bushes.

Pregnancy followed pregnancy. Not all the babies survived, and of those that did, no more than half lived beyond two years. If the granny was asked about all the dead babies she would reply 'Oh, she'll get used to it. It 's the same for all of us.' Inside she would think 'women are strong; they learn how to cope.'

The Birth

Sometimes, the parent or parents of a young child would die or disappear. Yet in Loufland, before the Uncomprehenders told them differently, there was no concept of 'orphans', that is, parentless children. The idea was inconceivable, and the word didn't exist. All the young ones were the responsibility of the whole community, and the whole community watched over and taught their children; some of them hardly knew who their blood parents were. Anyone in the community could praise or discipline any child. Any hungry or thirsty child was welcomed at any household and refreshed. And each child could contribute to the doings of the whole community.

Geena, who lived in the next smallholding to Elia and was her friend, had a child a year. The youngest baby was always slung close to her body. The one who was two could carry a machete to the woods, while she carried the firewood back on her head. Her child of three carried a hoe on its shoulders, while she carted the sack of potatoes she had harvested. Her child of four could carry a gallon of water on its head as they walked back together up from the valley. A child of five could look after a younger child - or two - while the adults were cultivating. The more children there were in a community, the more odd jobs could be done.

Elia was lucky. She grew old and worn herself, and her soft, soft skin turned grey and dry; then she would smile through her telling wrinkles knowing

The Birth

The Birth

that at fifty-two she had outlived her expected span of years. Her grown children were around her, doing the work while she told stories of the past. All the wisdom and experience she had collected would be a source of reverence and wonder among the community. They knew that all those births she had experienced had deepened her insight into things that were essential. Her loyalty was to the one King Ita, and she praised the One true god.

A FABLE FOR OUR TIME

Chapter Three : *The Marriage*

In all of Loufland, the women were beautiful. It was as if they had all the best assets of the women in countries round about, and none of the worst. Tall and dignified, or stocky and grounded, they walked with the balance born of bearing burdens on their heads since childhood. They moved with a lithesomeness that spoke of agile tendons and muscles. Before childbearing, they carried their breasts high and firm, and their bellies smooth and slim. The skin stretched over their limbs was soft and luminous, glowing with its blackness or shining with sweet caramel. And their faces: their faces were more beautiful than any in the world. With dark receptive eyes, high and wide cheekbones, their well-shaped noses were set above lips that curved in shapely definition. The whole face was mobile and full of expression; each one tapered from a broad forehead down to a neat and triangular chin. This elegant 'tapering' was characteristic, and marked out women of Loufland against those who lived in neighbouring lands.

Mattu was one of these beauties. As a teenager, she was entrusted by her parents to take their produce weekly to market. One day a stalwart young man from a few miles distant approached to stand and observe a young goat. He said he had lost a goat recently, and as it had been too small for the pot he had come looking for it in the near-by market. Mattu was worried - how could she persuade this young man that her goat,

The Marriage

although it was also white with large brown patches - was not the one he was missing? She looked round for someone who would vouch for her, and saw a headman of her village who was walking through the market to make sure of fair prices. He talked briefly to the young man, who turned out to be easily persuaded of his mistake. Mattu took to him. He said his name was Tuam, and he lived with his parents in a house not far from a plot where Mattu's cousin had recently worked.

The next step was easy. Mattu arranged to see her cousin and happened to call in at Tuam's house on the way, asking for a drink. Then Tuam had to walk back with her to make sure she took the shortest route - he knew the way well, he said. That was the first of several walks they took together, liking each other more each time they met. They agreed to ask the permission of their parents to marry. This was slightly, although not very, unusual. Ordinarily it was the parents who would agree amongst themselves which families would join together in marriage; but when two young people happened to fall in love without such adult arrangements, they were ready to consider the degree to which it was propitious, or not. As it turned out, the ancestors of each family were happy with the marriage, and so it was allowed.

Tuam's parents asked for a cow if they were going to accept Mattu into their family. Mattu's parents asked their brothers for help, and a cow was produced. In some places it was accepted that the bride's family paid a dowry, while in others it was the groom's family that paid a bride-price: either way it was considered to be a family responsibility. It was a fairly simple matter to add another mud and sapling room where the young couple could live onto the side of the parents' house. If necessary they could take the cow into it at night, and they all would warm each other. There was general agreement in the community that this was an acceptable union.

The marriage date arrived. Tuam and his family turned up in the morning at the home of the bride to collect her. The family of the new bride gave a party for them with all their neighbours. Then together they processed with singing and dancing across the fields to the home of Tuam's parents, where there was another party. His neighbours joined in with his extended family for the exchange of vows, and gifts were given from each side to the other, food and baskets and mats. And of course the ceremonial cow. Then Mattu was taken in as a permanent member of Tuam's family, and her own mother, father, sisters, brothers, cousins, aunts, uncles, and neighbours left her alone with Tuam. There was little privacy, but the marriage was consummated and life returned to its ordinary routine – there was just an extra mouth to feed in one house, and one less mouth to feed in the other.

The Marriage

Sex wasn't furtive. It was boldly every man's right and an every night occupation. Women concurred, and mostly did what their man wanted. If the man wanted it sharp and fricative, she would push sand up inside to provide it. If he wanted it short and repetitive, she would allow it. Houses were separated from one another in their own smallholdings, so the cries of pain or pleasure were contained within each household. A woman was there to serve. Her delight was to be a good wife. Mattu understood that if she didn't please her husband, prostitutes were easy to come by.

If friends dropped in, there were always the duties of hospitality. The woman chosen as hostess would cook several dishes one after the other over a small charcoal or wood fire in a shed outside the house. The cooking utensil was laid on three large stones which contained the fire. Rice, sweet potatoes, casava, yams, and beans were the usual dishes, and occasionally some meat from a goat or chicken. If they were lucky, there would be sorghum to drink. Mattu would slide silently into the room where the guests were seated carrying the dishes and serving them, but without talking or in any way calling attention to herself. She may have bought the seed, hoed the ground, watered the growing plants, harvested the food, prepared and cooked the meal, but it was not her place to receive thanks or accept compliments on her work. No-one talked to her, and she talked to no-one. Her 'presence' was to be invisible. She was there to look after others,

The Marriage

not associate with them, and although the food was hot, she didn't partake of it until later, when it was cold. That was the way of things.

Most days, the women of the households would meet and gossip. Many areas of life were transparent to them. Every action was known, and discussed between them, for they were a sisterhood; but not every thought. Secrecy over many feelings was the accepted rule; there was even a hidden strength in keeping some important emotions quiet. Public display of them was a shameful thing. The older women - of whom there were relatively few - held the crags of the rolling hills in their faces. Mothers of many children, survivors of many crises, they kept their knowledge inside until it was finely distilled. They would offer their wisdom when it was directly asked for, but never until it was solicited. Some things always remained closed. In Loufland the people knew when and how to draw a veil over certain recesses of the heart and mind.

Mattu worked, and fetched, and hoed, and carried. Soon her belly began to swell with a new being growing inside her, but she mentioned it to nobody. Maybe it would come to nothing, except a lumpy red puddle in a hole that no-one knew about, so it was best not to draw attention to her state.

One day Tuam said he had to visit an uncle some way away. He left

The Marriage

Mattu and went on the long walk. As he arrived he found that his aunt had prepared a large jug of sorgham beer, and he sat down to enjoy it with the young men, his cousins. They drank late into the night, singing and telling tales, exchanging stories of success. Next morning they slept late, and when his cousins asked Tuam to help them collect bricks from the nearby kiln he agreed. In fact he was away enjoying the company of his cousins for three nights. On his return home, he was surprised how much alarm Mattu had suffered at his absence. She said she had been afraid of the howls of wild wolves by night, and also had been exposed to the unwanted attentions of his father. She shook with relief as he held her.

Tuam was aware of remorse. 'O god' he called, 'Women are important; but they are also targets. Make me a good husband. Help me to protect and defend my wife and father her children. Send your spirits to make me strong and dependable. Give me fortitude so that I have the respect of the community. Make me to please you, O One god'.

What he didn't realize yet, was that the choices lay in the way he made his own decisions. That he would learn later, after some great trials.

A FABLE FOR OUR TIME

Chapter Four: *The Death*

This bit of the story is about Nutenga. In the days before the coming of the Uncomprehenders, death was known by everybody. Everybody knew that living things grow, flower, fruit, and die; then the remnants are hoed back into the ground and nourish it for the next season. In much the same way humans, having produced their best, return to the earth enriching the environment with their bodies. But humans who die have an added value: they enrich the world with their spirits. People knew that men, women and children died at all ages, and although it was never desirable, death was inevitable. There was little to be done to fight it. Death was alongside them all through their lives.

Nutenga was twenty-nine, a hardworking farmer and father. He was a good listener and knew well all that was expected of him in the traditions. One night he fell sick. The next day he was gravely sick. He told his wife to sell their precious goat in order to pay for advice from the medicine man. The medicine man advised Nutenga's wife to collect certain herbs from the forest, pound them in a very particular way, and feed them to her husband at specific times. Their neighbour suggested that his older children should look after Nutenga's younger children while his wife was away hunting for the herbs. But in that time Nutenga grew hotter, and sicker, and prepared to die. The children sat together in a corner of the hut, watching. On her

The Death

return his young wife was desperate. She decided of her own accord to take further steps and visit the witch doctor - the one surrounded with great mystery - to ask whether a curse had been put upon her husband. If anyone had felt wrong-footed by Nutenga, and had gone to the witch-doctor with enough payment to have a spell cast, then there was nothing that could be done but accept that death was ordained. But if the fee offered had been insufficient, or the witch doctor had disliked the supplicant, or if the wrong-doing had been with him and not Nutenga, then the evil could be returned to the sender. If that was the case, she could, maybe, save her husband.

The way to the cave of the witch doctor was hidden and long. When at last she arrived she was tired, frightened, and vulnerable. The witch-doctor's place had pungent and unfamiliar smells hanging about it, and ugly fetid shapes of unknown objects hung from poles round the fire. He shouted at her across the darkness even before he'd heard her questions, demanding that she should fetch him intimate parts of wild animals that were fierce and unobtainable by her. As he looked at her she felt naked and bewildered. She failed to reply and slunk back into the bushes.

It seemed a long time before she gathered enough strength to return to her hut. There she found Nutenga cold. He had been dead for hours. Their children were crouching, clutched together for warmth. There was

The Death

no food or water in the house. Death had infiltrated into their wellness. Death lived there, and had taken over her home. It was imperative to get her children out of the place and bar the door from the outside, so Death couldn't escape into the village. The small family sneaked out and huddled against the walls, where they waited. They weren't allowed to cry or shout or make a fuss, for that would only draw attention to Death and aggrandize him; but the wife quietly told the first person who passed, making sure everyone else would know in the shortest possible time. Then help began arriving. One person brought water; another a bowl of hot beans; another came with cooked rice; and still another brought some mats. Friends closed together around the outside of the house to keep watch. In silence they kept vigil all through the night, even the children knew not to cry or disturb the stillness. Next day gentle talk started, spasmodically, and now and again one or two people would leave for a while and return with more to eat or drink. Most people stayed squatting on the red earth to watch with Nutenga. Some strong men dug a hole where the people could see it, near the back of the house, and lowered the dead man's body into it before it started decomposing. They covered the cadaver, and continued the vigil. For four days the quiet vigil was kept, and then Nutenga's house was re-opened and Death, the interferer, was evicted; everything inside was ritually and painstakingly cleaned. Death had played his part and now it was time for him to go. Nutenga's wife and children returned to their places indoors,

The Death

and maybe, at last, could weep silently with each other.

Death had been an interruption, but daily life had to go on, it had to be re-asserted. The mourning was not allowed to last for long, During the next four days the whole extended family were in council, to decide whose lot it was to take on Nutenga's responsibilities. Whoever among them was chosen would accept possession of Nutenga's land, his house, his wife, and his children. The wife had no choice in the matter, and could not question the decision. Until the discussion was finalised, all male members of the family had 'rights' to her body, and she had to put up with their needs. Though in shock, and grieving, and at a loss, it was considered good and proper that she should be 'cared for'.

Eventually the matter was settled to the satisfaction of the relatives. They could go back to their smallholdings knowing that right had been done, and Nutenga's properties had all been secured within the family circle.

Just as in Loufland there was no word for 'orphan', so in the kingdom of the one king and before the advent of the Uncomprehenders, there was no word for 'widow'. Those women who lost their husbands were absorbed into the larger family and not left to fend on their own. To be left on your own was to be open to evil.

The Death

And Nutenga himself? He had known that Death and god had a lot to do with each other. The One god was Good, so Death would not be all Bad. God would make sure that the spirit of Nutenga would be around for many years so that his brothers could look after his life's work; his spirit would never be far away, it would be there to protect his family like those of his ancestors who had preceded him; and the children still unborn to him would be fathered by his brother and his wife. So at the end he could rest content, after all.

Later, very many years later when the Uncomprehenders arrived, they taught that Death should not simply be eased or accepted, but should be fought. They taught about lots of things that should be fought for, but fighting for things involved dying for them. It was strange, that although they taught that Death was to be opposed, they acted as though Life was expendable. They preached that death was to be put off as long as possible, although life after death was better. In practice they showed that lengthening the life of those who were not valued was not important. It all got very complicated.

Was Death a friend, opening the gate of a life lived closer to the One god, or a foe to be spurned and feared and hidden from daily experience? The Uncomprehenders seemed at odds with their own beliefs. What could the people of Loufland make of such opposites?

A FABLE FOR OUR TIME

Chapter Five: *The Property*

In the olden days of King Ita there was possession and non-possession; one at the same time owning and sharing; 'having', and supplying the 'have-nots'. There was a great faithfulness to boundaries of personal land, but this was held together with a knowing that the One god was provider of all to all. Walls and fences and hedges between smallholdings were unknown, yet theft was rare. Those in need were offered what they needed, they didn't have to take.

For an example, let's look at the life of the man called Peetah. Peetah was a young man, who lived in the same village as Tuam and Mattu. He kept house for his aging mother and cared for the small plot of land left him by his father. Younger siblings would run in and out, and take advantage of the fact that he hadn't as yet brought home a strong wife. For this, his mother nagged at him, and in a fit of exasperation Peetah threw a bowl of hot soup at her: she fell back and hit her head on the hoe. It was a large gash, and with no medical aid near by, she bled to death. In his shock and mourning, Peetah felt heavy guilt. It was he who had brought the hoe into the house out of the teeming rain, instead of pausing to store it at the back. His guilt grew and grew until it took on grotesque proportions and drove him into madness. Tuam and his neighbours didn't want to expose him to the judges, so they hid him and fed him. In the long years that followed,

The Property

Peetah became known as the local 'fool', and he was absorbed into the community as a wanderer, with no property. Sometimes he was laughed at by the children for his awkward antics, or shooed away by the men when he was angry; but though he slept in bushes, they held no grudge when he asked for food and water, and they shared what they had with him.

Peetah, the local fool, was the one man in the locality without property. Everybody else was attached to a smallholding. Smalholdings were indeed small, but everyone knew where their own ground lay. There were no office blocks or large department stores to take people away from the land, and each family had a share of the ground. There were no expansive fields or large farms, but over the hills and valleys lay a patchwork of personal fields, each with an individual crop and with a different colour and aroma. Loufland had a stunning beauty all its own. The land was not dissected by roads or railways or barriers; it was criss-crossed by paths winding through the groves of banana trees, and passion fruit vines, and the arches of oranges, mangoes and paw-paw. The rich variety of colours and shapes, sounds and tastes, were just about unparalleled by any other known country. The rolling hills ensured that every corner of the way was an adventure of new views, and new opportunities. Every now and again there would be a place of marketing, with a collection of a few houses with small shops, and a spring where the washing and bathing and collection of water took place

The Property

daily. The whole country was made up of small homesteads; there were very few organized villages, and towns were few and far between.

As Mattu and Tuam had more children, some of them moved out of the parents' house and built homes of their own. Elia and Geena and their families each had a smallholding and their property was typical: it consisted of a two room house which they had made from the mud on which it stood, supported by a framework of saplings gathered from the nearby woods. They thatched the roof with tall grasses, and as he prospered Tuam fired some roof-tiles made from his own mud. All these building materials were available without money, and neighbours would offer their labour to each other without cost. Each family had an outside lean-to in which to house the couple of goats or cows they kept - in cold weather their warmth would be taken into the home to help the people sleep. Also outside was a small shelter which acted as kitchen. Cooking was done with one pot at a time, supported over a charcoal or wood fire. Meals of several types of beans and manioc and potatoes would all be cooked in a serial fashion on this fire. The different homesteads were surrounded with a living fence built out of high bamboo-like plants, and were within easy walking distance of the fields where the families worked. The outside walls of the houses had openings which served to let air and light in, and at night they placed panes of wood over them to block out birds and bats which might disturb the sleepers. Inside were few possessions, and furniture was a luxury. Wedding presents of baskets and pottery made sufficient containers; and as the years went by these were easy to replace.

Family smallholdings were the basis of Loufland culture, holding within them the soul of the community pattern. Even when something bad happened (in times to come that would include <u>very</u> bad, such as the whole family being slashed and butchered ...) the home that had seen the lives of its forebears would be repaired, so that their stories were revered, and their lives honoured. It was imperative to each family that their story continued on the same piece of ground. Even after a very bad incident, a close relative will return to the house and wash blood from the walls, replace fresh red mud between the bricks, build up the compound fence, and once again take up the family story in the same place. Continuity was not based in the family name as in some other cultures - Mattu did not take on Tuam's name - but in the very earth of the land on which they lived. This was a first priority, that the family honour be upheld on the family plot of land.

Later on Tuam took another wife. He had cleared an adjoining piece of land and built another mud home on it; it was expected that Mattu would find in her another friend. There would be more hands to give to the work, more children to help with the carrying, and more chance that she could go away sometimes to visit her own family. Mattu's aunt, who

The Property

with her husband's other wives had had twenty-four children, had told her
'Now I have nothing to do! I can go out or sit back as I please; the children
do all that has to be done. I can stay at home or visit my relatives just as I
like'. It sounded good, very good.

People were so secure in their property in the old days, that other
things were stable too. Tuam's fourth cousin, Rawe, lived in the south,
while Tuam himself lived in the north. The cousin said, 'to-morrow I will go
to see Tuam. If I start early in the morning, it will take three days to walk to
his property. It will be no great effort, for I need carry no luggage, nor
worry about where to eat or where to sleep. Wherever I happen to be I
can call on any house for refreshment or for a space to sleep. No-one
refuses hospitality; I know well the saying "those who receive guests never
lose".' On his way Rawe passed through many different areas, but he was
never hungry or thirsty or tired for long as there was always welcome and
hospitality whenever and wherever he wanted to stop. He even received
gifts which he was asked to carry on to Tuam.

One day Rawe passed through an area of special fertility, where the
rich soil was prolific with food. Food was so plentiful that no-one wanted to
buy it, so the poverty in this area was extreme. Those who wanted to
barter and exchange couldn't, because there was nothing other than food
with which to barter and exchange, and everyone had plenty of the same

The Property

thing. It was up in the pointed hills, where roads couldn't exist, and no carrier arrived to cart the surplus to market. Piles of fresh food were left by the wayside, but having no customers, it rotted. There was no money to buy healthcare or schooling or improvements for their homes. Rawe carried as much fruit away as he could manage, but there was an overplus left. 'Why don't you move?' he asked his hosts. 'We could never do that' was their reply, 'our family and all the shades of our ancestors live in this place. This is where we belong and this is where we shall stay.'

After four days of walking Rawe reached the home of Tuam. He found no cardboard boxes, or plastic containers, or aluminium vessels in the house, but the pottery pots given him by his family of Tuas were indispensable. There were no imports from abroad in the homestead, but from the cattle of the Atus who lived next door they bought meat and milk and hides sufficient for their needs. There were Utas cultivating land nearby who brought a rich array of fruits, beans, grains and vegetables to market which added to everyone's diet. Each group had its own artists who crafted woodwork and artifacts with which to decorate their homes. Painted with natural dyes, these were as cheerful as they were convenient. All the things needed for everyday life were available without hassle or rancour. The Atus and Utas and Tuas had welded themselves into a people of mutual need and supply,

The Property

In this land of long ago, where things were stable, there was little house moving, so there was also no call to tell others about their surroundings. The flowers, trees, or birds which were all around them didn't need to be described or identified. Their unique beauty was simply a backdrop, often accepted un-remarked. It was a common heritage, it was all theirs, unchallenged (that is, before the advent of the Uncomprehenders) so it didn't have to be 'claimed' or 'classified', or 'possessed'. Such confidence was to last for centuries, but not for ever.

A FABLE FOR OUR TIME

Chapter Six: *The Sorrow*

The sorrow started imperceptibly. It crept in insidiously without anyone keeping track of it. Here and there was a scrap, and somebody filed a report, and things went on much as they had done before. But within a few decades there was such an influx of unfamiliar ideas and concepts coming in to Loufland, that the age-long stability of the people became honeycombed by unfamiliarity. Values and strategies imported from lands across the seas insinuated themselves between people. Things to do with comparison and competition; to do with being raised up and being put-down; to do with power and powerlessness. It was about loss, the loss of indigenous human dignity and neighbourliness. The loss of a well-knit culture, and its replacement by a hierarchical structure which produced grotesque images by reflection.

The sorrow started imperceptibly, but it grew alarmingly. Each alarm was glossed over, but as it persisted it seeped everywhere and undermined centuries old foundations. Its tentacles reached into every corner of the country, and every family in the land. It spread slogans that stuck, and its effects were searing and unimaginable. Its repercussions ricocheted round their world and later, round the outside world.

This is how it happened.

The Sorrow

Into the land of our fable, at first one by one and then by powerful groupings, came the ones who thought they knew it all. The Uncomprehenders. With not much attending, they misconceived what others knew already. With not much watching, they introduced wedges between the three occupations, the Utas the Tuas and the Atus. With not much listening, they misinterpreted the sounds they heard, and gave them new names, new and unmerited identities, new labels. They prised the three groupings apart. They set one against the other, preferring one against the others, favouring one above the others, fanning privilege and power, hatred and rivalry and ambition for the ends of Authority and Cheap Labour. All the age-long, well-tried, connectedness was disconnected.

The Uncomprehenders took upon themselves a special job. It was indeed to them a 'burden': they took it upon themselves to see to it that others knew what they knew, and did what they did, in just the way that they did it, because, after all the Uncomprehenders knew that they were the ones who knew best. They misconstrued the knowledge that already existed in Loufland, knowledge about how their people lived together. Where it wasn't the knowledge of the Uncomprehenders, the knowledge that the Uncomprehenders knew already, it had to be changed.

Over a few decades, the sorrow grew into the horror. This is how it happened.

The Sorrow

The layering that was imposed between people brought in attitudes that were strange: things like deceit, because it fostered resentment and secrecy among them. Old scores were remembered and stored; insults and injuries fermented; jealousies and injustices inflated. Long-held, well-tried traditions of tolerance and interdependence were overturned. Every slur became swollen with hatred, engorged by the means of propaganda and political slogan. The carefully inserted divisions and inequality bred loathing and disgust among people who had lived together amicably for centuries. The social structure that had stood up so well for generation after generation, imploded. The values and concerns and priorities that had been built around family and community were imperceptibly twisted from a pattern of "We are Us" into a pattern of "Me against You". The inter-woven wholeness fragmented; the sturdy branches of the tree slivered into sharpened splinters piercing each individual heart; tragedy upon tragedy and grief beyond grief.

Then came the final insult.

When the boil at last burst and the pus streamed out, the Uncomprehenders went away. They turned their backs on Loufland and said it was nothing to do with them. They detached their authority from the people they had 'taught' and withdrew to their own countries. There they rallied support for their departure from their wealthy collaborators.

The Sorrow

The factions and frictions that had been fanned by them were left to their own devices, ill-advised and swamped by the foul mess that had been left behind.

What followed was a rampage of horror, a free-for-all glut of atrocity. Every piece of personal putdown, every detail of subservience, every bit of inequality was converted into a justification for ravage. Killing, raping, burning, looting, even sadism had been seen in the world before, but seldom on the mass scale it was experienced in the Land of our Fable. There was not one family in the land that was left untouched. First it was one layer against another, and then the process reversed and those who had been violated became the violators. The informers who had become heroes in turn became the victims. There was no-one to trust, no-one who knew what was what. The turmoil and travail were not only about bodies and property, but about traditions and understandings, about hearts and minds and souls.

The evil was beyond 'human'. The lethal combination was made up of official exhortation to exterminate, of weapons made widely available by authority, and the belief that there was no-one to catch up with them - the rule of law absented itself. All this was fed through the public media, and boiled up into satanic savagery. Raw frenzy.

And the damaged, limping, bewildered remnant were left to work out their own salvation.

A FABLE FOR OUR TIME

Chapter Seven: *Negotiation*

Now here's a strange thing. And what is the nature, the value, the significance of this strange thing?

Time is not a thing of significance in Loufland. If an expected person does not arrive until two hours after their expected time, an explanation of the lateness would neither be called for nor given. What happened just happened. It was usual to say 'Well, our next appointment is due at midday. It is now an hour past midday, so we have plenty of time yet.'

But bargaining is a thing of significance. You offer this, and I will offer that. It can be fairly simple and may go something like this:

- You have two hens to sell, which I want to have; I have melons and lemons and sugar-cane to offer in exchange. But you want a window frame for your house instead of the fruit I have, so I must find some one who wants my fruit for his wood. Then we can negotiate.

- You want my son to marry your daughter, and I will require such and such goats, cows, hides, before I can allow it. You will find friends and relatives who are willing to help you supply the livestock, but in exchange for some help In their fields from this new wife. When you have settled that, we can negotiate.

Negotiation

Bargaining turned negotiation is important and can get a bit more complicated.

-   You are sick, and must be taken to the dispensary for medicine. I will give up my work today, and find three other friends who will help me to carry you in a bed-basket, as a walking ambulance, for six kilometers over the hills. But if you live, for one year you will be tied by debts of favour to repay me and my friends.

-   There is a road-block controlled by the rioting militia. If you have the right papers and identity card and money and the time to wait around, I will watch your every movement and calculate how you behave under acute anxiety; then I can pull power and I may, perhaps, let you go through. If there is any suggestion that you lack any of these vital essentials, I could negotiate holding you as a hostage while you 'find' the money; or I could torture you and kill you.

    It all depends on the negotiation.

Negotiating for life? It becomes horribly serious. That is the reality. When a killer comes to my door I will negotiate with him.

> 'Don't molest my wife and children, but you can kill me.'
> 'Shall I kill you by slowly reducing your body with my machete,
> or shall I shoot you?' .

Negotiation

'If I give you all the money I have hidden please will you consider
only shooting me?'

'That amount of money is insufficient. I'll come back tomorrow
with other killers and if you want to be quickly shot you must
have collected more money by then.'

'And if I can't get the extra money?'

'Then I will chop up your children as well as you.'

Quite coldly discussed with level voices.

If everything is up for negotiation, there is little left that is absolute. Maybe
the face will say one thing, while the guts are churning another. Maybe
there are different levels at which experience is sensed, and some of these
levels are undisclosed and kept secret. Maybe life becomes something like
a game of poker; but the pokers are surreal, while those who do the
poking are bone and flesh and iron. What happened to their brains and
sensibilities?

A FABLE FOR OUR TIME

Chapter Eight: *Horrors Beyond All Horror*

DANGER: THIS CHAPTER MAY ENDANGER YOUR MENTAL HEALTH. IF YOU NEED TO PROTECT YOUR OWN SENSIBILITIES, DO NOT READ IT.

In the space of a mere fifty years, or less, the world familiar to Elia, to Tuam and Mattu, their relatives and neighbours became unrecognisable. It burst apart. Congeniality and cohesion were twisted and pulled and reshaped into conflict and abomination. This bit of our story is about fomenting rage bursting into anarchy. It is hideous and terror-filled. If you are not prepared to be shocked to the core of your soul, don't read it.

It was open house; an unlimited invitation to act out all the hidden and hateful phantoms bred by repression. Men - and women - could go wild, with impunity. They abandoned discretion and compassion. Each violation gave access to further excess. It became a game to extend torture.

There was a gleeful power in the worsening of the horror, when the right to live became something to be negotiated. First, for the hunted ones, there was the terror of waiting. Hiding for weeks in a hole dug in the ground; in a bush; sunk up to the neck in a swamp infested with parasites; crouched in a cupboard; or above the ceiling - no movement, no sound, it might give away the secret; no food, no company, no water, no knowing when or how it might end - all in the slim hope of remaining 'unfound'.

Then came the approach of the crazed killers. The noise of those who were high on adrenaline, alcohol, drugs. The indiscriminate slash of sharpened machetes. The blows of clubs embedded with stones and nails. The wild beating of bodies, men, women, children, babes. The deliberate sexual debasement. It was not simply bestial and inhuman, it was much worse. The evil was beyond 'human'.

It wasn't just the destruction of life, and of everything that was familiar and recognizable physically or spiritually, that was so disturbing. It was the warped way of extracting it. It was the glee with which torture was measured, the madness and lust for inflicting terror. The new young mother, her heart frozen by terror, being chased by killers. The baby on her back cut at repeatedly with pangas, and screaming, dying, but the mother left to live. The diabolical imagining of new ways to violate the miracles that make up the human body - that host of miracles that together make up human life; and to castrate the priceless ability to live together in harmony. A degenerate ingenuity way beyond ordinary understanding.

Now, today, children go to school with wide and deep scars on their heads, their limbs, their psyches: reminders of wanton slashing on the part of those tormenting them. A woman stumps along the road on her heels -

the feet and toes have been cut off, one by one. Babies thrown down into the long-drop latrines to drown in excrement have been retrieved - what is left of them. Somewhere there is a coffin exposed for the veneration of a beautiful young girl who was raped publicly, a stake then passed through her vagina and up her body to come out through her head. Her hands were tied behind her back as she lay in the church square, while her child was systematically cut to pieces over her dying body. Then she was left alone to bleed to death, under the blazing sun and the gaze of her fellows. There is no memorial however, to the men whose genitals were macheted and then fed into their mouths so they could chew on their own reproductive flesh. Nor to the four day old baby who was pounded in a mortar taken from the kitchen of the parents who were forced to watch its murder.

Widow after widow, orphan after orphan, on and on and on. "…est tué, … est tué, …est tué"[1]. Perhaps a million people tortured and slaughtered like animals, by a maddened humanity. Crowds who were seeking sanctuary in the churches were engulfed in flames as they prayed; thousands cowering in 'safe' buildings were peppered with grenades and gun fire, beaten as they were dying with spiked sticks. The unleashing of the worst and most fetid imagination it is possible to conceive. There are no words sufficiently tortuous to describe the appalling atrocities of that hundred day rampage.

1   'was killed, was killed, was killed …'

And the whole world backed off, pretending not to notice, not to be aware, it was all simply an 'internal affair'.

And yet, and yet, in the thick of all the horror and wild sadism, something survived. How can the 'How's' of that survival be recapitulated? Friends emerged from bushes to discover carcasses left to die, and to drag them away into hiding; healing occurring, slowly and incredibly and without visible medical means. Acts of astonishing heroism taking place in secret. The human ability to simply survive is over and beyond all expectation or reckoning. And, more extraordinary than anything, the survivors turned to praise God.

O God, come into the deepest recesses of my soul
   And bring your Light;
   The light of Understanding, and
   The light of your Hope.

A FABLE FOR OUR TIME

Chapter Nine: *From Despair into Praise*

Ancient ways of birthing and marrying, owning and belonging, dying and restarting, had made connectedness among the people of Loufland. Living connections within the family, within the community, among the shades of the ancestors, and with the created world around them. It was familiar that life was about continuing the habitation of their own heritage.

The Horror disconnected it all. As a hurricane separates roofs from houses, trees from their roots, possessions from their possessors, connectedness was blasted. Yet the few who remained in Loufland, those who had been unable to limp away, continued to live on.

Connectedness was blasted but not erased. Primal sources of energy that had been overlaid were uncovered, deep springs of life that had been overgrown were re-opened.

*****

A miracle is a frame of mind. It's a way of seeing things in a different light. It is a marvel to move away from a place of despair to a place where God can be praised. Sometimes it's a work of personal choice; sometimes it is the work of the Holy Spirit. The cost is remembered, but somehow the parts of it take up different places, and it can be seen with a different light.

- If it hadn't been lost, it could not have been found

- If you hadn't been hurt, you could not have been healed

- If Jairus' daughter hadn't died, she could not have felt her life return

Maybe a bad situation has to exist before it can become restored.

Nietzsche is famed to have said 'a person must first experience chaos within them to be able to give birth to a dancing star', which is something akin to aphorism 'at the heart of every act of creation there is a shriek'. It's about staying within the bitterness and the waste and the hurt of it - or galvanizing some movement from inside it. The woman in the gospels had haemorrhaged for endless years: she could have held on to her remorse over the babies she hadn't conceived, the sexual delight she hadn't known, the stuntedness of her relationships, the communal activity she had missed; or she could move ahead into the marvel that once again she could feel dry and clean.[1]

Unless I am familiar with the cost - as few of us are - I can barely begin to appreciate the magnitude of the miracles about to be related. It is a total astonishment.

And the astonishment grows with every story related.

1 See Mark ch.5: 25-34

From Despair into Praise

These stories are real. Some of them are difficult to absorb because the terror is so great, and the turn-around within them is almost too strange for the hearer to digest. Many of the following stories tell of experiences which are already seven years old, and of what has happened since that time. One person said: 'Unless you have been a victim, you can't know about how a victim feels. Only those who have recovered from such despairs can know how it is to praise God, for life'.

[How can I, from the comfy position of never having been through it, possibly guess at the depth of their gratitude for still being alive?]

We are left simply to do our best to hear what they want to be heard.

*****

- Anny today is a young woman of great beauty; it is as if gentleness and patience and courtesy make up every cell of her body. She has soft smooth skin, large glowing eyes set wide apart in her caramel forehead. Her limbs flow quietly and gracefully whenever she moves, and her taste in clothes is calm and uncluttered. It is only when she sits under a strong light that the gaping scars of seven slashes of a machete can be seen across her forehead.

As a second-year student of nursing Anny is looking for further funds to complete her course. Most of the war she spent hiding in the forest -

literally 'living in a bush' - on her own. Her whole family was killed, and her home had been looted and fired. As a young teenager she had had to forage, in secret, for food and water, waiting for her wounds, physical and emotional, to heal. Anny's voice is difficult to decipher as she tries to get the details out. It is her trust and calm confidence that are unforgettable; her acceptance and thankfulness that reach deeply into the heart of the hearer.

*****

The journeys of changing utter despair into praise are told and re-told, always with great simplicity. The grisley tragedies are sometimes dwelt upon, and sometimes described in bare truth but quickly. The details are neither denied nor disguised; they are seldom repressed. But those same details are somehow re-arranged. 'My right hand was cut off. That disabled me because I lost my livelihood. But by the grace of God my left hand was spared. Some people have remained bitter and oppressed and distraught, but I have Jesus. Knowing him changes everything. I praise God every hour of my life.'

*****

- Immediately following the triggering crisis, Matahera said, 'Now, we'll die'. Everyday, they waited to die, that was the way of life. But where to wait? Trapped in their own homes? In the road, running away? Sheltering in the classrooms of the school, in the company of their friends? Or taking sanctuary in the well-loved church? Surely that last was the safest, the most certain place of security, thought Matahera. She collected her family of eight children and together with her husband, mother, sister-in-law and aunt they crept out after dark into the open door of the hushed church. They took a basket of cooked corn cobs and sweet bananas and tucked some money underneath. The water tap was just outside the church so there was no worry about the children being thirsty. Anyway, she said, the crisis wouldn't last for long, soon help would come from outside the country.

But the scare did last. That night, the next day and night, and into the following day. The building was so crowded that few could lie down. The small supplies of food soon disappeared. The self-styled 'militia' prowled round the outside shouting menaces and beating those who tried to get in, so there was no question of going out to fetch water. The frightened children didn't even have to be told to keep quiet, as they cowered. Making themselves as small and unobservable as they could, their terror stoppered any noise, they kept it all within. Threats and yells and jibes were thrown in at them all through the night, but they hugged a trace of hope that help would arrive. Spasmodically they tried negotiation. One woman collected some money - including the sum brought by Matahera - which she offered gingerly through a crack in the door hoping it might be taken as pay-off. But her arm was nearly pulled out of its socket by three men who hauled her into the churchyard and gang raped her, while taunting her husband and brothers inside for not protecting her.

In the morning the men came in, just a dozen of them, and chopped off the hands of those who could not give them more money. In passing they smashed a few of the children's skulls to give a taste of their power. Another day and night passed, while ammunition was collected outside. The attackers' frenzy mounted. So did the terror inside.

On the morning of the fifth day rocks came through the windows, and then at last the shrieking exploded outwards. The rocks were followed by grenades, and people's clothes caught fire. The 'men' outside broke through the barricaded door and with whoops of brutality slashed their weapons at anyone within reach. As the bodies fell, everyone became reachable. Matahera's youngest daughter - she was three years old - was caught by a sharpened stick through her mouth, and it penetrated through to her temple. Matahera pushed her down to the floor and covered her with her own body to protect her. But the caring mother was speared through the back and died. The little girl passed out, unconscious.

It took the rest of the day and most of the night to complete the work of killing in that church. Then the corpses were searched for anything that was lootable, and discarded over one another. At last the killers moved on, and only the deathly hush was left. In the early hours of the following morning, underneath the body of Matahera and those on top of her, there was a stirring. A little girl of three looked out, her face swollen unrecognisably. She eased her tired, hungry, thirsty, sickened body from under the mass of cadavers, and huddled in a corner where she could breathe more easily. She stayed there until another nightfall, hurting and waiting and wondering; as the light faded she painfully picked her way across the debris to the small back door, swinging on its broken hinges. Outside, the open space was mercifully short, so she managed to reach the comforting shadows of the bushes. By now her tiny young face had been blackened by gangrene; she came across some people hiding, but in the shade of the bushes no-one knew her. They pulled out the stick in her face and fed and warmed her. It wasn't until weeks later that those who had found her realized that they were cousins of Matahera, and that they were related. It was a miracle. Now, seven years later, the little ten year old girl with a scarred face is doing so well at school she is determined to be a teacher. 'I want to grow up to tell people that God does miracles' she says, 'and to praise him with me'.

*****

From Despair into Praise

- Tillatu told this story: her husband was away on a study course, so she was living on her own in their small house in the town while her first baby grew inside her. When the crisis erupted she climbed above the cane ceiling, knowing that her time was getting close. She stayed there for a week in a cramped position, afraid to go down to find food or water.

Then her husband returned and joined her in the ceiling; together, both unskilled, they managed her labour and a son was born. The killers found out her husband was with Tillatu, and they came up murdered him across her own body. She pleaded that they should kill her and her baby as well, so they could stay together, but they opted to leave her alive. The day old baby survived.

Now Tillatu and her seven year old son are settled in a different house. She has a new husband and the family are flourishing. They honour God every hour of their lives.

*****

- Lomina told her story rather differently. She has a very mobile face, and gestures with her hands as if she is re-enacting the drama right before your eyes. 'I had ten children before the war', she says, 'but three of them died of disease when they were very little. When the killers came my husband

and I decided to runaway separately, hoping one of us would survive. He took the sons and I took the daughters and we went by different secret paths over the border. In the refugee camp we met again, and that was a big miracle. But there was no food and we all were starving. Then I had an idea! The lorries came to collect the dead bodies and take them away somewhere else, where there weren't so many starving people. If we wrapped ourselves in mats and lay by the side of the road, we would be collected too and taken away. We might find some food wherever the bodies were dropped. My husband agreed with the plan, so we wrapped the children in the old mats and laid them by the side of the road. I was just about to roll myself up, when a different lorry passed. As I watched it, I saw a bundle of papers drop off the back. My husband went to pick it up, but I said we must pray before we looked at the papers because there was a lot of witchcraft around. I was very frightened and suspicious.

'When we looked at the bundle, it was money!! At once everything was changed: we had had a sign God wanted us to live! So we bought food and drink, and praised God and got strong. Now everything is alright: he saved us because he had a job for us to do for him. We never stop praising.' Lomina had to sit down, she had become so excited in telling her story.

*****

From Despair into Praise

- Then an older woman asked if we wanted to know her history. She was quiet, but her cragged face spoke loudly of the trials she had met. She said she knew that she was among the people who were going to be killed because her husband had gone to join the opposing force over another border. When the killers came to her door she played for time, and offered them her cow. They took it away. The next day the killers returned and said 'now we are going to kill you'. She prayed, and bargained with the men; 'if I get you some money please don't kill me'. They demanded too much, but for ten hours she walked round her neighbours' houses, asking them for money to save her life. When the men returned she had just enough to give them. They took it and went away. She was left with the oppressive worry how she was going to repay the money to her neighbours, it was much more than she could ever earn with no cow. She made herself sick with this new worry. She prayed. The next day the killers returned, with both the money and the cow! They left them, went way, and never came back. She says she will sing praises for the rest of her life. She knows who the killers are, but there is nothing between them now, and they are good neighbours to her; she passes them on the road and greets them daily. 'That is what praising God has done for me', she finishes.

*****

- Ranatha's story was echoed in the atmosphere as she told it. At the beginning, the day was bright and ordinary. Sitting with her in her mud house, and being there with her poverty, the sky began to darken as did the story.

'This is my first home since the war', she said, 'the neighbours helped me re-build it for this is where my brother and his family had lived and died, they were all destroyed in the war, the people and the house. You can use my name, it is only the truth.'

She was wringing her hands, but wanting to be heard.

'Before the war my husband and our four children were all living together at the tea factory. We had work and a house and we were very happy. My husband was a driver, so he had to be away a lot. He took two children with him to try to escape the killing, but they were all cutted. They all died. I was hiding in the bushes near the factory with my ten year old son and my ten month old baby but they found us; my son was hit on the head with a stone and the baby slashed across his face; look, you can see the bad marks here, now. He is seven but very teased at school because of his face.' The air around us became heavy with an approaching storm: as the light darkened it felt thick with menace.

'The children were taken to the hospital, until the government declared

From Despair into Praise

the hospital was unsafe. So we went to a refuge to be cared for, but there was no food. The refuge was attacked; the men were armed and dragged me outside and beat me. I lost consciousness and was left lying in my blood for two days. When I woke up - I don't know how - but I dragged myself back to the refuge'. Ranatha's voice became so dim it was difficult to hear. The rain started pounding on the tin roof, drowning out the soft words.

'They tell me I was in a coma for two weeks. The killers came but didn't kill me because they thought I was dead, I seemed to be dead. But they took all our clothes. When I recovered I found the two children were still alive, and I praised God. It was then they told me that my husband and other children had been killed.'

Her voice was flat. The flat roof shook with the pounding of the rain and the thunder was straight above us. There was no light in the house, but the lightning occasionally shone on Ranatha's dark skin and then her lips could be read. She insisted on getting the words out, hardly noticing the storm raging outside. She was struggling through the turmoil inside.

'The doctor prescribed medicine for me, but they didn't give it to me. I was very sick. The liberating soldiers took the children and looked after them, giving them the food and drink they needed. But when I was well enough to meet them again, I saw they were handicapped. We were refugees, and we were told we would be rescued by lorry. Three times the lorry called, but I couldn't get on. My limbs were too weak and the crowd was pushing. I carried the baby and the limping child and held them until the next day. Then someone I recognised helped me up onto the lorry, and we were taken to a safer place. It was safer from the killing, but we all three got malaria. It was a very bad time.'

The whole house was enveloped in darkness. But the storm was passing, and the noise on the roof lessening. My breath was easing.

'Then someone gave me the money for a taxi, and we rode back to this house. The walls were only two foot high off the ground, so my children and I slept outside while the neighbours helped me rebuild it. They were very kind, and the children gradually got stronger. We moved into our house and a young cousin came to help me, and I had an orphan to live with me to help too. My elder son has very bad times of heaviness; he is very depressed. But we try to talk about what is worrying him and then in a while he goes back to school. I go to the hospital to sing and pray with those who are around, because I used to sing in the choir before the war. It is difficult seeing the other children singing and playing, because neither of my sons can join in,'

From Despair into Praise

The worst of the storm is over, and we can all breathe again. But night is drawing in and there are no lights in this house. Ranatha brings in one candle, and hot cups of tea for each of us.

'There are still no relations near me, and the sorrowing goes on. The fear is still there, and denunciation still threatens us. Some people can forgive, but some people cannot receive forgiveness and the bitterness lingers. But I am making new friends on Sundays at church, and I praise God he has kept me alive. I still have life.'

*****

Another statement: 'I used to practice witchcraft. My husband fell sick, very sick, and I was frightened. So I sold our cow to pay for the witchdoctor. But my husband died so I know it was wrong and the sorcery was bad. Now I've thrown all witchcraft away and I praise God. God looks after those who pray to him, it's the only way.' She beams.

*****

- 'My husband beat me' said Dibuni; 'so I beat him back'. He died a year later 'so I am the head of the family now. But the attackers got me. While they tied me up to beat me, I sang to the Lord and prayed for them. They went away. It took a year to forgive them properly, the picture of the soldier who beat me haunted me day and night. But the picture went when I had praised God, and now when I see him I really like him!'

*****

- A really old lady burst in. The others laughed at her - out of embarrassment or with familiarity? 'My husband died a natural death, but my son was killed in the war. I haven't found the secret of victory. I wish it was me who had been killed, not my son.

'There are widows around who now look like mad people -

'There are widows around who leave their children to go and look for another man -

'There are widows around who leave their children to go to the town for work -

'Does it do us any good to say "Praise the Lord?"'

*****

A story for light relief: a spectacular welcome was given to the first white woman to be seen in that remote village. We were taken to have tea with the village pastor and his wife. His mud brick house was the best in the area, and its walls had been whitewashed. On each of the walls of the living room was a brightly coloured poster, all identical, with the picture of a traditional house and a traditional family chatting round the house. Each poster had the same announcement, in the local language. When asked what the slogan on each wall was, the pastor interpreted: 'What a good thing it is to have a clean latrine'!

*****

- Laurentia was explicit. She was old before her time, shorter than many, and her face was dark not simply because of its pigment, but on account of the suffering it held. 'God', she said, 'you know me very well. I give you everything because everything belongs to you. Sometimes there is hatred and bitterness inside me; I am troubled and sick and wounded in my heart, I am hungry with need and full of grief; but my fortune is in your hands'. Laurentia had borne twelve children. Her husband and seven of the children were killed in the war, at places where they had looked for refuge, three more died from malnutrition, and the last two were taken from her with malaria. She went to her father in a remote village for help, but his new wife mistreated her. Neighbours would lend her clothes when she had to go to market, or she would have been wrapped in rags.

Later, when she had the strength, she returned to her old place and her old house. The roof had been stripped of the iron sheets, all the animals taken, and the plantation destroyed. No-one was there. Her asthma got bad but she had no money for medicine. A brother and a sister helped her re-build the little house, and she took in five orphans for company. 'Life is a great burden,' she says, 'especially when you can't breathe. But I no longer blame anybody, everyone has their own troubles. I give mine to the Lord and I make friends at church and that is how I manage'. She falters. Then Laurentia geared herself: 'could I have some clothes please, so I won't have to borrow them to come to church and praise God?'

*****

This is another strange thing: the words 'DESPAIR' and 'PRAISED' are anagrams. Their makeup has simply been rearranged, the elements set in a different order, and new meanings emerge. What goes into them is still the same, but they are placed in a different order. Look again at this:

Each of the narrators speaking their stories above have moved, maybe consciously or unconsciously, maybe deliberately or influenced by the priorities of their community, they have journeyed from a place of utter despair, towards a place where God himself can be praised. A place where they can feel more positive, supported, hopeful, and valued. What they have in their hands, they are building with for their tomorrows. Apparently, they can face the reconstruction of their lives and relationships with patient optimism, without any firm time frame.

Would we take that journey? Would we have the courage, the abandonment, the trust? Is our faith that strong?

A FABLE FOR OUR TIME

Chapter Ten: *Celebration*

Almost as suddenly as it came, it went. It was as if the satanic savagery had bottomed out, exhausted. Fury and bestiality left Loufland. Evil had emptied itself, and it went back to cowering in corners. It wasn't annihilated, but it no longer swaggered in open spaces. It ceased to boast.

There wasn't much left behind. The terrified people had nowhere to go; there were lost children with no families; homes were burned-out, water had been polluted. The old neighbourliness was in shreds. Little by little the bush extruded its secrets - emerging from its shadows came the hungry and mutilated people hanging on to life; bit by bit the dying and the dead were extracted. Limbs and bones gave up their evidence of the tragedies that had been played out in its wilderness.

At first there was little hope that things would get better. Or could. What energy was left? Most of the male strength of Loufland had been annihilated or had haemorrhaged away with the refugees. There was a government which had been pulled together from the remnants of eight different parties to take over a shattered economy, and international relationships were in shreds.

So what was there to celebrate?

Celebration

Now this is a staggering thing. Almost universally in Loufland the people turned to God. Not so much to their old One god, but to the one God. Some said the One god had left the land, but they found the personal presence of the one God close to them in their trouble. They said things like -

Thank God! He has kept me alive until today. He has a job for me to do for him!

'Praise God - you have existed up to this moment!'

'If I've been condemned to live, I shall live alive/alive, not alive/dead!'

'Glory to God for the very air of every breath I breathe'

'Give glory I still have my left hand; it was spared when they cut off my right'

'IMANA ISHIMWE .... OUR GOD BE PRAISED'

Just being alive, alive at all, was a cause for celebration.

Places of worship had been desecrated, abused and vandalised; so the people chose to worship the Christian God in fields, under trees, in village squares. Nationally the people gave thanks, in greater numbers than known before.

Slowly food trickled back among the people. Houses began to be repaired – at least mud didn't cost anything. Cabbages grew, birds continued to

Celebration

sing, and the sun rose into the sky each day. Children made friends with each other, and when their families were nowhere, they set up households in abandoned shacks and foraged for each other. In due course many of them were reunited with the remnants of their extended family groupings, and many of them were taken into the homes of widows who had lost most of their own children. The children made up more than half the population of the country, and on them depended the future of Loufland.

Celebration is primeval. It is the glue that keeps people together in the darkest times. Not just an antidote to trouble, but a deep joining and enmeshing. In simple physiological terms, getting together to celebrate raises the 'feel good factor'. In social, psychological, spiritual terms it is the spring from which hope rises, where delight and play and laughter combine to prove that life remains worth living. It was traditional in early Loufland; so the people returned to what they knew, what belonged to them. Celebration goes a long way in affirming connectedness, and rejoining things that have been broken.

Someone said 'God is in pain; and every so often he sends us a hint of heaven.'

In Loufland people found ways of getting re-connected. Picking up the old ways of listening, accepting, bonding, celebrating. There was nowhere further to go down, so they started up by revisiting the old times of laughter and song, dance and play, praise and worship.

The great grandchildren and great-great grandchildren of Mattu and Tuam knew this. When there was no home, no school, no money, no food provided for them, between the times of scavenging they would scamper and chase each other, kicking the pebbles and delighting in funny faces and angular antics. Some decided they could care for each other without adult oversight at all. They set up 'households' in tiny crumbling huts, the young teenagers being 'heads of families'. These groups of children who lived together without adults, organized their households into different chores. One child would forage for food, one went to find firewood, another to fetch water. A boy said his dream was to educated as a teacher, "to tell others about the goodness of God".

In modern day Loufland the women-without-men get together to recount their tragedies to each other, taking comfort from each other's sympathy. Tillatu and Lomina, Ranatha and Dibuni, meet with Laurentia. The way they talk and share and work in together helps them live through their sorrows. They have in their homes children of others who have been disconnected, and they all join the neighbourhood in laughing and joking and singing. Where the plots of land that they cultivate adjoin each other, groups of women and men work together as a team, and their songs ring

Celebration

Celebration

across the valley as they hoe and plant. Men going out across the lake to fish in slim dug-out canoes chant in harmony to beguile their catch. Anny joins in as groups of young men and women jog down the road singing "Loufland is a good place to be! I love my Loufland!"

Wherever people meet in numbers, whatever their stories, whatever they have been through, there is clapping and dancing and chanting. Arms outstretched to each other in the movement, carried away by the beat of the homemade drums and the tins shaken with beans, chuckling and smiling. They all join in, whether skilled at the steps or as learners; whether child or mother with baby or granny; whether known to be virtuous or known to be unrestrained; whether tuneful or just trying; everyone together celebrates the fact of being ALIVE. In the villages it is the old men with crinkley white hair who burst into the aisles shaking their shoulders, bending their knees with intricate steps, weaving their hips in rhythm as their years fall away. The celebration is vibrant, vocal, flashing with a vitality that poverty can't put down. Aching bones, diseased bodies, ragged clothes, but gleaming, shining, sparkling eyes. And wide, wide smiles.

They have found a clear slate on which new choices can be made.

There is so much to learn from Loufland.

A FABLE FOR OUR TIME

Chapter Eleven: *Not to Question, or to Question?*

Wonder is such a strange word: to wonder at something, or to wonder about something, is a strange contrast: they are almost opposite to each other. To be taken over by wonder at an event full of marvel, or sight filled with beauty, or a person of great achievement, is one thing; it is about almost unbelieving acceptance. But to wonder about something implies a questioning, with a possibility of several answers. In the Land of Our Fable Loufland, the first was common, the second was rare.

There is a subtle difference between negotiating and questioning. The first comes up with a solution and the second remains unending. They each have a typical mind-set. In Loufland the first was prevalent everywhere, the second was less recognizable. It may be that there was a submerged faultline in the Land of Our Fable. Maybe in those rolling hills of antiquity, such a flaw existed; it may be that when that faultline was put under pressure, it gave way to breakdown and collapse.

Remember, in Loufland children who were strapped to their mothers' backs felt so secure that crying was seldom heard. Nor was questioning. Very early in their lives infants learnt that, without question, it was easier for them and best for everybody to do as they were told.

Not to Question, or to Question?

- When two-year olds are asked to carry machetes to the fields, they do it. Where children are taught by rote and chant, there is little room for questions. Later, they discover values and meanings through stories and folklore, but these are not for questioning. Knowledge and understanding are passed on through myths and legend, symbol and dream, convincing not by logic but by fascination and absorption. Choice was not taught.

- The young ones didn't question their family's occupation, and they seldom left to search for an alternative. They did what they were asked, People were secure in accepting what they were taught, it didn't occur to them to doubt.

- In that land wives accepted whatever behaviour their husbands handed out to them, and husbands did what was traditional without questioning.

- In Loufland, responsibility was a matter for the community, and not a matter for personal decision. Where 'authority' was set in the ways of the olden days, not in an individual's response to them.

Questioning didn't seem to fit in Loufland, it didn't find a place there.

In the Land of Our fable, two phrases were often heard. One, was 'they're told to do it, and they do it'; and the other was 'they're used to it'. They came up again and again. They came out of a solid and steadfast assumption that responsibility is deeply centred in the community, rather than in individual choice. They're used to it - the street children with nowhere to wash, or to sleep, no change of clothing: they were 'used to it'. The school children who walked six kilometers to school and back again each day; the house-girls working long hours silently and efficiently; the wives keeping their pregnancies secret; the men pushing huge loads of bricks and iron sheets and sacks of grain up long hills on unstable wooden scooters. All of them, it was said, were 'used to it'. Whatever happened, happened.

The people of Loufland acted from goodwill towards the whole, they weren't taught to analyse and discriminate between differences. Yielding to the community ways was paramount, and always considered to be best if it was considered at all. It was how everything and everyone fitted together and got on with the business of living. Maybe the time came when they forgot how to question.

Birds and flowers were abundant all over the country. Foreigners came in and asked questions about their differences and names. But Elia, Mattu and Tuam, Nutenga and Peetah didn't need to know the significance of each of the species; they were all just part of life, the unquestioned background to life. Accepted and trusted.

Not to Question, or to Question?

Outsiders would come across those hills and mountains and exclaim 'Look at those mountains! The shapes and distances and colours!' And the Loufland reply would come 'What mountains? What shapes and colours? Oh those! We're used to them, they're normal.' Enquiring or exclaiming was redundant, irrelevant.

When new ways and new ideas arrived with the Uncomprehenders, they were met with acceptance and trust and compliance; they were followed without the hassle of too much embarrassing enquiry.

When the priests came from other lands, they weren't questioned much either.

******

Nor did they question Satan, even if they recognized him.

A FABLE FOR OUR TIME

Chapter Twelve: *The High Ground*

Much of the 'under-mind' of King Ita's time - those common assumptions upon which their daily life was based - became grossly undermined during the time of the Uncomprehenders. The concepts which were brought in from the outside branded the people in Loufland: these brandmarks burnt into their very being. The horror would never have happened in the days of King Ita. When it had passed, ideas emerged which connected with the old days of the one king and the one god, the one country and one language and one culture. Principles forged in those days were restored and used to decorate a new High Ground. These are some of them -

* Alus, Tuas, and Utas once again mingled freely. Ethnic equality again became a first priority.

> *The Responsible man said: "No-one asks about anyone's identity any more. It is not significant. Over the generations we have mingled and intermarried, and 'ethnic purity' is a mirage. Even I, who am one of the people, can't tell who is what. How can outsiders tell?"*

* New leaders brought home again the process of community responsibility. They systematically trained officers in the army to go into the villages and form teaching groups In the groups it came to be accepted there that every person in the land had been damaged by the atrocities. Everyone had lost; all had been implicated; the hatred had affected each individual, and everybody in the land was in need of forgiveness. Neither professionals nor officials nor dedicated religious were excluded. Not businessmen nor stallholders nor farmers; not women nor children nor men had remained untouched. Neither academics nor artisans had stayed outside. Killers and victims had alternated roles and came from each area of the community at different times. And so the people came to understand that personal recrimination was out, it had no future; that parceling out individual blame was pointless; and that trying to take personal reprisal was counter-productive. New laws insisted that efforts to repossess property that in the owner's absence, had been lived in by survivors, was illegal. A blanket impunity would have been an offense to all: but among those not actually taken into prison for trial, every inhabitant of Loufland was to start afresh. Those in prison would, in time, be tried; but just like Peetah, when prisoners were charged and released it was to be back into their local community, with appropriate restrictions. The local community was expected to receive them and care for them even when they knew full well what they had done.

A widow said: "That man – I knew him as a neighbour, his market stall was close to mine; he invaded my house and slashed two of my children; then he beat me and killed my husband. I couldn't mourn for them because it was happening to everybody, it was 'normal'. After the war I was angry, very very angry. But there was no future in hating. So I forgave the killer. I still see him in the market, and now I quite like him. If it came to it, I would eat with him. He did what he was told to do. If he hadn't killed my husband he would have been killed himself.

There is no future in clutching on to my hatred."

* In the days of King Ita, many things were held as having higher priority than the needs of any one individual. Things like hospitality, sharing, respect for elders, and the good of the community. In a remarkably short time after their cataclysmic war, fear and mistrust and terror gave place to an extraordinary welcome, one that was forged from their early culture. They looked for things which would root them to the high ground, so rather than retreating into a covert to lick their wounds, they were out there with arms outstretched to hug and embrace and include anyone who happened to come along. It was a wide welcome, with an acceptance of what they call 'Oneness'. Difficult to believe, nearly incredible to see, this 'Oneness' is creating a level playing-field of forgiveness and common sharing.

What a story!

Children used to starvation pressed around the visitor. She was handing out sweets, to them rare treat. It was difficult to place just one into each of the massed hands as they pushed and pulled towards her. Then there came a tug at the visitor from behind: a seven-year-old girl lifted up a hand, which held two sweets. The child solemnly asked that one should be given to someone who had none.

* The One God was now named; the powers of the old One god were theologized into their experience of the One God. The One God expects allegiance and loyalty through thick and thin. The people said "If you love God and follow him through bad times as well as good, he will look after you". They found that the One God did not simply allocate favours and protection, but was the One who is there and whose wisdom is absolute whatever life throws up. Amongst those who came through the bad times still holding on to their lives, the intense excitement and marvel of being alive was potent.

Sedoro tells this story: 'I had a job in a supermarket after the war. My father and mother and brother and sisters were dead so I had to look after myself. The supermarket sold beer and wine and other things which troubled people and I knew it was wrong. I had no job to go to but I didn't want to have a job that was wrong. You can only do what you want to do, what you feel is right to do, what God wants you to do. So I gave up the job and hid in my room and cried and prayed for

two days and two nights. "Oh my God" I cried "Oh my God. I have no
family, no friends to go to. Oh my God" I cried, "Oh my God" for two
days and two nights. Not going out, no food, no friends. Then my
brother turned up from nowhere. He knocked at my door and said "I
have a job for you." So I praise God I am alive. I praise God I have a
job. Not all people are like that, but you thank God. Stay close to
God; he will keep you'.

* Loufland was rich in children. At least half the population had lived less
than eighteen years, and had all the energy and determination and
imagination that young people possess. Loufland valued her children,
whether they were survivors, whether they were with their families or
without families, and whether they were formally educated or too poor to
get to school.

Everyone in the community was responsible for the upbringing and
'good' behaviour of the children. This included those living on the
street or in the bushes; all were praised or reprimanded as the need
arose. Any adult who was around and familiar with them automatically
took part in the system that moulded their behaviour. The forming of
their childrens' character was seen as a shared obligation, and no
particular relative had the exclusive duty of reinforcing good behaviour
or condemning bad.

The High Ground

* The women had been left with a crucial part to play. Not only were most of them left without husbands and fathers and sons - the men with skills and knowledge and leadership had been amongst the first to be targeted in the killing times; not only were they left with the re-fashioning of property and homesteads; not only were they left to mourn without tribal ceremony; but where their children had been killed they filled their small houses with children whose parents had themselves been killed. At first the grief and reactive suspicion of the women held them apart, but as they started to depend upon one another for practical help they began to tell each other their stories-

> *There was the time when three whole days were dedicated to corporate remembering. The women of the cathedral went together to a neighbouring genocide site: it was a church set aside to honour the five thousand men, women and children who went in for sanctuary, but where they had been systematically slaughtered. The ghastliness of these places un-utterable. The women stayed at the site for a whole day; there were too many stories to absorb and 'exhibits' to respect to take less time, so they watched and mourned. The following day they met again to weep and to hear from each other. They discovered that not one of them had had no share in the genocide: either they had been personally harmed, or suffered a loss; or they had labelled or harassed or informed on supposed 'enemies'; or they*

The High Ground

had simply stood to one side. Fear and savagery had touched them all, and they all needed forgiveness. The third day they came together and spent the hours in forgiving one another, sharing the total burden, and releasing the guilt felt by individuals. Divisions melted, and from that melt-down emerged a bonded sisterhood that refused to blame. It grew into mutual care for each other, and an enlarged comprehension of the effects of the genocide. This group now holds a cohesion and sense of personal support that would be difficult to match anywhere. They say they are now teaching the men.

A woman from the University said: 'Our women have a boundless capacity of compassion for humanity … their strength flows like a warm current. We won't lose hope; amid all the horror, hope is possible. It is better to try smiling than be always crying. When we have fun, it tempers the fury.'

* The new government was left with major decisions. Retribution or Restitution. It was discovered that Retribution was non-feasible and impractical, and that it furthers hatred and destruction. Restitution - if it could be made real - would make space for something of healing to take place.

Throughout the land, a practice developed of mounting an annual day of Communal Remembrance. The people of a whole area put down their tools and walk (for several hours if need be) to the genocide memorial site of their region. In one, it takes the form of great concrete vaults buried deep in the ground. These vaults hold the bodies and parts of bodies collected after the war, some identified and placed in coffins, but many not. Once a year the manhole covers over these vaults are removed, and the gathered people process around the opened doors and gaze inside as they remember. The procession then continues with weeping and mourning until all the people have passed by the holes in the ground. Then the covers are closed and bouquets of fresh flowers placed on them. The procession passes around a second time, this time singing songs of hope and corporate resolution. 'Oneness', again, is the theme.

* The old practice of waiting has been resurrected. A waiting, without fussing, with an insistent conviction that from just waiting, not demanding, not pushing, something essential will 'arise'. Something new but pertinent, something worth struggling for, but without struggle as we know it in the West, something of the heart and guts, that is more grounded and rooted than is possible when relying only on the roving mind. Waiting with patience and hope, waiting with an obstinate sense of resisting disillusionment.

If it doesn't happen today, it will happen tomorrow, or the next day, or the week after. Meanwhile the groundwork of relationships and connections will be strengthening, and then what happens will happen better after all.

* A hope was born in the ashes of despair. It is a hope structured upon a different quality, one that is more rooted than simply sticking to the bright side. Nothing, no-thing, can defeat it for it has been through the crucible of total loss and come out the other side. It consists of a passionate knowing, that when there is no further to go down the only redeeming alternative is to get up.

> *When the rapist broke into the house he accosted the small boy before attacking his white mother. The young eight year old stood up to him and said "Go on, do what you like, you can't hurt me because God is here; He is with me, and He is stronger than you". Two years later, in the face of the horrific aftermath of this nightmare, the mother said "I am still living on the power of that moment. God was with us in that room, and it is the knowledge of that Presence that has held me up through all the terrible consequences that followed. It has never left me."*

At the closure of a conference a new pastor who had been working with disillusioned young people at the very bottom of the heap spoke up and said:

"NO, I DON'T KNOW THAT GOOD WILL OVERCOME EVIL; I DON'T KNOW WHAT THE FUTURE HOLDS, OR THAT GOOD WILL EVEN SURVIVE. WHAT I DO KNOW IS ONE THING: WHATEVER HAPPENS, GOD WILL BE WITH ME, THIS HERE, THIS NOW, THIS ACTION. AND THAT IS WHAT MATTERS ABOVE EVERYTHING".

The High Ground

Looking back over the stories of Loufland, we can find the seeds of this remarkable recovery sewn right through them. The 'one-ship' of King Ita; the hidden strength of Elia and her deep interiority; the mothering that was natural to Geena; the keeping to tradition of Tuam and Mattu and his plea to the One god; the acceptance concerning death shown by Nutenga and his wife; the community care of Peetah in his bewilderment; the travelling and dependence on others for hospitality of Rawe; each had its part to play in the ordering of daily life.

Then came the Horror.

As the people of Loufland re-assessed their priorities and told their stories, some surprises emerged. The practical surrealism of the women narrators; the long-term positive outcomes, such as that for Tillatu, who with her new husband has a good job and a nice house near the city; the sharing trust of Lomina and the old women, and Ranatha who related her story in the storm; the ego-strength and forgiveness of Dubini; the courage within pathos of Laurentia. Each and every one of these ingredients have been part of the fashioning of their new national character; a significant strand in the re-making of the whole.

The underpinning and overriding conviction is one of inter-relationship and interdependence. 'I am as I am because you - and the others - are you as you are'. The people are thinking not just of themselves as individuals, but as bound up in networks of relationships which hold their entire people together. It is formidable to compare this with the self-concerned and fragmented attitudes held in the West: it shows up how much our individualism risks extreme personal loneliness. The late John Taylor insisted that the Western view of individualism is a 'very new phenomenon', and is a 'monstrosity of human history'[1]. What mischief to humanity are we in the Western industrialised world doing? Are we even conscious of it?

Possibly the most significant and notable of all:

THEIR EBULLIENCE[2] and EXUBERANCE[3]

IS NOT A BIT OF RESPITE,

A TEMPORARY FORGETTING, A MERE COPING SKILL;

IT IS THE RESOURCE FROM WHICH THEY GAIN, AND REGAIN

THEIR STRENGTH TO FACE AND DEAL WITH ATROCITY.

---

[1] John V. Taylor; *The Primal Vision*, SCM Press, 2001 p.60
[2] ebullient: effervescent, bubbling over: Oxford Etym. Dictionary
[3] exuberant: abounding in health and spirits, growth and fruitfulness: OED as above

A FABLE FOR OUR TIME

Chapter Thirteen: *Postscripts*

A fable is about the general shape of the wood, rather than the exact configuration of each of the trees. But to have any truth about it, a fable must relate to reality. Our fable is now concluded; the following are postscripts to it. And where is the real experience on which this Fable is based? Rwanda. That remarkable country of highest beauty and deepest torment. The country at the centre of Africa that in recent history has been the centre of complexity, pulled about by political intricacy. The tiny country that has been subjected to inhumanity as much from external sources as of its internal making. But the fable is not confined to Rwanda; the principles drawn together in the fable are not limited to that country by either place or time: they have a wide, even global, application. Now, through the generosity of their people, we have a critical opportunity of learning from what they learnt, of changing as they are changing, and all this without having to go through in real life what they have gone through.

These postscripts are about some issues that are special to Rwanda, and to us, now.

Postscript A

In a single period of one hundred days, the country had an estimated eighth of its population slaughtered, seven-eighths of its population dislocated, and a half of its population fleeing their own homeland as refugees. It has endured an almost total amputation of skills, funds, and energy. And yet, in the short space of seven years later, more than in any other country in the world that has experienced even a small portion of their devastation, the people of Rwanda are once again turning towards hope and regeneration. They are sharing, forgiving, moving forward together. How have they done it? Let's look behind three particular concepts, each have wide significance.

Firstly, the concept of *sharing*. In the West it has become a much-used word. As an adult, when I 'share' something, in general it means I am spilling out experience felt deeply in my guts, something of significance in my own interior life. It's different in countries of great poverty. Sharing means a practical, physical and external spilling: it implies I am willing to share my house, my bed, my beans, my sweat, my water and my family with you.

Secondly, looking behind our concern for what is *best*. We in the West have an innate assumption that our ways are 'best'. Before leaving for Rwanda I made enquiries about the type of fertilizer that was appropriate to give to the smallholders out there. In Britain, it was pointed out to me that in the light of our advanced technology and the high state of our research it was sensible to approach the Ministry of Agriculture in London for details.

Postscripts

As it turned out, they were difficult to access and in the time left to me they were unavailable. Out in Rwanda itself, I discovered that the local people knew just what was applicable, appropriate, and achievable immediately. It could be bought in any local market.

The third concept is contained in a letter I received from a young Rwandan woman now living in Britain.

' Yes, my people are quite special and I am very proud of them and many thanks for visiting them; that means more than anything else for them. For us, it is very important to have visits during bad times, times of sadness, you can't imagine what your visit means, as you are and as they are. Yes, don't hesitate to publish your story. Many people think that what our people need from them is money and things and they forget that that is secondary and really people can even do without if they have loved each other with people alongside them. One of the reasons that I think Rwanda fell into the deep pit, is because the devil got very jealous of God. Rwandan people were getting closer and closer to God; they were religious since long ago before they were 'discovered'. They always believed that God loved Rwanda more than anywhere else in the world. We have this saying - IMANA YIRIRWAHANDI IGATAHA I RWANDA: that means "God spends his days roaming the world, but he returns home each night to Rwanda."'

Postscript B

At this stage readers may well be wondering why this book has been designed in the form of a 'fable' rather than a straightforward diary or commentary. The form of the 'fable' used here has enabled us to take an overall look at some of the possibilities without inflicting labels or judgements where they don't belong. Further rationale for presenting a story in this way is expressed succinctly in a recent book[i] which explains it like this:

> The description of the spiritual 'inside' of something which is nevertheless essentially connected to a material 'outside' is a very powerful mental tool, because it allows us not only to speak of groups or institutions as a whole in spiritual terms, but also lets us use spiritual language for aspects of their life and behaviour, which might be quite transient.

Wink takes us further in the application of analogy and fable to communicate, making use of the illustration of a football crowd[ii]:

> A 'mob spirit' does not hover in the sky to leap down on unruly crowds at a soccer match. It is the actual spirit constellated when the crowd reaches a certain critical flashpoint of excitement and frustration. It comes into existence in that moment, causes people to act in ways of which they would never have dreamed themselves capable, and then ceases to exist the moment the crowd disperses. This way of thinking is helpful for two reasons. In the first place, it allows us to recognize how powerful certain patterns of behaviour or institutional

arrangements can be. Individuals in the football crowd would describe themselves as having been 'taken over'. Similarly it is not accidental that we talk about 'market forces': nobody chooses to close a factory and put people out of work, they feel compelled to do so. Our normal language tends to assume that when people do things, someone somewhere is in control; but this is not always true. Sometimes 'the powers' are in control. And to acknowledge this is not to abdicate responsibility (it's not my fault – I was just taken over'); it is to realize how deadly it may be to put oneself in the hands of 'the powers'.

The second reason why it is helpful sometimes to concentrate aspects of people's behaviour rather than people as whole individuals is this: it allows us to label behaviour of certain kind or institutions in certain respects as demonic or 'beastly', without labeling the people or institutions as demons or beasts ... and without judging people in themselves to be evil.

It could be argued that that point is from the outside, looking in. Perhaps it has to be borne in mind that if the same principle is applied from the inside, looking out, we come across a paradox simply stated by the Bishop of Byumba [in Rwanda] in a personal conversation. The jist of it went something like this:

"It is easy and comfortable to 'blame Satan'.

While we blame Satan we can keep our own hands clean and ourselves relatively blameless.

Satan therefore prefers to be blamed; this is how we can keep our invulnerability alive, our consciences clear and intact, and still believe we have not been implicated.

Satan is cunning, devious, underhand. Watch out!"

A quote from the recent postscript to John Taylor's classic book on 'The Primal Vision'[iii] is very apt here:

If the word 'myth' is properly applied it should not denote truth or untruth, but a universal relevance such that all who hear respond not with 'That was their story', but with 'This is our story'.

But if this really was 'our story', what then?

* If I had no education, no job, and no training, and a high authority told me to kill or be killed - how would I act?

* If my culture shaped me to not question my neighbours, but to negotiate with them, how would that affect my relationships with them - would we get on better or worse?

* If the responsibility for my behaviour and that of my children was not mine alone but belonged to the community, would I judge others less?

* Is my own heart big enough to listen, accept, forgive, and bond in 'oneness'?

John Taylor writes further that our current sense of the importance of the individual is in stark contrast to their 'unconditional readiness to share'; this builds a 'totality of being', and an 'aggregate of the ancestral soul'.

Postscript C

Rwanda is unique in many ways, but perhaps none more so than in their brand new development of political philosophy. While the eyes of the world were focused on the Truth and Reconciliation Commission in South Africa, Rwanda was working out her own way of looking ahead from the place of an even more battered economy, and an even more blanket experience of horror and destruction. As I understand it this has been brought about with government foresight and deliberation. The old way of inclusion was to be re-established : the early ethnic origin of a person was of no significance to their education, housing, social standing or employment, and all identity cards were to be destroyed. 'One-ness' was the aim both philosophically and in practice, based on sharing, forgiveness and regeneration. Has anything similar been promoted as a political policy anywhere before?

This process of communal intention is likely to lead to wiser choices and more appropriate decisions as the country regains its vitality.

The Rwandan people are precious to God. Their desire for 'Oneness' and regeneration should lead the world, and for the sake of our poor broken world we must listen continuously, hoping their example strengthens and deepens and withstands everything else. Together, they are building something so crucially important, that we must attend to it for our own growth. The potentcy of their hope and sharing, the confidence of political reconstruction, is humbling, and yet it is largely unheard in the West. This is happening, now, at this very moment, and day by day it is gaining momentum, but unpublicised. We in the West need to learn from their resilience.

The people of Rwanda have faced the abyss. Personally. Socially. Materially. Politically. Spiritually. They have survived with their inner resources of resilience and mystery still alive. They say it is because they rely on God, and God alone. Outside help is badly needed, <u>but not the interference</u> that too often goes with it[iv]. The people are working out a new morality, rooted in their own experience and cultural wisdom: those who go in to 'help' must do so with ears that listen to the gains that have been made. Outsiders have to desist from dragging back onto the scene the old dependencies, from sucking the Rwandan people into the current of Western desires for materialism and 'efficiency'.

Finally, a few lines from 'The Poisenwood Bible': Barbara Kingslover[v] writes -

> 'And only now, after working this land for ten years, am I coming to understand the length and breadth of the outsiders' failure to impose themselves on Africa. … You can't just sashay into the jungle aiming to change it all over to the Christian style, without expecting the jungle

to change you right back. … Poor Africa. No other continent has endured such an unspeakably bizarre combination of foreign thievery and foreign goodwill.'

They do not need our false gods imposed on them again. Every one of those peopling this fable have so much to teach us - can we find the courage and humility to learn from them? Can we learn from Rwanda as Rwanda re-learns herself? Or are we too proud, and power-crazed, and plum patronizing to hear what they are saying?

If we have ears, then for God's sake, let's use them to LISTEN.

i   Christina Le Moignan; *Following the Lamb*; 2000 Epworth Press UK. p.41 ISBN 0-7162-0537-8

ii Walter Wink; *Naming the Powers*; 1984 Fortress Press UK. p.105

iii John V. Taylor; *The Primal Vision*; re-issued 2001 SCM Press, London.

iv Martin Conway: *Journeying Together Towards Jubilee*; 1998. See 'In place of booklist' for details.

v Barbara Kingsolver: *The Poisenwood Bible*; 1999 Faber & Faber.

Postscripts

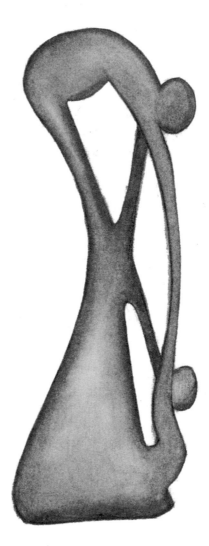

A FABLE FOR OUR TIME

Chapter Fourteen: _After the Nightmare . . . September 11th; Where now?_

The emotional combustion that was ignited on September 11th 2001 set fire to the world. It was not so much that the reaction was what it was, but that it was the world that reacted. Every community on our globe heard about the event, and every heart was affected. It is not possible to begin to calculate how many individual attitudes have changed as a result of the actions which took place on that day; it would be virtually impossible to measure the publicity it was given; no-one can evaluate the surging compassion from all over the world that enveloped those afflicted. It would be pointless to even try to figure out such quantities.

*****

It is patently obvious that September 11th 2001 was not the first time a few thousand people were horrifically killed in a short space of time. But it is the first time that a few thousand white, powerful, moneyed people have been slaughtered at one time, other than during a mutually declared war. And the whole world rallied.

Most of us just stood amazed at the speed and the astounding energy of the coalition. The galvanising of international leaders; the rhetoric and negotiation which went into obtaining their commitment; the fantasy-sized sums of money which were mobilised; all this as a result of an attack on two office buildings in New York[i], which it itself took up barely half a day. Larger numbers of people have died more protracted and atrocious deaths on other occasions, but for this incident the whole world was moved.

At different times, in other parts of the globe, more than several thousand people have been extinguished, but with considerably less reaction. Ordinarily the consumer on the High Street barely notices whether there has been any special exertion of effort or finance or resources or diplomacy or threat or warfare resulting from mass death. There has seldom been such a rallying of world opinion, or such caustic consequences as that which followed on "9/11/01". On these other occasions the killed have been seen as among the powerless, the poor, and as having a different colour of skin. Seldom have the victims been among the wealthy, the property owners, the politically erudite, and the financial elite. They have lived in Bangladesh, Tibet, the Balkans, in Cambodia, the Sudan, Rwanda – places where the savagery against people was at its greatest when they were seen to be without resources (or, at least, without those resources most desired by the West). These peoples' plight has passed scarcely articulated or acknowledged by the world of which they are also citizens. If so much energy can be collected and projected as the result of a single event in a place of high-rise profile, what might happen if it was dispatched to the benefit of those with less voice?

Above all else, the aftermath of September 11th has proved once and for all what is possible if the gall of the 'right' people – those in 'power' – is sufficiently roused.

Prof. Dr. Kirkaldy-Willis[ii] has put it like this: 'The real news now is not concerned with politics and places but with the ways in which quite ordinary people like ourselves interact with one another all over the world. It has opened up completely new material and spiritual vistas. If only we can grab the courage in both hands and make the most of these new opportunities for <u>change</u> in inter-conflict and international behaviour'.

What sort of change? I have found something of it in the writing of this book, and it has been totally engrossing. I hope that you, the reader, will feel something of the same. There are things out there that could prove the way for all of us; some of the experiences of so-called non-influential peoples could lead the world on a course of different, new and exciting ways of behaving. I like to think of it as – *the How's of Hope.*

Many observers and commentators have reached similar places of wonder. In preparing the fable offered here, things have unravelled that could be applied anywhere in the world.

- The way in which the government leaders realised that each side had alternated between being oppressor and oppressed;
- the way of acknowledgement that everyone in a country needs forgiveness, and to forgive;
- the realization that to apportion 'blame' is impossible, both morally and in practice.

The implications of these principles are colossal and epoch-making. Can we stretch our love and compassion and mutuality enough to meet them? Looking at other areas of conflict in our distressed global village, how much of this could be appropriated?

Today, in the 'developed' world we are encouraged to make sure of our 'Rights'. When we feel wronged, we can legitimately seek for compensation or restitution. It is open to us to assert - and sue for - our Rights. As a political initiative, the people of Rwanda have turned this premise upside down. They have chosen to give up keeping account of their 'Wrongs'. There is no denial that everybody has been wronged, and hurt, and suffered losses. To keep account of them or compare them one against another would result in a further deadening of life, it would make for a total degradation of relationship and goodwill. But in accepting this, people in Rwanda have found the energy and enthusiasm to move forward together, from an equal starting line. They have reached out towards each other and towards their future, in the excitement of their saying *"Turi Bamwi – We are all One".*

Has this acceptance that retaliation is self-defeating, married to a mutuality of forgiveness, ever been a political principle before? Narrative shapes the way in which the world understands itself; a fable designed for adults to read touches upon deep levels of philosophy and morality. In story form, these are not tied to one place and time, but are true for other places, different times. They speak of values not trumpeted in our daily media. Ordinarily, much of the content of our newspapers is based on logic, legalism, control and competition - those tired and tiring values to which we have given such high profile in the 21st century. Things which properly belong to a left-brained robot. In contrast, fable and story can light up the qualities of a right-brained harlequin, the image of laughter and tears, dance and love, forgiveness and delight, empathy and 'oneness'. The story told here is about a way to new birth: even out of despair we can move into a place where God can be praised. IMANI ISHIMWE. A place of dramatic, powerful, expanded reality.

Sometimes we forget that Jesus himself appeared in a forgotten place of obscure poverty, yet from that obscurity the world was changed. Perhaps the manger can <u>still</u> show us the way, and with it we will have more truth and hope and insight than is commonly to be found in the bomber's cockpit.

Do you remember that old song? It went something like this:

'There's a place for us;

A time and space for us'

Where we'll find a new way of living -

We'll find way of forgiving -

.... somewhere .... sometime ....'

HASN'T THAT TIME ARRIVED? IS THAT TIME HERE AND NOW?

i   plus other attacks in Washington and Philadelphia
ii   Dr. W.H. Kirkaldy-Willis, MD, FRCS, LLD, FICC of Victoria, Canada. Personal correspondence.

A FABLE FOR OUR TIME

ADDENDA NOTES

The Cover Picture

A portrait sculpture of a Rwandan child by Robert Hunt. Robert and his wife, Belinda, were part of a group that visited that country with the author in February 2000.

This small boy was one of several children taking a break from picking tea at the Gisakura tea plantation near Cyangugu, south west Rwanda. Robert took photographs of a number of them but this little boy stood out from the rest. At the moment of the photograph he was looking up at one of the visiting group of Europeans handing out Tic-Tac peppermints. He had seen his friends being given one and he was standing patiently in the hope that he might be given one too. While his companions clamoured noisily for attention he stood silently - staring up with this bewitching, far away look on his face.

His patience was, of course, rewarded.

It seems likely that his jersey, or what was left of it, was more of a status symbol than a useful garment and he clearly wore it with pride.

1. In the Beginning

'King Ita' could have lived anywhere between the end of fifteenth and nineteenth centuries. His successor was still in place in the mid-twentieth century. The state described here is not necessarily so very long ago. In the C15th, when the Portuguese adventurers crept up river into central Africa, among their written reports were accounts of the tools, skills and lifestyle they found there, already well established. The chiefs and their families wore clothes made of fabric formed from beating the bark of specified trees, or weaving the fibre of palm fronds. Finely crafted woodwork decorated their houses, including exquisite pieces of ebony. Iron-age farm tools, spears, musical pipes, buckles and brooches were apparently in everyday use. The people of the chief's court included tax-collectors, administrators, musicians, judges and poets. Even in the face of this evidence, the Europeans hung on to their confidence of being innately superior.

In addition, it is known that vestiges of Christian metaphors and images from the early church had permeated down from North Africa and become embedded in their familiar religious ritual. The following hymn is said to have been in Africa in the tenth century:

'The cross is the way of the lost
The cross is the staff of the lame
The cross is the guide of the blind
The cross is the strength of the weak.

The cross is the hope of the hopeless –
It is the freedom of the slave;
The cross is the consolation of the bonded labourers –
It is the cloth of the naked.
The cross is the water of the seeds,
It is the source of all those who seek water.

The cross is the healing of the broken;
The cross is the healing of the church.

2. The Birth

The secretiveness of women in this region has a strong tradition. It affects many parts of their lives. For instance, if a wife is beaten by her husband, only rarely will she tell her friends. As one lady said to me '- she is expected to beat him back!' This evasion of confidences can be taken to extremes; even if a woman is forced by a man other than her husband and raped, she traditionally keeps it to herself until her dying day. With only two of them at the event - who will believe her story? It seems to be assumed that 'the least said - the soonest mended.'

3. The Marriage

The stately movement of these women is almost allegorical. It has been described with wonder by every visitor from abroad who observes them. From infancy, it is taken for granted that their deportment should be so stable and upright that no weight or surprise or blunder should upset it; they 'defy gravity while wearing the ho-hum aspect of perfect tedium' [Kingsolver]. Sitting, standing, stretching and reaching, are all done without disturbing the weight commonly carried on their heads. Whatever their mood, it is never betrayed in their posture.

Addenda Notes

Marriage itself is more often about the extension of family bonds and influence, and its continuation with children, than it is about personal feelings. John Taylor put it this way:

'The transfer of a girl and all her unborn children to become a wife in another kinship group represented a very serious loss of the life-force of her family which must be compensated by some exchange. The classical form of Bridewealth was a transfer of cattle. ... Urbanization and a cash economy have smashed the intricate balance of dependence and obligation within the family, and Western education has undermined its sanctions. In the face of this destruction of its outward forms, can the primal concept of "Man" survive?'

4. The Death

Later still, when the Uncomprehenders had turned away in disgust (did they secretly suspect what they had done?) there rose another problem: what was to be done when one mother lost her husband, four sons, three daughters, two parents and five siblings, within a few days of each other? How could each of them be properly mourned? If bits of their bodies were scattered around among bits of others' bodies, how could each dead body be honoured and grieved over?

Somebody asked 'Surely you felt bitterness, or anger that the One god had let you down?' After a long pause the answer came: 'How could I? How could I grieve?' she paused, 'it was normal. It was happening to everybody. Nobody could mourn, there wasn't time.'

5. The Property

The story of Peetah is about toleration, but there is more to it than that. Is it something about communal forgiveness? Rwanda today is a secure place for visitors. The only fragment of fear I felt during my whole stay was being pushed off the narrow path by Peetah, in a petulant gesture of surprise. My guides immediately moved to 'protect' me, but Peetah himself was barely scolded.

Addenda Notes

6. The Sorrow

The means whereby the different groups were identified and set apart had been used before. There was a particular instrument of calibration which was applied to each person's face; it was to measure the exact length of the nose. The result was recorded on their identification card.: It separated Tutsi from Hutu and Hutu from Twa. This ID had to be taken everywhere at all times. The instrument of calibration was not new: it had been used previously during the Holocaust: to differentiate 'Jew' from 'Gentile'.

7. Negotiation

In common English conversation there is a significant difference in 'bartering' and 'negotiating'.

When 'bartering' is discussed, it is implicit that one side will come off better than the other. A certain element of craft, trick or fraud may be acceptable, and the offered equivalents may be transparently unequal. Bartering is a popular and expected form of exchange in many parts of Africa.

In negotiation, the action or object (or combination of actions and objects) to be exchanged are considered of equal value to both parties. Mortgages can be negotiated, business deals, fees, and wherever people 'swap' services.

But when a person's life is as stake, acceptable equivalents are not possible.

8. Horrors Beyond All Horror

It wasn't just the killings. Nor simply the depopulation - they fled away through fear of murder and mutilation or of discovery. But it was especially difficult for women with young children to move; many of them simply had to stay where they were. So after the 'war' the remnant population was made up of five grieving widows to every one man. There were additional twists to all this tragedy:
- those who remained could recognize the killers. Most of them were former neighbours.
- many of those who fled their homes, could only go as far as the bush. They barely lived, surviving on grass and roots.
- news of the liberation from the killers filtered through to those hiding only very slowly: many died of starvation before it reached them.

Addenda Notes

9. From Despair to Praise – stories in detail

This book very deliberately takes the form of a fable. But at this point it is important to include some stories that were narrated to me personally. These stories are about the perception of their narrators. They, too, were wanting to get a point across. It is not their actual accuracy that counts; it is the accumulated desire of each of the narrators to convince their hearers that despair is not the end. That from the breakdown of compost - the mix of live and deadened material - new life can grow. The stories recounted here have been compacted; but their phraseology is as it was offered. The emphasis on replacing the potential for self-pity with positive reconstruction was applied to their life circumstances even unrelated to the 'war'. For instance:

* *'I lost my husband, but now God is my husband and I can serve him wholly. I think of him and thank him all day long. He has kept me alive, praise him.'*
* *'When I was three I had a hot charcoal iron ground into my cheek. But I was not burned elsewhere: it was a sign God loved me and wanted me to live and do a job for him. Now I can help others who have suffered and I praise God!'*

There is so much that has been written about forgiveness. My personal favourite definition was described by Otto Kernberg [the author of 'Love Relations' Yale University Press, 1995]. It goes like this:

Forgiveness comes from a morality that has matured.
Rather than stemming from naivete, or narcissistic grandiosity, it is made up of:

* an acceptance of the pain that comes with the loss of illusions about the self and others;
* a faith in the possibility of the recovery of trust;
* a belief that love will be recreated and maintained; and
* all this in spite of, and beyond, the experienced aggressive components of love itself.

A way that stands in sharp contrast to retribution or instant reactivity.

10. Celebration

It has been estimated that up to 97% of the entire population of Rwanda worships the Christian God, whether it is through traditional forms or in indigenous churches. The part that different churches played during the atrocities has been well documented. It ranged from pastoral heroism through to shocking betrayal. Nonetheless, even where officers or officials of the church carry blame, 'God' is not blamed. People still flood into the churches each week, and prayer is vocally part of everyday living.

It is difficult with our tired ears to hear the spontaneity of some of the things that have happened. We in industrialised countries have grown weary of horror, fatigued by the recounted tragedy of others in so many places. When we haven't been through it ourselves, we are dulled to the extraordinary possibilities of resilience, we can get suspicious of rose-coloured spectacles, and too soured to recognise genuine celebration. Perhaps we can learn to listen, with clean, unclogged, ears.

11. Not to Question or to Question?

A brief note: 'complaint ' and 'compliant' are also anagrams. In the days of King Ita in Loufland, complaints and complaining were seldom heard, while compliance was the very webbing of society. A feature of compliance is a dearth of questioning, and where resistance is rare a people will be pliable and conform. In general this can strengthen the bond of community; nevertheless the way of questioning leads to critical analysis and increased discernment. Maybe, at times, these were in short supply in Loufland.

Compliance has some very attractive features; for example: piles of fresh merchandise are left unattended by the roadside, such as firewood, cabbages, bricks, bananas. When there is no-one around to state the price, no-one appears to take them. Trust, compliance, obedience, acceptance.

There are other, less easily acceptable traits to non-questioning:

- When the vehicle stalls, no-one asks why, what has happened? The driver simply gets out and fixes it, and we move on. And when we are stopped by the police, no-one asks 'Why?' The driver gets out and shows his papers, and we stay in the car ("It's unwise to get out") and wait. We wait for an unidentified length of time, for an unidentified reason, until we are told to move on.

- Occasionally a pastor is asked by an outsider "Why did the people do that?" The answer is always "It's tradition, we've got to do it."

- A wonderful non-West incident: as each item in a day's program is altered, in the typically flexible way, I would be informed: 'You just stay here and relax. I won't tell you when I shall be back because that would give you too much suspense. You eat and rest and prepare yourself for the meeting and when the time is ready I will return to fetch you.' What happens, happens.

Addenda Notes

12. The High Ground

Identity cards have been abandoned, and it is now against the law to enquire professionally about the ethnic origins of an individual.

The notion of leveling all individual accounts of grievance is extraordinarily potent. A sort of equalising of need, hard to put into words. Ordinarily, and largely due to today's culture of individualism, we are acutely aware of the wrongs done to us by others. We are all riddled with our own ideas of our 'rights' and 'dues', leading into a consciousness of each infringement of our own personal requirements. We take note of, and often keep an on-going account of, what we see as being personal injustices and harassments and wounds. Added to that, we learn that things for which we can claim damages are a valuable and rightful source of compensation. It seems that in the modern world hurt can be converted into cash.

What is being shown in Rwanda is that where the will and the courage are available, it is feasible to set all 'righteous' grievances to one side, in order to reach a place where we can see the affects they have on the other. And then a strange thing happens: we begin to see the similarities between my needs and the needs of the other.

> At one of the foremost prisons in Great Britain, special work done in restorative justice has dug deep and discovered issues that resonate with what has been happening in Rwanda. They have found that what a hurt individual needs to know is something more buried than anger. It is something much deeper and more difficult to access. To address it calls for compassion and patience and dedication. It is something about how I see my own victimhood, and how this can be put next to how the other sees their victimhood. If I can come to some understanding of how my actions affected you, and what they meant to you, it will start to unravel the whole process of the harm. The person on each side of the injury can touch into a new realization about what happened and why it happened. Each person involved may come to sense their own part in the incident, and consequently want to contribute to the way of regaining what has been lost. Both sides will want to take part in restoring relationships that are more tolerable.

The almost superhuman levels of mutual acceptance that are being demonstrated in Rwanda have also been experienced in individuals exploring this sort of restorative justice. Coming to terms with who I am and the levels of atrocity of which I am capable - together with who you are and of what you are capable - goes hand-in-hand with an acknowledgment of the fantasies of revenge that have affected them. The fundamentals of 'rights' and 'grievances' melt as both parties to the event agree that what happened wasn't meant to happen in the way it happened, and then think through the grief for the loss of whatever it was.

From this, an astounding state of mutual self-forgiveness and other-forgiveness can germinate; when it is matched with the will to start again with a different pattern of understanding, new life can begin.

It can happen at the personal level, and as in Rwanda on levels that are political and social. Is it applicable to other times and places, peoples and nations?

For further discussion see

Robert Beckford; God of the Rahid: redeeming rage. 2001, DLT London. ISBN 0-232-52331-2.
Brian Frost; Struggling to Forgive: Nelson Mandela and South Africa's search for reconciliation. 1998, Harper Collins, London. ISBN 0-00-274002-8.
Mary Grey; The Outrageous Pursuit of Hope. 2000, DLT, London. ISBN 0-232-52319-3.

Postscript

Of course there are many thousands in prison who are properly awaiting trial for instigating and perpetuating the genocide.

This notion of simply returning to 'the old ways' in a stupor of nostalgia is of course insufficient in itself, but it needs to be incorporated in the future vision of the country. The urgent danger is that ancient ways will be dismantled as a result of industrial influences and commercial encouragement from us in the West, in order to misguidedly ape our lifestyle. Perhaps we need to publicise our failures too!

CONCLUSION

Obviously, I have no idea if my visits made any difference to their lives. What I do know is the difference they have made to mine. If only we could learn from Rwanda, as she re-learns herself. And I pray, with the Bishop who prayed with me "God, help us to trust that You're there, keeping at it. Amen."

Addenda Notes

This doesn't mean, of course, that we have only a hope of future joys: we can be full of joy here and now even in our trials and troubles. Taken in the right spirit these very things will give us patient endurance; this in turn will develop a mature character, and a character of this sort produces a steady hope, a hope that will never disappoint us. Already we have some experience of God flooding through our hearts by the Holy Spirit given to us.

Romans 5:3-5. Trans J.B. Phillips

A FABLE FOR OUR TIME

In Place of a Booklist

In speaking of fable, strict historical accuracy is irrelevant. In telling the story of the hare and the tortoise, who wants to know the exact place and time of the race?

But for those readers who want to expand their knowledge of Rwanda itself, the following are seminal books, each with an extended booklist of their own. They are listed below in chronological order.

John V. Taylor: *The Primal Vision*, SCM Press, London 1963.
      Re-issued 2001   ISBN 0-334-02837-X
Fergal Keane: *Season of Blood - a Rwandan Journey.* Viking/Penguin,
      London 1995   ISBN 0-14-024760-2
Antoine Rutayisire: *Faith under Fire: Testimonies of Christian Bravery.*
      African Enterprise, Essex, 1995   ISBN 0-9529312-0-6
Philip Gourevitch: *'We wish to inform you that tomorrow we will be
      killed with our families' – stories from Rwanda*, Picador,
      New York 1999   ISBN 0-330-37120-7
Martin Conway: *Journeying Together Towards Jubilee: the World
      Council of Churches meets in it's 8th and 50th Anniversary. Assembly
      in Zimbabwe*, Dec 1998. Oxford 1999
Barbara Kingsolver: *The Poisenwood Bible*, Faber & Faber,
      London 1999   ISBN 0-571-20175-X
L. R. Melvern: *A People Betrayed: the role of the West in Rwanda's
      Genocide*, Zed Books. London, 2001   ISBN 1-85649-831-X
Rowan Williams: *Writing in the Dust*, Hodder & Stoughton, London,
      2002   ISBN 0-340-78719-8

ACKNOWLEDGEMENTS

The scheme of this book is sufficiently unusual that I needed to gather confirmation from others that it 'worked'! Personal friends and those professional in producing books were both asked for advice, and the following is a list, in chronological order, of the people who were kind enough to spend time with the draft. To all of them I owe a debt of great gratitude for their generosity of time and comment; I learnt from each and every one of them and if the reader finds the story smooth going it will largely be due to them.

Ann Coggan   Christine Smith   Jim Cotter   Tessa Till
Teresa de Bertandano   Brigid Pailthorpe   Trina Rankin
Bishop Michael and Lou Scott-Joynt   Kay Kershaw   Morag Reeve
Valerie Makin   Jane and Peter Mason   Canon Barney Milligan

Plus, of course, my professional co-workers: Barbara Butler, Robert and Belinda Hunt, and Phoebe Roman. I am extremely grateful to Archbishop Rowan Williams for his very gracious Foreword.

Especially, I want to voice my appreciation to those people who enabled my empathy with Rwanda:
- to the invitation of Archbishop Emmanuel Kolini and his wife Mme. Frieda, and also to her parents;
- to the patience, tolerance and inspiration of my guide, mentor, and friend, the Rev'd Agnes Mukandoli;
- to the care of those I knew as Emmanuel, Samuel, Sonja, Dorothee, Dorothy, Console, and the Rwandan women who hosted me in Byumba; to Marie-Claire and all those many people I met through her; to Esther, Immanuel and Patrick.
- to Robert, Patrick, and to Charles and Juliette and the hospitality of many pastors and their families in the diocese of Cyangugu.

Acknowledgements

Members of the church hierarchy wonderfully taught me and were tender with my questioning. They were:
Bishop Ken and Jill Barham, my very first contacts and teachers;
Bishop Onesphore and Josephine Rwaje of Byumba;
Bishop John and Harriet Rucyahana of Ruhengeri;
Bishop Augustin and Virgine Mvunabandi of Kigeme; and
Bishop Geoffrey and Mary Rwubusisi of Cyangugu.

Perhaps, most of all, my personal tribute is at its deepest towards those many, many women who opted to tell me their stories. If readers have been moved to a fraction of what these women did for me, this book will not have been produced in vain. Thank you.

Wanda Nash

Globalizati...

Internation...

ONE WEEK LOAN

Globalization and International Relations Theory

Ian Clark

OXFORD
UNIVERSITY PRESS

OXFORD
UNIVERSITY PRESS

Great Clarendon Street, Oxford OX2 6DP

Oxford University Press is a department of the University of Oxford.
It furthers the University's objective of excellence in research, scholarship,
and education by publishing worldwide in

Oxford New York

Auckland Cape Town Dar es Salaam Hong Kong Karachi Kuala Lumpur
Madrid Melbourne Mexico City Nairobi New Delhi Shanghai Taipei Toronto

With offices in

Argentina Austria Brazil Chile Czech Republic France Greece
Guatemala Hungary Italy Japan South Korea Poland Portugal
Singapore Switzerland Thailand Turkey Ukraine Vietnam

Oxford is a registered trade mark of Oxford University Press
in the UK and in certain other countries

Published in the United States
by Oxford University Press Inc., New York

British Library Cataloguing in Publication Data

Data available

Library of Congress Cataloging in Publication Data
Clark, Ian, 1949–
Globalization and international relations theory / Ian Clark.
Includes bibliographical references.
1. International relations 2. World politics. I. Title.
JZ1305.C49 1999 327.1´01–dc21 99-21478

ISBN 978-0-19-878209-4

10 9 8 7

Typeset by Hope Services (Abingdon) Ltd.
Printed in Great Britain
on acid-free paper by
Biddles Ltd., King's Lynn, Norfolk

To Janice once more

CONTENTS

DETAILED CONTENTS

PREFACE

This book has developed directly out of its predecessor *Globalization and Fragmentation* (Clark 1997). That earlier work was an attempt to historicize globalization and to 'put the state back in', while not simply succumbing to a revamped realism. By employing a number of devices, such as corporatism, it sought to argue that the ebb and flow of both globalization and fragmentation could be linked to powerful shifts in domestic balances of social forces, and consequent transformations in the social functions of states. These, in turn, both reflected and impacted upon new configurations of inter-state relations. The core argument was intended to politicize the analysis of globalization and thereby to rescue it from the banalities of economic and technological determinism that threatened to engulf it.

Within its own historical terms, I am broadly satisfied that it served its purpose. However, even before the work was completed, it became painfully obvious to me that, in certain respects, it was considerably under-theorized. For potential readers of a historical bent, this was no doubt a redeeming virtue. It was also a practical necessity to accommodate, without undue distractions, the historical analysis that was its principal *raison d'être*. But this demanded that a large number of theoretical issues had to be passed over, either in silence or with only token treatment accorded to them. In passing, for example, the book (Clark 1997: 5–6, 201) highlights the deficiencies of neo-realism as being unable to account for globalization within the dualistic theoretical frame of reference it chooses to deploy. Unfortunately, that argument could not be pursued in any detail and hence the opportunity was missed to develop the many related ways in which an analysis of globalization impacts upon the manner in which we theorize about international relations.

The present study is an effort to fill some of these theoretical gaps and is, in that sense, an integral part of the former exercise. In retrospect, if not in original conception, the two books should be read as the elaboration of a single and sustained argument, albeit that the burden of the first is heavily historical, whereas that of the present is predominantly theoretical. It is the hope that both parts of the argument will serve to complement each other.

A number of debts have been incurred in the writing of this book and I am delighted to acknowledge them here. My move to the Department of International Politics at Aberystwyth has placed me in a most congenial and stimulating intellectual environment that has helped me to think my way through this ambitious project. Its speedy completion was, in turn, largely due to a period of sabbatical leave granted by the University of Wales Aberystwyth. I am grateful both to the Department (especially its Head, Steve Smith, and its Director of Research, Colin McInnes) and to the College authorities, for making this possible. The work has been considerably improved by the suggestions of the anonymous readers for Oxford University Press, and I am indebted to them. I particularly acknowledge the helpful comments of Richard Devetak at Warwick University. In addition, individual sections have benefited from the comments of many of my departmental colleagues and I thank, in particular, Ken Booth, Tim Dunne, Nick Wheeler, Colin Wight, and Howard Williams. Toni Erskine, in Cambridge, kindly read a draft of Chapter 7. Parts of the argument appeared in an earlier version in 'Beyond the Great Divide: Globalization and the Theory of International Relations', *Review of International Studies*, 24 (4), 1998.

This is the fifth of my books to be published by Oxford University Press. It would be extremely remiss of me not to use the opportunity to acknowledge the tremendous editorial support and encouragement I have enjoyed in my many years of dealing with the Press. Tim Barton inherited me a decade ago and has been a tireless campaigner on my behalf ever since. I remain permanently in his debt. Dominic Byatt was kind enough to respond enthusiastically at a critical moment to my first foray into this particular subject. I would also like to thank Angela Griffin and all other members of the OUP team for their friendly professionalism once again.

The book has been written in circumstances of unusual domestic dislocation. Janice has borne these with unfailing resilience and good humour. That I have been able to write it at all is testimony to the strength of her support. I dedicate it to her in loving appreciation.

I.C.
Aberystwyth and Llanarmon Dyffryn Ceiriog

INTRODUCTION

The title of this book might strike some readers as an oxymoron. If we accept that globalization is taking place, there cannot be, nor do we have any need of, a theory of international relations. Starting from the other end, if theorizing international relations is the core intellectual enterprise, this immediately casts doubt upon the claim to globalization. The tension appears acute for the very reason that, by most accounts, globalization takes us well beyond that world of self-contained states and their mutual relations with which the discipline of International Relations has been centrally preoccupied, if by no means exclusively so. The remainder of this book is an attempt to demonstrate that this seeming contradiction is more apparent than real, and that globalization and IR theory can profitably speak to each other.

During the past decade, there has been a proliferation of studies devoted to the general theme of globalization, so much so that it has become a highly visible sub-field encroaching in a major way upon the traditional terrain of International Relations. Indeed, it currently serves as the latest rallying cry for those who would pronounce the demise of International Relations and its replacement by world politics or global society.

Much of this writing, whatever its distinctive disciplinary orientation, addresses concerns that are relevant to the student of international relations. However, it does so incidentally rather than as its explicit intention. Moreover, the coverage tends to be partial and selective. There is no single volume that attempts to take stock of the range of writing on globalization, and to set out in detail its potential impact on the full spectrum of the IR theoretical agenda. It is the objective of this book to provide such coverage and to do so by developing a theoretical framework itself drawn from an understanding of the process of globalization.

Most of this writing is concerned to document the evidence for the existence of degrees of globalization, and then to explain both its causes and its various impacts. It is understandably seldom interested in globalization primarily for what it might reveal about theories of international relations. This is the task of the present volume. In that sense, it is a study of globalization at one remove, less preoccupied with the extent of, and evidence for, globalization as such and more so with the ways in which its occurrence might require adjustments to the theoretical apparatus of International Relations. While it does not take the case for globalization in any way for granted, it is less intent on making a direct contribution to the understanding of globalization for its own sake. That said, it is scarcely possible to do the one without devoting some attention to the other.

This book argues that globalization is a pervasively unsettling process which needs to be explained not only as an issue in its own right but for the insight which it affords into cognate areas of theory. In short, it advances an analytical model whereby globalization itself can be understood, and utilizes this as a theoretical scheme that may be applied more generally to other aspects of international relations. Above all, it seeks to move the discussion beyond the confines of much of the present debate. At the moment, the dominant tendency is to treat globalization as an external set of circumstances that constrains the autonomy of states. Substantively, as a result, the focus has been upon whether or not the state has been in retreat. Rather than participate in this particular debate, the present work sets out to reject the framework within which it has been located.

Globalization and IR theory

Because of core disagreements about the nature of globalization, its impact on IR theorizing can be understood in a number of different ways. To employ analytical schemes that are standard within the field, globalization may be thought to impact upon the nature of the actors, or upon the environment in which they find themselves; it may be transforming the processes of international life or its structures. For purposes of preliminary exposition, and by employing a conventional classification of theoretical approaches, the potential impact of globalization might be surveyed in terms of its meaning for realist, pluralist, and structuralist perspectives on the subject (Little and Smith 1991). This will be done with the intention of demonstrating why such a scheme is not suited to the analysis of globalization.

According to the first perspective, globalization would be seen to be transforming the processes of international relations by diminishing further its 'power and security' dimensions. By its very nature, globalization draws attention to the economic and technological aspects of life, and to deep-seated change at the level of culture or identity. In all such cases, the very emphasis on the global highlights the integrative aspects of social life, and thereby lessens the validity of any view of inter-state power politics as an autonomous sphere of activity.

Secondly, globalization might be regarded as an intensification of the pluralist challenge in that it draws attention to the variety of international and transnational actors. Because of its questioning of the relevance of inter-state borders, it seems to problematize further the primacy of states, and the idea of their unitary nature. Indeed, in some cases, it seems to question the ability of actors to 'act' at all. Much writing on globalization draws attention to the role of transnational corporations in creating a global market and system of production; to capital markets in creating an integrated financial system; and to bodies such as the

International Monetary Fund (IMF) in disseminating a particular view of the state's role within the international economy. In these various ways, globalization poses afresh the actor question in International Relations. As part of a pluralist paradigm, globalization may also be conceived as an intensification of the conditions of interdependence, with all the supposedly transformational associations that flow from such a condition.

Finally, globalization might be discussed as part of a redefined structuralist paradigm. At first glance, this would mean simply a reordering of the environment in which states operate. But just as much of the dominance/dependence literature, and world systems theory, argues that states are formed by their location within the capitalist world system, the significance of a structuralist perspective goes beyond that of environmental change alone. It projects a new era of state formation, as part of a quasi-deterministic account of the material system within which the state is generated. Equally, globalization might be viewed as giving rise to a refined structuralist framework of this kind.

In short, the exercise of locating globalization in contemporary IR theory appears, initially, merely to entail an assessment of the part of this theoretical scheme on which globalization has its most pronounced impact. Does it change the structures, the processes, or the actors of international relations? Accordingly, this book could have been organized on that basis with an unfolding investigation into each area in turn. This has been rejected for the simple reason that it would have resulted in an approach that was radically at odds with the core argument. It would, by necessity, have resulted in a *partial* analysis instead of a *holistic* approach. In turn, this would have missed what the book contends is the essential point to grasp about the nature of globalization, and hence about its theoretical implications.

Instead of resorting, *seriatim*, to such existing IR theoretical categories, the book poses a deeper form of question. Does globalization not call into question the very analytic schemes upon which such categories are themselves based? How much of the globalization challenge can IR theory incorporate within its existing schemes and still pretend that it is business as usual? Alternatively, does the study of globalization itself offer us a different approach that might be employed in other facets of IR theory? These matters will be explored in the following chapters.

The complex of issues associated with globalization already impinges on a number of areas of IR theory but the connection has often remained implicit and understated. This is so, for example, with regard to some fundamental problems within International Political Economy (IPE); the debate between neo-realism and neo-liberalism; and the central arguments of structural realism itself.

As regards IPE, globalization raises key questions about the relationship between the economic and political domains, and indeed about whether they can be so sharply distinguished. There is a latent theme in some of the literature that economic globalization will 'spill over' into the political, and that social and political organization will follow where the economic has already led. As against this, there is the well-established view—itself central to the liberal tradition—that the economic and the political are separate, and respond to differing dynamics. In the version made famous by Polanyi (1944), and now an icon within so much of the globalization discussion, the two are dialectically related as part of a 'double movement'. Politics exists as a corrective to the excesses of the free market and as a form of social protection. Implicit in this is the prognosis that there is no linear development of globalization, but that instead recent neo-liberal trends in economic policy will eventually be recontrolled by defensive political strategies. In this way, contested interpretations of globalization lie at the very heart of the most interesting controversies within IPE (Stubbs and Underhill 1994; Strange 1988).

Secondly, globalization is not normally called to give testimony in the exchanges between the neo-realists and the neo-liberals. And yet its testimony appears highly pertinent. This familiar debate is essentially about whether—in framing explanations of outcomes—the international structure can do all the work, about what is to be included within the structure, and about the extent to which institutional density alters definitions of interests (Keohane 1986). Even in these limited terms, there is a fair case to be made for including globalization within the discussion. How does globalization compare with the effects of interdependence? What impact does it have on state interests and the prospects for cooperation? Does it compel a reconsideration of the nature of international anarchy?

Thirdly, and by direct extension, globalization goes to the heart of the analysis offered by structural realism, as globalization might be understood to mean simply a redefinition of the international structure. As will be seen in due course, there are indeed, approaches to globalization that do interpret it as a reconfiguration of anarchy. Since anarchy is taken to be the principal structural constraint upon state behaviour, any reshaping of it would then portend important theoretical shifts across the field as a whole. Globalization, in this way, has the theoretical capacity to challenge key aspects of neo-realism.

In each of these areas, respectively, the potentially unsettling theoretical effects of globalization can be discerned. All such claims, however, seem to rest upon some posited distinction between globalization as part of a changing structure, and the state that is then left to find its way as best it can. In fact, it will be argued in the next chapter that globalization stands as a challenge *in toto* to all the analytical schemes that rely upon a separation of this kind. This book works towards a fundamental reconceptualization of the state–globalization relationship. This, in turn, provides the basis for the discussion of other aspects of IR theory.

The emerging literature about globalization is characterized by marked diversity, and its nature and scope will be reviewed below. However, as a broad introductory generalization, it can be said that it is very much engaged in a debate about the retreat or resilience of the state. In some accounts, the impact of globalization is thought to lie in the progressive incapacity of the state to manage its own affairs; according to others, the process of globalization has been wrought by state action and continues to be sustained by it. Viewed in these polarized terms, the state is either the object or the subject of globalization.

The argument to be developed in this book seeks to avoid this stark choice by suggesting the mutually constitutive relationship between globalization and the state, within which change occurs in both. It will be demonstrated that this interpretation emerges from an analysis of the historical process of globalization, and that the resulting framework is the most satisfactory way in which to think about the topic. Such an approach is not intended to diminish the significance of globalization—it is not yet another empirical defence of 'the primacy of the state'—but instead is a plea for an adjusted analytical framework which eschews some of the more misleading political representations of globalization.

To avoid an unduly abstract account at this stage, we can begin to establish such a framework by examination of a specific historical period. The end of the cold war serves as a convenient illustration. Much of the debate about the aftermath of the cold war proceeded as an investigation into the polarity of the emerging international structure, construed as the distribution of capabilities amongst the principal actors. But this remained an exceptionally narrow, and largely unenlightening, focus of enquiry. It lacked that wider perspective which would have recognized that both domestic and international changes were taking place, and were inextricably interwoven. The extent to which the end of the cold war represented a major transition derived, in consequence, from this mutual enmeshment and from the multiple layers into which the cold war structure itself had penetrated. This is the thrust of one historian's insightful claim: 'Precisely because the cold war was an order, a settlement that integrated international relations, the framework of the world economy, and domestic political arrangements, its passing is of truly world-historic significance' (Cronin 1996: 238). What this suggests is that the 'domestic' is as much a part of the fabric of the international system as any abstracted 'structure' of the relations between states. Accordingly, if we seek to make sense of the post-cold war world, we cannot do so by dissociating changes in the international system from the purportedly separate changes in domestic state forms. It is precisely in the synergy between the two that the dynamic of change is to be located. Concisely expressed, the change induced by the end of the cold war lies in the nature of the accommodation between 'domestic' and 'transnational' forces, rather than in the specifics of either. The change is *relational* to both rather than *particular* to either.

By extension, it would be a distortion to address the impacts of globalization upon each of these areas separately and in isolation from each other. An alternative framework is required. Instead, it will be suggested that what is challenged by globalization is the *interconnection* between these various elements as a whole, rather than any one component on its own. Without question, and as will be argued in detail below, the cold war order was one in which there was a remarkable interpenetration between the international and domestic spheres, such that 'international' stability was predicated on measures that had been taken to ensure increased levels of 'domestic' stability. In this sense, the international and the domestic became truly mutually supportive. When we speak of the resulting order, it must be understood to embrace both.

It might be objected that this has always been the case in terms of the formalities of the international system, wherein the state derives impressive legitimacy internally from its external membership of a wider system predicated on principles of sovereignty and non-intervention. However, this creates the linkage in formal, not substantive, terms. What was distinctive about the settlement after 1945 was that this mutual reinforcement went beyond the formal principles of the system to include also the substance of policy. States—at least those within the extended Atlantic community—and the international system created each other in their own changing images, both characterized by higher levels of government intervention, planning, management of the economy, and provision of welfare. These became (variable) elements of domestic policy, but also practices of the international system as well, albeit to a lesser extent.

Could it then be that it is this mutuality, rather than the state itself, which is threatened by globalization? An attractive version of this argument has been developed by John Ruggie, and his work is central in much of the following discussion. In Ruggie's analysis, it is exactly the international/domestic trade-off that is destabilized by changes in one part of the international system, namely the international economy. The consequence of this is that the economy has become increasingly 'disembedded from the domestic social compact between state and society' which had been the foundation stone of the multi-level stability engineered after 1945 (Ruggie 1995: 525). What is so instructive about this presentation of the issue is that it draws our attention to the integration of the domestic and the international, and to the political accommodation between them. This suggests the outline of the framework to be developed throughout the remainder of this book.

Globalization and the 'production' of international relations

Although the concept of globalization will be reviewed more fully in Chapter 2, the following remarks need to be made at the outset. Globalization, it will be argued, is not itself a substantive activity or area of human behaviour, either material or mental. Instead, it is a quality, condition, or form that such behaviour or activity might take. Accordingly, the focus of interest within this volume is the sum of activities involved in international relations, and globalization will be examined for the effect that it has upon their quality, condition, or form. In that sense, the discussion of globalization in these pages is conducted as a means to an analytical end—an assessment of how much, and in what ways, globalization demands change in IR theory—rather than as an end in itself. Although it is to be hoped that this volume will enhance our understanding of globalization, that is not its principal objective.

The methodology of this study will then be to create what might be called an analytical template for globalization which, when developed, can be superimposed upon key areas of IR theorizing. When this is done, it will be possible to demonstrate how various, seemingly disparate, debates actually have a great deal in common with each other. As a result, we should also be able to develop a better understanding of each topic individually precisely because of the common framework that has been generated. What is it that might be changing about state performance on economic, security, and ethical matters and why are conceptions of its democratic structure under challenge? Why is the notion of sovereignty so deeply contested and how, if at all, are all of these issue-areas interconnected? The answers to these questions have much to tell us about a range of topics currently under intense scrutiny within the discipline.

The approach might be illustrated by a simple analogy. Various industries or services engage in distinctive spheres of human activity, such as the running of railways, the production of coal, and the generation of electricity. Within the UK in recent years, these industries or services have been privatized. This does not mean that all these activities have become the same. It means only that these activities, formerly nationalized, operate within an altered legal, financial, and regulatory structure and that they now have this much (more or less) in common. In the same way, this study will concentrate upon discrete areas of IR activity, but through the unifying lens of the (more or less) common condition of globalization within which each is now conducted. However, the analogy is most revealing precisely where it breaks down. To the extent that these industries have been transformed, this has been because of the context of privatization and the new 'external' regulatory environment in which they have been placed. Privatization recasts the units of production, as it were, from without. Globalization, by contrast, is more than a framework imposed from the outside: it is also an outgrowth of the restructuring of the industry of international relations from the inside.

The literature on economic globalization tends to argue that systems of global production have radically altered the world economy, especially as far as its units of production are concerned. For presentational purposes, this book will look at the state as a unit of production operating in new circumstances. It will review metaphorically the provision of a variety of 'goods and services' in which the state is currently engaged—sovereignty, economic management, security, 'the good life', and democracy—and assess how its productive capacity has changed under the new conditions of globalization. By extension, it will be argued that globalization is not merely a context in which the state operates but a new form that it takes. The focus then shifts to the *globalized state* as a single unit of analysis, rather than upon globalization and the state as two distinct fields of intellectual enquiry.

The problem, of course, is that there is little agreement within the literature about the essential qualities of the condition of globalization, let alone about the extent to which such qualities have actually emerged in the world. As will be seen, substantial arguments are going on about what globalization 'means', about its causes, its historical lineage, its empirical extent, its normative or ideological status, and its trajectory and potential for reversibility. And yet in spite of these uncertainties, there is nevertheless a pervasive impression that this much-contested globalization is reshaping the provision of a number of 'goods and services' thought central to the discipline of IR: the production of sovereignty; the production of economic goods and welfare; the production of security; the production of normative community and identity; and, finally, the production of good democratic practice. The discussion of each of these topics, during the past decade, has been carried on in the shadow of globalization. But is it possible to construct an agreed template about globalization that, while emphasizing what all these functional areas have in common, also throws each into relief in an illuminating way?

Given the intensity of the disagreements about globalization, it is unlikely that such a template can simply take the form of an agreed definition, and such a solution will be eschewed. If for no other reason, this dissension partly reflects the emergence of globalization as a topic of study within distinct disciplinary settings—sociology, economics, International Political Economy, cultural and communication studies, geography, political science, and International Relations, to name a few. Each of these disciplinary perspectives brings its own agenda to bear in such a way that common ground is difficult to establish. A single definition is unlikely to travel well between these disciplines. Accordingly, the strategy to be pursued in this book is to develop a template which says less about the substantive evidence for globalization and which focuses instead upon those social and political dynamics that, historically, have accompanied its development. In particular, these derive from the subsumption of both the domestic and the international domains within a single field of political forces. This generic quality of globalization can then be set against the various dimensions of IR theory and the latter re-examined to take it into account.

Whichever way globalization is conceived, it has major implications for our understanding of International Relations. At the very least, some of the globalization literature makes the claim that the 'space' between states is being transformed (or eliminated) and that, as a result, what is taken to be the *international* is itself being radically redefined. Elsewhere, the concentration is less upon the changing environment in which states find themselves and more upon a reconstitution of the states: globalization does not merely change the context of state action but transforms the essential nature of the state itself. In such accounts, even if we continue to have inter-state relations, we have relations between different kinds of state. Either way, it must be readily apparent that these debates have immense implications for the way we approach and define the subject of International Relations.

Globalization and states

No doubt some readers will think it strange—not to say perverse—to devote so much attention to the state in a book about globalization. We are told that, across the social sciences collectively, the intellectual fashion is for 'a new era of "state denial" ' (Weiss 1998: 2). Given that the bulk of the globalization literature calls into question existing territorial concepts of politics, of which the state is the paramount instance, it must seem counter-intuitive to present much of the argument, as below, with such a sharp focus on the state.

This, however, should not be misconstrued as some revivalist state-centric account of the discipline. The reason for the emphasis on the state is that, if the globalization thesis is compelling, then it is in the functioning of the state that its transformative effects will become most readily apparent. Nor should this be taken to imply that globalization affects states alone. Any such claim would be preposterous. Globalization impinges, both positively and negatively, on a whole range of social movements and actors. We can readily admit the claim that 'contemporary world society cannot be meaningfully understood—nor can it be effectively regulated—as if it constituted only the sum total of those activities originating within states and which states can control as between themselves' (Poggi 1990: 183). Even so, Poggi concedes that states remain '*the* political protagonists' and the degree of their continuing viability provides the best measure on offer of the presence of globalization. Hence, by examination of the state, the consequences of globalization can be traced and measured. The focus on the state is thus a means to an end rather than an argument about the primacy of the state as such. Succinctly expressed, we need to concentrate upon the state since that is the principal site of globalization. Additionally, however, the moot question is whether globalization alone induces a reconstruction of the state, or whether it is the reconstruction of the state that, reciprocally, gives globalization its historical opportunity and character.

For the moment, it can be suggested that IR theory engages with globalization within two types of broad context. The first might loosely be described as globalization and the theory of states. The parameters of this discussion are the extent to which globalization is itself interwoven with, and reflective of, the major trends and events of international history. By way of illustration, and as previously argued (Clark 1997), globalization can be understood to be, at least partly, a function of the play of international politics and is variously encouraged or impeded by the balance of power and the clash of ideologies. Events such as the World Wars, the Depression, decolonization, the Cold War and its end—all have left their traces on the ebb and flow of globalization. This is not to argue that international relations is an autonomous realm and that globalization is the creature of a hermetically sealed set of international activities. It can be readily accepted that international relations is open to 'deeper' forces of economic, social, and technological change but that these are still, to some extent, mediated through the play of inter-state activities.

The other predominant conceptualization of the issue within International Relations might be referred to as globalization and the theory of the state. From this angle, the debate has been structured between the proponents of state redundancy versus the champions of continuing state potency. In turn, these arguments rest upon an image of the capacity of states being eroded by external (globalizing) forces, or alternatively, of external (globalizing) forces being generated by state action. In either case, there is the assumed duality of the state(s) set off from, and ranged against, a seemingly external environment. Instead, the present argument is that the state occupies a *middle position* between the internal and external and is itself both shaped by, and formative of, the process of globalization.

The following illustration may be helpful. Numerous writers point out that sovereignty represents both a set of domestic political arrangements and a set of principles of international order, which are mutually reinforcing and mutually redefining (Giddens 1985: 263–4). Within a changing international order, it would follow, it is possible to think of sovereignty as being transformed rather than eroded (Sassen 1996a: 30). The transformation takes place, as it were, on both fronts. In the same way, it is instructive that we regard globalization not as the mere environment in which states find themselves but as an element within the (shifting) identity of the state itself (Armstrong 1998: 476). If this argument is allowed with respect to globalization specifically, what might be its more general import for theorizing within the field?

There are a number of areas within IR theory which have been undergoing substantial repositioning for a number of years, mostly related to the more permeable nature of the territorial state. These have questioned the idea of a national economy (within IPE), the viability of the state as provider of security (within security studies), the moral identity of the state (within normative IR theory), and the sustainability of democratic institutions on a territorial state basis (within political theory). Generically, this has raised questions about the utility of the notion of sovereignty, or about the extent to which it is now obsolete. The issue of globalization permeates all these problems, and is to varying degrees portrayed as the cause of them. It follows that the manner in which we debate them is very much dependent upon our conception of globalization itself. At the same time, the way in which the processes of globalization are analysed may provide us with a model for moving forward along a broad theoretical front. While each separate issue-area carries its own substantive agenda, they collectively share common analytical frameworks. If globalization compels us to revise the underlying framework of existing approaches to the subject, it should assist us to think anew about the spectrum of issues on the IR theory agenda.

According to one definition, globalization 'refers broadly to the process whereby power is located in global social formations and expressed through global networks rather than through territorially-based states' (Thomas 1997: 6). This formulation emphasizes the antinomy between state and globalization. Rather than approach these issues from within such a dichotomized state-versus-external-forces perspective, this book argues instead that they can be better understood as denoting a reconstitution of the state within the vortex of social forces that surround and suffuse it. Indeed, the very progress of globalization demonstrates this transformation at work. This is the core of Cerny's claim that globalization 'is a *domestic* as well as a transnational and international process' (1996c: 91).

If this can be understood in relation to globalization in general, it should also assist us in thinking about specific areas of state activity. These will be surveyed at length in the book and require only a preliminary exposition at this stage. For example, there are a number of issues within normative theory that continue to be addressed within familiar structured polarities, such as particularism and universalism, or communitarianism and cosmopolitanism. The relevance of the above analysis of globalization to these normative concerns is that it begins to move us away from the notion that those categories are fixed and static, and towards the idea that their content might be shifting: what is particular at any one moment in time is fluid in its relationship to what is universal. This is akin to Linklater's argument about the fluidity of community. 'Too little is known', he feels, 'about the ways in which communities come to be bounded and distinct from one another and too little is known about how boundedness and separateness change over time' (Linklater 1995: 183). Adapting Walzer's (1994) terminology, we might then argue that normative theory is not a dialogue between two settled categories of the 'thick' (embedded in the state) and the 'thin' (challenging from outside). Rather, the two are engaged in endless mutual adjustment that constantly redefines the state itself. Just as the state (as national economy) is re-created by internal and external forces of economic globalization, so the normative state is pushed and pulled by the fluid interaction between shifting degrees of cohesion, domestically and internationally. Symptomatically, it has been suggested that such quintessentially 'thick' conceptions as those of citizenship and national systems of rights are themselves in process of transformation. As Sassen remarks, the 'latest bundle of rights that came with the welfare state does not constitute the ultimate definition' (1996*a*: xiii; see also 96–7). Hutchings has attacked the 'logic of the mutual exclusiveness of particularity and universality' (1996: 129) from the perspective of ethical contextualism. This book attacks it on the basis that particularism and universalism penetrate the state as shifting categories, not as reified or static bodies of normative thought, and that they therefore have the capacity to reshape the state accordingly.

The contemporary discussions of democratization provide another telling illustration. In common parlance, democratization refers to the spread of democratic forms to individual 'national' political systems. However, within the context of globalization, the much more interesting question concerns the potential for democratization of those capacities that might be seen to have leaked out of the individual states into the transnational or non-territorial spheres. Accordingly, the contradiction that is commonly depicted is that between systems of authority governed by democratic procedures, and those globalized activities that operate outside the ambit of any democratic surveillance. This is the nub of Scholte's observation that 'contemporary globalizing capital presents a challenge not to the survival of states, but to the realization of democracy' (1997: 452). Similarly, the point has been made that 'the contradiction between the emergence of a clear preference for democracy in national political units and the lack of means to ensure accountability in world markets is a central feature of world restructuring' (Mittelman 1997: 79).

But as any number of commentators has testified, the problem cannot be solved simply by extending 'domestic' democratic practices to multilateral activities, not least because many areas of globalized activity lack any observable institutional form, or seem remote from any political control (Zurn 1995: 156). The problem then for political theory is not that of fitting the existing off-the-peg democratic state into a changing external environment, but rather that of conceptualizing the changed nature of the democratized state in conditions of globalization.

Organization

The book is organized on the following lines. Chapter 1 begins by suggesting that much theorizing within the field of IR rests upon an implicit Great Divide between the internal and the external, or between the domestic and the international. Within such a framework, the state is thought to embody the internal and, thus constituted, to embark upon external activities. The international system may subsequently present a constraint upon its behaviour, but it is not the source of the state's identity in the first place. It will be demonstrated that such an initial framework is deeply misleading and has pervasive, and unhelpful, consequences for the way in which we think about the subject. Chapter 2 will then review the burgeoning literature on globalization to establish the extent to which it further destabilizes many existing theoretical assumptions. While by no means accepting all the claims of the globalization literature, the chapter acknowledges that there is a case to be answered.

If we are to achieve a clear appreciation of the impact of globalization upon IR theory, then it seems obvious that the place to begin is from within an historical interpretation of the phenomenon of globalization itself. An insight into the dynamics of globalization will, in turn, shed light upon the manner in which it unsettles the accepted categories of IR theory. Accordingly, Chapter 3 will seek to establish a theoretical framework for comprehending globalization. It repositions the state away from a view of it as the mere embodiment of the 'internal', the 'communitarian', or the 'particularistic'—as if these were static in content—and towards an understanding of it as historically dynamic. Part of this dynamism derives from the state's reinvention of itself in the face of challenges both from within and without. This position recognizes a transformational logic shaped by the interplay with the 'external', the 'cosmopolitan', and the 'universalistic'.

With this theoretical framework in place, it will then be the task of the remaining chapters to apply it to a range of issues that are central to IR theory. The point of this exercise will be to demonstrate how a modified initial set of theoretical assumptions can develop new and revealing ways of thinking about well-worn topics. Chapter 4 will deal with the aggregate of issues under the heading of the sovereign state. Chapter 5 will illustrate how this logic plays itself out from the perspective of International Political Economy by discussing the debate about the nature of the competition state.

However, this is in a sense the easiest stage of the argument. Successive phases in the evolution of IR theory have engendered disagreements about the extent to which the substance of international relations has been transformed by changing economic and material realities. In the 1970s, discussion focused upon the implications of interdependence, whereas in the 1980s attention moved to the effects of regimes and the new institutionalism. Of course, the standard response to these arguments has been that, however important that evidence might be for understanding economic or functional aspects of international life, this affects only low politics. It does not impinge upon security issues and the high politics agenda. We have thus been left with the somewhat sterile debate as to whether or not the essentially anarchical condition of international life has been changed, and whether the prospects for co-operative behaviour have been improved as a result (Baldwin 1993).

The issue underlying these debates is whether economic/functional change is representative of other areas as well, or whether it should be regarded as the exception that proves the rule. Accordingly, much of the transnationalism/interdependence argumentation of the early 1970s was attacked by a reassertion of the prominence of the state, and by an appeal to the continuing exceptionalism of high politics. Whatever might be said of low politics, this was thought not to encroach on core state activities in the sphere of security, and hence of sovereignty.

Similar perspectives underlie the discussion of globalization. While some commentators are happy to acknowledge that the processes of globalization continue apace in various economic and functional areas, they make a distinction between this and the mainly political spheres where globalization is thought to have made fewer inroads. Indeed, attention is frequently drawn to the increasing disjunction between the economic (material) domain, and the domain of the political (identity).

To some, the economic is indeed the exception and it is asserted that it functions in accordance with its own logic: politics, however, marches to a different drum. To others, the issue is rather one about the variable velocities towards globalization or, otherwise expressed, one of sectoral time-lags. From this point of view, globalization is most marked in the realms of communications technology and financial movements; it is less so in the realms of production, social life, and value systems; organized political life lags yet further behind those other areas. But it makes a world of difference whether we are to construe the leading edges of globalization as the trend-setters of tomorrow, or rather as the exceptions that are more likely to reinforce than transform the traditional contours of political life.

In short, if an alternative theoretical framework is to be helpful as a more general tool of IR theory, it must be able to deliver the goods beyond the realm of the economic alone. This is all the more so given the economistic nature of much of the globalization literature. What then needs to be established is that globalization is a process extending into domains apart from the economic. Accordingly, the remaining chapters will discuss a variety of state attributes and functional activities. The rubric of globalization, and the analytical framework associated with it, can then be used to revisit a series of debates in IR theory. These will be addressed in Chapters 6–8 under the summary headings of the security, normative, and democratic state. Collectively, this survey covers a representative sample of the key areas currently of concern to IR theory. It demonstrates how common analytical issues lie at the heart of each, and also suggests a possible way forward in discussing them.

Globalization has become too prominent a topic of scholarly analysis, and of public rhetoric, to ignore. At the same time, there has been a strong tendency to present it as an alternative to thinking about international relations. The hope of this book is that it may make a small beginning to a more constructive engagement between the two.

THE GREAT DIVIDE

The notion of a Great Divide provides a pervasive framework for theorizing within International Relations and lies at the heart of its claim to being a separate academic discipline. One survey has recently summarized its basis:

Domestic society and the international system are demonstrably different. The latter is a competitive anarchy where formally similar states rely on self-help and power bargaining to resolve conflict. Domestic society (not system) is, by contrast, rule-based. (Caporaso 1997: 564)

This points to empirical differences between the two distinct realms: we can describe the respective political processes taking place from what we know about the differing structural conditions that prevail in each. It also, by its appeal to society and rule-based behaviour, posits a normative distinction as well: there is a value difference between the separate domains. In normative theory, this Divide is accordingly reproduced in the debate between communitarian and cosmopolitan perspectives, the former resting on the principle that values are grounded in the 'domestic' constituency (state, *polis*, community, citizens) whereas the latter makes 'external' appeal to universal rights and values attaching to humankind. These and similar schemes abound in the literature but find cogent expression, for example, in C. Brown (1992) and Linklater (1982). Otherwise expressed, the division between the *polis* and the *cosmopolis* manifests itself in what Walker takes to be a fundamental contradiction. 'Inside the particular state', he suggests, 'concepts of obligation, freedom, and justice could be articulated within the context of universalist accounts . . . Yet these claims to universal values and processes presumed . . . a boundary beyond which such universals could not be guaranteed' (1990: 165).

A house divided?

Thus the Great Divide encapsulates a profound series of assumptions about the radically differing empirical and normative provenances of the international and the domestic. But what happens to this framework when it is asked to incorporate tendencies towards globalization? In what follows, it will be demonstrated that globalization challenges head-on the claim to structurally differentiated behaviour in the two fields. If it did not do so, it could reasonably be concluded that globalization is bereft of much of the substantive content claimed for it by its proponents. One might say that the validating test for globalization is precisely its success in eroding those separations on which the Great Divide has hitherto been predicated. If it fails to do so, we might legitimately dispense with globalization as a concept, at least as far as International Relations is concerned.

Unease with the Great Divide is by no means new. At least since Kant, writers have felt uncomfortable with the assumptions on which its separations are based. The argument of these pages is that the concept of globalization requires that the Great Divide be overcome and also offers a theoretical strategy for doing so. It will be shown that globalization poses fresh challenges to the normative agenda by unsettling the facile distinction between the many instantiations of the universal and the particular on which so much existing IR theory depends. One of the salient characteristics of globalization is precisely the manner in which it transcends or subsumes the separation between the internal and the external political realms. If this is what globalization does, then it provides an analytical template that can indeed take us beyond the Great Divide.

It is in this sense that Kapstein (1994: 5) is right to insist that globalization of the world economy 'poses a major challenge . . . to students of international relations'. The question is how radical this challenge is, and we are faced with the choice of either abandoning traditional conceptions of International Relations altogether, or redefining them in such a way as to accommodate the changes that are taking place. Strange sketches the argument for abandonment: 'The conventional rationale for the separate study of interstate politics and domestic politics disappears. Exit International Relations' (1997: 242). The alternative strategy, and the one advanced in this book, is to reformulate International Relations in such a way that it retains some purchase on the transformed nature of its subject matter.

The idea that International Relations is based on an assumed Great Divide is a fairly standard notion within the literature, as is the associated expression of dissatisfaction with this state of affairs. There is then no originality in yet another recitation of this situation. However, the chapter will not only document the existence of this division, but will also attempt to demonstrate how it structures our thinking in important, and misleading, respects. Above all, it will be argued that the Great Divide creates a fault-line within theories of the state and in so doing creates a distorted picture of the state and of the way it behaves. Above all, it renders it impossible to grasp the significance of globalization. In other words, the attempt to theorize the state in conditions of globalization must itself begin by subverting the framework of the Great Divide. The chapter will illustrate how the Divide has arisen, and how pervasive it is throughout the literature. It will then explain why it has become a source of widespread dissatisfaction, how some writers have attempted to bridge it, and why a problem still remains. It points the way to an engagement between globalization and state theory.

If the 'international' represents a field of political and economic forces distinct from the 'domestic', it follows that it needs to be studied within a separate framework, and by means of its own tools of analysis. Traditionally, these have included anarchy, states-as-actors, balances of power, and the resort to war. The occasional appeals to domestic 'analogies' (Suganami 1989), intended to soften this separation, have, if anything, served further to reconfirm it. In the very suggestion that there might be an analogy between the international and the domestic there is, of course, a denial of homology: the two cannot, in actuality, be the same thing. Neo-realism reinforced this tendency by a formidable reassertion of the autonomy of the international as a domain with its own, and distinctive, political structure. As a contrast, the following discussion presents the state as the common but contested ground that brings the international and the national together, rather than as the barrier which marks the line of separation between them.

It is commonplace to note that in its intellectual development, International Relations has been beset by a number of related dualities. In a crude sense, the discipline has operated an explicit division of labour whereby political science or comparative politics deals with the 'internal', whereas International Relations is the study of the 'external' relations of the state. Thus, even when presenting his own qualified challenge to it, Jackson acknowledges that the 'distinction between domestic politics and international politics is of course an important one which theorists should take note of' (1996: 204). The separation is encountered equally in Keohane and Milner (1996), and while they themselves seek to counteract it, they do so only in a qualified sense.

Such a division of labour lies at the heart of the distinction classically made by Martin Wight (1966) in which political theory, devoted to the 'good life', is sharply marked off from international theory, which has not been able to move beyond the instrumentalities of survival. In the former realm, political theorists have long since discussed the values to which the individual polity might aspire, while in the latter, theorists have had to content themselves with strategies for protecting the security or national interest of these polities. As Wight's position has been summarized, 'Political goods are therefore a given for international theory, whereas they are an end for political theory' (Jackson 1990*b*: 262). In fact, and as Jackson demonstrates (1990*b*: 265, 267), Wight was by no means consistent in maintaining this distinction and, in most philosophical respects, was hostile to it. Nonetheless, it appears to find paradigmatic expression in that famous article.

Walker is only the most recent commentator to have made much of this dualism. There is a tradition of political theory where 'it is possible to proceed to discussions of justice, freedom, and progress'. Set alongside it, but distinct, there is also a tradition of International Relations within which there is no more than a 'concern with the management of order in a system bereft of overarching power or authority' (Walker 1990: 171; see also 1993). On this basis, International Relations has been accused of contributing to the myth of 'two distinct and separate realms of activity, the domestic and the foreign or international' (Saurin 1995: 252). The domestic, wherein the search for the good life may proceed, is a manifestation of state; the external has to content itself with the non-authoritative management of order for the reason that it is literally stateless. As explained in a typical commentary on this form of reasoning, the 'key assumption is that political community requires enclosure—that politics proper is impossible without a protected space where ideals can be realized and interests ideally adjudicated' (Magnusson 1990: 49). Once locked into this dichotomous logic, it is virtually impossible to escape its built-in conclusions. Some analysts, even in the very way that they express their unease with the Divide, end up by reaffirming it. One critic lays the blame on International Relations theory for 'a wholly inadequate understanding of inter-stateness', in contrast to the 'relatively sophisticated concept of stateness' to be found in theories of the state (Taylor 1996: 100). This does not lament the division of labour as such, only its unequal fruits: it thereby reaffirms the essential idea that there could be, in principle, a theory of inter-stateness, separate from theories of the state.

The central claim of this work is that any such theoretical separation is misconceived. The implication of the Great Divide is that while we may theorize the state, this does not carry over to how we think about relations between states. There is a theoretical disjuncture between the two. Applied to the context of globalization, such an apparatus becomes meaningless because, as the book will seek to demonstrate, a theory of the global is itself an integral dimension of a more plausible theory of the state.

The varieties of the Great Divide

The basic dichotomy of the Great Divide has been replicated in various aspects of the discipline. As indicated, it can be found throughout many types of normative and 'positivist' theory. What follows is a representative sample of illustrations, intended to demonstrate how deeply entrenched the Divide has become. These will indicate some key debates in a wide spectrum of contemporary IR theory and show that, generically, they derive from common issues associated with the Great Divide.

While this may seem to lead us some distance from matters pertaining to globalization, the connection will soon become clear. Globalization does much more than force us to question the extent to which, as a matter of policy, the 'foreign' and the 'domestic' might be thought to interact. It also raises profound issues about the nature of political community and the manner of its transformation. To this extent, just as it challenges the idea of the state as having a historically 'fixed' identity, it also questions claims that the community is a stable repository of collective values. If globalization's engagement with IR theory is to be fully explored, the spectrum of issues to be reviewed is wide indeed. This section will trace the Great Divide in some of its various manifestations: a morality of states and a morality of people; communitarianism and cosmopolitanism; communitarianism and liberalism; thick and thin; democracy of the *polis* and cosmopolitan democracy; foreign policy analysis and International Relations; and reductionism and systemic theory. A theory that is to make sense of globalization compels us to look again at the traditional manner of presentation of many of these issues.

Let us briefly review the standard dichotomies, as symptoms of the extent of the Great Divide. These are, first of all, a generic division between the world of states and the world of people. Faced with the harsh realist judgement that international life is the realm of necessity, not of moral choice, the delicate toehold that morality can alone secure is in the limited sense of the state as moral subject. This is the 'morality of states'. What flows from it is the view that 'states, not persons, are the subjects of international morality, and the most fundamental rules that regulate their behavior are supposed to preserve a peaceful order of sovereign states' (Beitz 1979: 65). This sets it apart from the 'morality of people', and in turn spawns a long series of questions about the nature of the state as moral subject— such as its agency, responsibility, and role of trusteeship.

This basic dichotomy develops along two distinct lines of argument. The first is that, if it is indeed the state that is the bearer of rights, it enjoys a right to autonomy and this is generally sanctioned under principles of sovereignty and national self-determination (Graham 1997: 5). For an effective morality of states, the state must have freedom to determine its own good life. Secondly, it extends to the notion of the value of preserving the international order that is the instrument of this self-determination, and hence to the international society perspective, often presented as a 'third' or 'middle' way (C. Brown 1995b; Dunne 1998). The international society and its institutions, including non-intervention, thereby become morally sanctioned as the means to preserving the fabric of the individual states. The paradox, of course, is that the morality of states requires that 'states should be desensitized to each other's domestic wrongdoings in the interest of order among them'. It is this tension that reveals the gulf between it and a morality of people, since the latter tends to heighten 'the sensitivity of people in one place to wrongs done in another in the interest of the achievement of global justice' (Vincent 1986: 118).

This approach slides conveniently into the second, and much-favoured, dichotomy between cosmopolitanism and communitarianism (C. Brown 1992; Thompson 1992). The former holds to the assumption that all people, by dint of their common humanity, inhabit a universal moral order and people are the overriding moral subjects within it. The latter dissents from the notion that the 'disembodied' individual can be any kind of moral actor at all, and insists that it is only through community that values are generated. In consequence, community has intrinsic value. Cochran makes the contrast in the following, albeit overdrawn, terms:

To the cosmopolitan, who regards the person as morally free to choose her social attachments, the autonomy of states has no normative relevance. For the communitarian, it is within the sovereign state that ethical duties are made possible, where the individual may achieve freedom and self-realization   Thus, the sovereign state is morally relevant because it is necessary to the development of the individual as a free person. (Cochran 1996: 37)

This is the normative counterpart to the arguments about the structural effects of anarchy on state behaviour in international relations. From a cosmopolitanist perspective, there should be no distinctive international moral anarchy, since the universal moral order obliges all actors, persons as well as states, to conform to it. The normative 'international', as such, has no structural constraints distinct from those operating in the domestic realm as well. Alternatively, from a communitarian point of view, morality is constituted within communities, usually deemed to be represented by states. The moral universe is partitioned into separate political communities and international relations are conducted in the moral void that falls between them. At the very least, communitarians subscribe to the notion that moral ideas cannot sensibly be abstracted from context as 'it is the necessary embedding of these notions through and in the actual existence of communities, that creates the values to which communities adhere' (Rengger 1992: 355).

A cognate debate, with its home in political theory rather than in International Relations, is that between liberalism and communitarianism. This reveals how elements of the Great Divide have been imported into International Relations from political theory more generally. Much of this debate has been generated in response to the arguments of John Rawls' *A Theory of Justice* (1972). That book is taken to be the quintessential liberal statement that justice is discernible by all right-thinking people, wherever they might be found. They can, as rational citizens of nowhere, agree to the principles that should govern any just society. As has often been pointed out, Rawls did not apply his theory to international relations, although subsequently others have done so by elaboration or extension (Beitz 1979; Pogge 1989). But this entire line of argument has been challenged by the communitarians. The two sides are in disagreement, both over the validity of the rational individualist methodology employed by liberals, and about the intrinsic value of community itself (Avineri and de-Shalit 1992*b*: 2–3).

Methodologically, they clash over what kinds of moral choices the individual can make, and about the extent to which the atomistic individual can be considered a moral agent at all. Sandel summarizes the liberal position, although not personally subscribing to it: 'For the unencumbered self, what matters above all, what is most essential to our personhood, are not the ends we choose but our capacity to choose them' (Sandel 1992: 19). In sharp contrast, it is the communitarian belief that 'human beings become "individuals" only by the process of relating to one another in societies' and 'the kind of individuals they become will be a product of the kind of society within which this takes place' (C. Brown 1995*a*: 103).

Substantively, this disagreement results also in differing views about the nature of the community to which humans belong, and about the kinds of moral codes that function within and across them. All of this, as will be seen in due course, is of immense significance for arguments about how globalization might be inducing societal change, and about the extent to which a genuinely global society might be emerging in its train. For the communitarians, shared values are themselves the expressions of an already extant society. The spread of seemingly common values cannot take place, in disembodied fashion, where society does not already exist, and any suggestion that a world society might be constructed on the basis of 'free-floating' common values fundamentally gets things the wrong way round.

For the liberal and, in Sandel's words, the just society must have a 'just framework' and in this sense the 'right' is prior to the 'good' (Sandel 1992: 13). We might refer to this as a kind of instrumental or procedural ethic. When Sandel makes this point, he seems to have in mind constitutional and other decision-making procedures that allow for the exercise of individual wills. Similar in spirit, if not in mechanism, is Linklater's conception of justice as opportunity for dialogue, and the creation of the universal 'communication community' as the central goal. Under this view of the normative ideal, 'the emphasis shifts away from universalisable conceptions of the good life', he observes, 'to the procedural universals which need to be in place before true dialogue can be said to exist in any social encounter' (Linklater 1998: 40–1). In short, proponents of a global society need to be precise in their claims about the type of society that is in gestation, and about its relationship to moral values. Is it one that shares notions about the right, or about the good? Do the values create the community, or do they presuppose its existence?

All these matters are critical to any discussion of normative globalization but tend often to be brushed aside in favour of the crude stereotypes of the Great Divide. Broadly speaking, we might need to make some kind of distinction between communities entered into by free-standing individuals who already know what is just, and those thought in some sense to be ontologically prior to the moral capacity of their members. On this basis, we might reach differing judgements about the extent to which globalization can bring about change to existing moral communities. In the same way, such conceptions will also determine whether we can begin to assign moral significance to global communities. Are these brought gradually into existence by the cumulative acts of autonomous individuals, or do the individuals become moral agents only if the global community (of a certain kind) is already in existence? This point lies at the heart of much communitarian philosophy (and especially of its rejection of moral homogenization), and also pertains directly to key themes in constructivist theory. While individuals may well form a community, they are in turn formed by it. But what kind of community is it and, in consequence, what kind of moral individual emerges? One possible basis for distinction is detailed by Sandel, as follows:

Only if the self is prior to its ends can the right be prior to the good . . . Understood as unencumbered selves, we are of course free to join in voluntary association with others, and so are capable of community in the co-operative sense. What is denied to the unencumbered self is the possibility of membership in any community bound by moral ties antecedent to choice; he cannot belong to any community where the self *itself* could be at stake. Such a community—call it constitutive as against merely co-operative—would engage the identity as well as the interests of the participants, and so implicate its members in a citizenship more thorough-going than the unencumbered self can know. (Sandel 1992: 19)

What this means, in effect, is that there are two sets of issues dividing the camps. The first is whether or not the individual, stripped of social context, is in a position to make any kind of moral judgement at all. The second is whether the atomistic individual can make decisions about the good, even if it is conceded that he or she can make decisions about the right. How does this pertain to globalization? It suggests that we must be careful not to confuse the limited provenance of a co-operative society with that of a moral community already in being. In short, the issue goes to the heart of the diverse assessments about whether the interconnections represented by globalization are indicative of an emerging global moral community or not. As we can now see, this issue is even more complex than at first imagined, as liberals and communitarians proceed on the basis of different conceptions of community, and of its relationship to its members.

Finally, and before leaving this discussion of communitarianism, it should simply be noted that its critics have expressed varying degrees of unease about its perceived conservatism. In this regard, the concern is that it necessarily conducts its moral discourse within the terms of the extant community. The danger here, it is felt, is that it entails a morally reproductive logic which is immune to any outside reflection or critical distance. Typically, the charge of conservatism is made on the basis that, in communitarian terms, 'the good society . . . is one of settled traditions and established identities' (Gutmann 1992: 121). Any such conservative bias would, of course, make it difficult to sustain the argument that a global society might be in process of emergence. The emphasis on what is already in place is methodologically inimical to fundamental transformation in the nature of community. As an instance of the Great Divide, this debate lines up over whether people and values are herded into pre-existing communities from which there is no escape, or whether new moral identities can be created by a 'free-ranging' humanity.

Another normative pairing, of much the same kind, is that developed by Michael Walzer (1994). Walzer, within the above-mentioned categories, would normally be deemed to belong to the communitarian camp. His defence, albeit qualified, of the presumption in favour of non-intervention (Walzer 1977) was largely based on the premise that the community knows best what it wants, and should be allowed to go about its business without undue let or hindrance. The qualification that he enters to this, and the source of much subsequent criticism of his argument, is that this broadly communitarian argument is made to co-exist with a principle of human rights that is seemingly cosmopolitan in inspiration. It is the latter that undergirds his exposition of the war convention. To this extent, there appears to be a tension between the universalistic and the particularistic elements of his moral philosophy.

It is to this theme that Walzer returned in his *Thick and Thin* (1994). Here he openly acknowledges the co-existence of the two moral spheres of human society, 'universal because it is human, particular because it is a society' (1994: 8). His suggestion is that there are indeed certain 'thin' universal principles that can be found in many particular moral codes. As against this, 'thickness' can be found only within the context of a specific community. Such a dualistic conception might appear commonplace but Walzer's originality resides in the manner in which he seeks to relate them. The common, and common-sense, argument would tend to hold that the starting point for all moralities 'is the same in every case' and that universal beliefs come to be elaborated within specific social contexts: 'they start thin, as it were, and thicken with age' (1994: 4). But Walzer is at pains to deny this commonsensical position: 'the moral minimum', he adjudges, 'is not a freestanding morality' but instead 'simply designates some reiterated features of particular thick or maximal moralities' (1994:10). Elsewhere, he is similarly insistent that 'the minimum is not the foundation of the maximum, only a piece of it' (1994:18). Either way, there is a divide between the thick and the thin: the only argument is about how these two might relate to each other, and not about their existence. Since thick moral codes are to be found only in particular communities, the dialogue between the thick and the thin becomes another powerful expression of the normative Great Divide.

More recently, and as a variant of the same essential theme, theorists of democracy have begun to question the viability of a closed conception of democracy that is self-contained within an individual polity. As opposed to a world of democracy in parts, theorists are attempting to devise schemes for a cosmopolitan democracy of the whole (Parry 1994: 11; Held 1995). Such a development is felt necessary because much governance is now international, or transnational, in aspect and yet it 'is not tenable to maintain that an aggregation of democratic states produces democratic multilateralism' (Scholte 1997*a*: 451). The root problem goes back to the same essential bifurcation within the discipline: 'because democracy has hitherto been understood as a form of *state*, it is difficult to know what "democratisation" of the *international system* can mean' (Holden 1996*b*: 138).

This same divide runs through what has become one of the most widely discussed theories of the 1990s, namely that concerning the democratic or liberal peace. This is the point at which explicitly normative theory meets would-be positivist theory. The substance of the arguments need not be rehearsed here but the structure of the analysis is revealing. In essence, following Doyle (1983, 1986), the suggestion is that changes in the international order towards peace and stability are contingent upon change at the domestic level: the more democratized the members of the international community, the better the prospects for international peace. Although there is a causal link between the two domains, the internal and the external, the form of the argument is such as to reinforce the notion that they are separate and distinct, even if interactive. In the same way, the optimism found in Fukuyama's analysis derives largely from his account of domestic changes, particularly with regard to the relative weakness of states as against civil societies in the second half of the twentieth century (1992: 12).

Finally, this binary opposition reveals itself in the general fault-line which runs between the study of foreign policy (looking from the inside out), on the one hand, and the study of international relations (looking from the outside in), on the other. This compartmentalization permeates all the discussions of 'levels of analysis' and 'images' within the subject, and also overlaps with the more generalized agent–structure motif to be found in the social sciences as a whole (Hollis and Smith 1991). And yet we must take care to distinguish the various ways in which the conflation of levels can take place. In his defence of 'double-edged diplomacy', and his elaboration of a two-level-games approach, Moravcsik remarks that it 'challenges us to revisit the level-of-analysis problem, throwing into relief the many instances in which the levels collapse into one another' (Moravcsik 1993: 33). But the way in which the levels collapse into one another in his formulation is not the same as the way they collapse when viewed through the lenses of globalization theory. Thus elsewhere it is claimed that the 'central novelty of globalization as a concept . . . lies in the fact that it defies traditional conceptions of levels of analysis in political science and international relations' (Cerny 1996a: 620–1). This latter view can be endorsed but we need to note that, while the wording is deceptively similar to that of Moravcsik, its import is significantly different. The distinction will be elaborated in the arguments to follow.

The most influential manifestation of the Great Divide is the now deeply entrenched Waltzian scheme of 'reductionist' and 'systemic' theories. According to Waltz's much-discussed formulation (1979), a systemic theory postulates a structure as well as interacting units. By contrast, a reductionist approach concentrates on the units alone. In his quest for the development of a genuinely systemic theory, Waltz was driven by the realization that similar outcomes, generated by dissimilar units, implied the possibility of a structural constant. The attraction of the focus on structure was that, after the pluralist critiques of the 1970s, it restored a semblance of analytical coherence to the discipline (Little 1985: 82). Fundamental to his enterprise was an insistence upon a sharp distinction between systemic and unit levels:

The claim to be following a systems approach or to be constructing a systems theory requires one to show how system and unit levels can be distinctly defined. Failure to make and preserve the distinction between structure, on the one hand, and units and processes, on the other, makes it impossible to disentangle causes of different sorts and to distinguish between causes and effects. (Waltz 1979: 78)

In order to preserve that distinction, it then became necessary to omit certain elements from the structure and, amongst these, Waltz listed the units' social and political institutions and their ideological commitments (1979: 80). It is on the thinness of his residual category of structure that he has received most criticism (Keohane 1986; see also the attempted reformulation in Buzan, Jones, and Little 1993). As Waltz elaborates his position, he resorts to another image to refine it. He likens his structure to 'a field of forces in physics' on the grounds that interactions 'within a field have properties different from those they would have if they occurred outside of it' (1979: 73). This carries with it a number of serious implications. Since he also maintains that the international and the domestic possess different structures, the former with an organizing principle of anarchy and the latter one of hierarchy, it follows logically that the international and the domestic constitute *separate* fields of forces. Indeed, he states this categorically: 'A systems theory of international politics', he avers, 'deals with the forces in play at the international, and not at the national, level' (1979: 71).

What is so deeply misleading about this exposition is that, even if at the extremities the fields of forces appear distinct, the fields intersect and the state acts within this area of intersection. Moreover, as Waltz concedes, it is not the field alone that affects the objects, but conversely 'the objects affect the field' (1979: 73). This is assuredly the case and must mean that the state affects both fields simultaneously, and is in turn affected by them. Accordingly, International Relations must now try to elaborate a framework that recognizes this fact.

One possible objection needs to be cleared away at the outset. Waltz relegates interactions between the units to the unit level. At this level, he certainly accepts that unit actions are influenced by interactions with the external, by the 'international'. Accordingly, Waltz's scheme does allow for interaction between the domestic and the international. Could it not then be counter-argued that the present discussion misses the point? We can recognize internal–external interaction while still leaving intact his claim to a reductionist/systemic division of labour. So what is the problem?

The critique developed here goes beyond any such defence. It does not simply restate the uncontroversial position that the international influences the domestic, and vice versa. It goes further in insisting that the 'domestic' is what it is because it constitutes a part of a specific international structure. Likewise, the international structure is what it is, at discrete historical moments, in consequence of the nature of the polities embedded within it.

The point at issue emerges clearly from Waltz's own diagrams (1979: figs 5.1 and 5.2, pp. 99–100). Two features of these are striking (Clark 1998: 487–8). The first is Waltz's decision to find different notations for the state in its internal and external aspects, thus visually confirming the radical separation that he portrays. Secondly, it is evident that states are regarded by him as givens, wholly outside the international structure: even if 'affected' by that structure, states are certainly not constituted by it, nor is the structure constituted by them. They are ontologically separate domains and this tends to confirm Devetak's complaint that 'neo-realism cannot address ontological issues such as the constitution of the state and states system' (1995: 23). Thus it has been said of Waltz's argument that, while ostensibly outside in (as a matter of causality), it is in fact inside out (existentially) since it 'views the state as an already complete, fully formed, unitary whole, which subsequently enters into interaction with other like totalities' (Devetak 1995: 24). It is as if the state is genetically coded to behave in certain ways and does so regardless of historical circumstances, the resultant behaviour being attributed to the structure but in fact being a consequence of deeply embedded assumptions about the nature of stateness. Such a perspective leaves out of account, as repeatedly noted by historical sociologists, the outside-in pressures on the formation of states. In Halliday's summation, 'states . . . develop as a result of international processes, and not the other way around' (1994: 35).

Equally, in the Waltzian formulation, the characteristics of the structure are simply taken for granted. As against this, there is now a wealth of evidence and argumentation from within the IR literature to suggest that the structure is itself reflective of a number of (historically specific) practices. Thus neo-realists are berated for their failure to recognize, in conceptualizing structure, 'how extensively the socially constructed practices of sovereignty—of recognition, of intervention, of the language of justification—contribute to the structures of international society that exist beyond the realms of neo-realist analysis' (Biersteker and Weber 1996*b*: 5–6). This accords with the historical perspective that the structure so constituted is not a uniform structure, naturally attaching to any group of states, but instead is a creation of specific circumstances 'reflecting the passage of European history and the structure of European societies and their political thought' (J. Williams 1996: 47–8).

If the preceding analysis is valid, it establishes a considerable deficiency in the Great Divide as articulated in neo-realist theory. It also suggests that there must be a generic weakness in all such derivative forms of structural realism. For instance, within the realms of globalization analysis, there has emerged an adaptation of the Waltzian position. Instead of a structure, the key attribute of which is anarchy, there is now a *genre* of globalization theory that posits a structure characterized by capital mobility. This likewise induces uniformity of state behaviour. 'The central claim of these theorists', Andrews clarifies, 'is that when capital is highly mobile across international borders, the sustainable macroeconomic policy options available to states are systematically circumscribed' (1994: 193). If Waltz's systemic theory fails, so must those derivatives based upon it, and for essentially the same reason, namely the artificiality of the Great Divide that lies at its heart.

Beyond the Great Divide

The above examples provide some of the more prominent manifestations of the Great Divide, drawn from a broad spectrum of IR theory. There have also been repeated expressions of dissatisfaction with such an analytical procedure from many parts of the discipline, a number emanating from perspectives that have little to do with globalization as such. However, the globalization literature collectively seems to encapsulate the existing concerns. In its most general form, the complaint is that a narrow focus upon the history of the international system has precluded IR from developing 'a framework which can fully embrace the evolution of world history at a global level' (Little 1994: 10). Expressing the same concern more positively, Linklater and Macmillan feel confident that this deficiency is on the point of correction, as IR is 'poised to overcome its peculiar separation from Political Theory' (1995: 14).

Those working from the traditional political theory end of the spectrum are making essentially the same appeal. This emerges clearly in David Held's attempts to update democratic theory to take account of the circumstances of globalization. Held's critique of the Great Divide is that, as expressed in realism and neo-realism, it lacks 'a convincing account of the enmeshment of states with the wider

global order, of the effects of the global order on states, and of the political implications of all this for the modern democratic state' (Held 1995*a*: 25). His concerns
are matched by those working from within IR. Typically, Ferguson and
Mansbach, in their historical investigation into the nature of polities, have
appealed for the same wall to be torn down. 'Historical consciousness is also
necessary to escape the false dichotomy between "domestic" and "international"
politics', they insist, on the grounds that 'Separating the two arenas distorts analysis at the outset and precludes thinking about politics as a seamless whole' (1996:
24–5). Their main objective is to bring the polity, rather than the state, back in to
the analysis, encompassing all its historical manifestations.

Not surprisingly, similar complaints have been made by those seeking to establish a global society paradigm. In his own account of the end of the cold war, Shaw
insists that such a perspective becomes essential. The end of the cold war was
brought about by a conjuncture of 'social' and 'international' transformations,
and these must be merged into a single analytical scheme. They are to be viewed,
in his terminology, as 'two major constellations within global society' (Shaw
1994*a*: 68). At the same time, in the apparently far-removed field of international
economic regulation, Sassen has challenged the 'global/national duality', and
the zero-sum notion of diminished state capacity which it induces, because for
her that is not an accurate assessment of what is happening. 'I view deregulation
not simply as a loss of control by the state', she contends, 'but as a crucial
mechanism to negotiate the juxtaposition of the global and the national' (Sassen
1996*b*: 46).

If the IR literature has for some time been sensitive to the problems created by
the artificiality of the Great Divide, it has also advanced a number of purported
solutions (Caporaso 1997). Four principal contenders will be reviewed briefly, all
of them integrated attempts to combine international and domestic politics: a
decision-making framework; historical materialism and world system theory;
theories of international society; and finally constructivist theory.

The attempt to overcome the Great Divide is currently fashionable in a range
of decision-making literature, especially that seeking to relate the domestic elements to the international. A prominent example is provided by Keohane and
Milner (1996). It is the central claim of their work that 'we can no longer understand politics within countries . . . without comprehending the nature of the linkages between national economies and the world economy' (Milner and Keohane
1996*a*: 3). To the extent that this is the case, it follows that any theoretical model
must attempt to link the two. The linkage that these authors make is of the kind
that they themselves describe as 'second image reversed' (1996*a*: 6), which means
that it is an attempt to demonstrate how internationalization impacts upon the
political economy of the individual state and becomes, in turn, an aspect of
domestic politics. From such a brief account, it should already be apparent that
while Keohane and Milner seek to create linkages between the two domains of the
domestic and the international, theoretically they assume their continued separation. The same can be said of other quests for a 'Realist theory of state action
which bridges domestic and international politics' (Mastanduno, Lake, and

Ikenberry 1989: 459). It is precisely because they differentiate the two that the quest for linkages, interactions, or bridges between them can be conducted. If such approaches express dissatisfaction with the Great Divide, they do so in much more modest fashion than the literature on globalization.

Others, working within essentially rational-choice models, also appear to challenge the Great Divide. This emerges clearly in the literature on 'two-level games' and the resultant concept of 'double-edged diplomacy'. In his own commentary upon this, Moravcsik insists that 'the question facing international relations theorists today is not *whether* to combine domestic and international explanations . . . but *how* best to do so' (1993: 9). In this literature, the core assumption is that actors make international choices to manoeuvre domestically, and make domestic choices to influence the nature of international bargaining. 'Diplomatic strategies and tactics are constrained', Moravcsik elaborates, 'both by what other states will accept and by what domestic constituencies will ratify' (1993: 15). To this extent, the state embodied in the chief executive is a strategic actor capable of making choices which 'cannot be reduced to reflections of domestic constituent pressure' (P. Evans 1993: 401–2). Instead, the pull of the two competing logics opens up 'an area of autonomy' within which the chief executive can make free choices (Moravcsik 1993: 15). By those means, there is indeed two-way interaction. However, as argued above, this remains very much at the level of mutual influence between the two domains which remain separable in theory, even if not always separate in practice. As one commentor has noted, they 'take the domestic and the international levels as given and inquire about the connections between the two in terms of strategic interaction and cross-level processes' (Caporaso 1997: 579). In short, the challenge presented to the Great Divide from this quarter is much less radical than the one that emerges from the analysis of globalization.

A second attempted submergence of the Great Divide takes place through historical materialism/world system theory. This confronts the divide between the internal and external by reducing both to functional properties of an integrated system, within which the state is no more than a contingent epiphenomenon. The state is not an independent actor and its sovereignty is illusory. By extension, there is no inter-state system apart from the economic structures of which it is a by-product. As Halliday observes of historical materialism generally, 'there is no "international system", or any component activity, be this war or diplomacy, abstracted from the mode of production. Indeed, International Relations is the study of the relations not between states but between social formations' (1994: 60). In similar vein, we are told by adherents to this perspective that 'geopolitical systems are not constituted independently of, and cannot be understood in isolation from, the wider structures of the production and reproduction of social life' (Rosenberg 1994: 6). It follows from this that there can be no problem about a Great Divide, since states have no autonomy with respect to wider social formations and these, by definition, transcend the division between the domestic and the international. The logic of world systems theory is similar, as far as this issue is concerned. 'A world economy, by contrast,' Little summarizes, 'has a polity which is fragmented into independent political units; these are located within an integrated economy, defined by a single division of labour' (1994: 13). Within such an integrated framework, any Great Divide is more apparent than real. In any case, in the works of such writers as Wallerstein (1991), cores and peripheries can as easily occur within states as between them: the fault-lines are not drawn along the division between the internal and external since these, within a world system, are essentially meaningless concepts. For purposes of a world system, everything is 'inside'.

Thirdly, there is the prospect of a solution through the medium of international society (Armstrong 1998). Although a generic approach to the theory of international relations, this is normally identified with the 'English School' (Dunne 1998). Its key premise is that 'states have rights and duties', and that this realization is a 'concrete reality in the minds of those who think and act in the name of states' (Wheeler 1992: 466). In short, underlying the notion of international society are the common objectives to which its members subscribe. They may not share 'substantive goals and values' but, at the very least, they attest to 'a common code of co-existence' (Dunne and Wheeler 1996: 94–5).

How might such a conception be thought to contribute to a bridging of the Great Divide? As with constructivism, it does so in so far as it posits a particular connection between individuals, states, and the international society within which they are represented. Indeed, in this sense the international society approach should be viewed as a subset of constructivism more generally (Dunne 1995; Armstrong 1998). What this amounts to in practice is that while the 'world of people' seems to be divorced from the 'world of states', the two are brought into important connection by the similar ends that they serve. This is Jackson's point when he argues that international theory is a part of political theory, since there would be no value in state survival unless that goal were to contribute to human well-being as well. 'If there were no basis for the good life in states,' he acknowledges, 'there would be no point in their survival' (Jackson 1990*b*: 265). This is echoed in the assertion that 'the moral value of a pluralist society of states has to be judged in terms of its contribution to individual well-being' (Dunne and Wheeler 1996: 96). Thus international society is 'constituted', albeit at one remove, by the moral needs of individual human beings.

This is not to say that the idea of international society is itself unproblematic. Its severest critic, N. J. Rengger, has charged it with being incoherent. He does so on the basis that the theory of international society cannot provide a compelling reason for state observance of its rules, beyond that of self-interest. In effect, Rengger uses the logic of communitarianism, as earlier explained, to attack the coherence of the notion of international society. Such a society, like communitarianism more generally, is predicated on the prior creation of norms within a social context: obligation is incurred by the fact that these norms are socially created. Pointing to the parallel between the two, he remarks that 'each assumes a degree of cultural homogeneity which generates certain shared concerns, interests and values which, in their turn, create, encourage and maintain a set of obligations' (Rengger 1992: 361–2). However, in the case of international society, this argument does not work: it cannot provide a value-based reason for compliance, beyond self-interested prudentialism (1992: 366).

Finally, the attempt to overcome the Great Divide has been made by various forms of constructivist theory within which the interests and identities of states are not fixed or given but themselves represent historical contingencies. At the same time, neither does the system have permanent attributes, deriving from abstracted structural properties. Instead, the state and the system of which it is a part (not narrowly conceived as a state system alone) must be regarded as being in a mutually constitutive and permanently adaptive relationship. However, lest this sound as if the mutual constitution is one of idyllic harmony, this adaptation imposes costs, measured in degrees of real-life human sacrifice, hardship, and suffering. This is what gives rise to the dynamic of change that some critics have complained is lacking in constructivist theory (Mearsheimer 1995: 91).

The broad contours of a social constructivist approach to IR theory have been set out in a number of other works, although there are as always differing emphases within this genre of writing (Kratochwil 1989; Wendt 1995; Armstrong 1998; Ruggie 1998)). Many of the essentials have been usefully summarized in Ruggie's recent contribution (1998). His position is that constructivism differs from both neo-realism and neo-liberalism (both of which he bundles together as types of neo-utilitarianism), in that its distinctive quality is not to take state identity for granted: theory must commence before the state finds itself in its 'anarchical' or 'institutional' setting. Thus Ruggie employs the distinction between the regulative (rules of the road) and the constitutive (rules of chess), to make the point that neo-utilitarianism, in both its variants, lacks any notion of constitutive rules of international relations. 'Its universe of discourse', he maintains, 'consists entirely of antecedently existing actors and their behavior, and its project is to explain the character and efficacy of regulative rules in coordinating them' (1998: 23). Generally, and in useful summary, he portrays the salient qualities of constructivism as those going beyond neo-utilitarianism: 'by problematizing states' identities and interests; by broadening the array of ideational factors that affect international outcomes; by introducing the logically prior constitutive rules alongside the regulative rules; and by including transformation as a normal feature of international politics'(1998: 27). Wendt is more succinct in his summary. 'Constructivists', he writes, 'think that state interests are in important part constructed by systemic structures, not exogenous to them; this leads to a sociological rather than micro-economic structuralism' (1995: 72–3). Both accounts point to strategies that are helpful in understanding globalization.

The problem with much constitutive theory is that it can appear politically uninteresting: indeed, it is often so sanitized as to leave much of the politics out altogether. Accordingly, what the following argument will seek to do is to reinstate the costs, sacrifice, and pain into the otherwise seemingly sterile process of mutual constitution. In order to do this, it will also have to be understood that, historically speaking, the process of mutual constitution is asymmetrical: at times, the 'external' pressures operating upon the state will be dominant and will discipline the state to behave in internationally acceptable ways. At other times, domestic forces will reassert themselves and the form of international order will be reconstituted from the inside out. If the idea of mutual constitution is to be made historically interesting, ideas of political cost and asymmetry must be built into the analysis. Politically speaking, the advantage of this is that the domestic and the international will at least be brought into the same field of forces, something which neo-realism is resolutely inclined not to do.

Globalization and the Great Divide

The purpose of this book is not to show that individual policy decisions are shaped by a combination of domestic and international concerns. It is rather to posit a mutual restructuring of state and system in such a way that the context of political choice is itself transformed. The argument builds upon ideas already set out by others but attempts to extend them to a more general analysis of international relations in a context of globalization. Thus, in his own work, Hobson has been concerned to redefine the relationship between state and economy. After detailed historical investigation, he offers as his 'key insight' the claim that 'states shape the economy and society for domestic (as well as international) reasons and that state action can be reduced neither to the inter-state system nor to the domestic social structure' (Hobson 1997: 4). What is the specific import of such a suggestion for theories of international relations in general?

The Wightian separation between the 'good life' within states, and mere survival without, has been questioned on the grounds of the greater intrusion of outside forces into states. Thus it has been said that the distinction is being eroded because 'the good life is affected more and more by events external to states' (Jackson 1990b: 270). This is precisely not the case that should be mounted from globalization. As will be argued in detail, it is not something that is 'external to states'. If we are led to question the good life/survival dichotomy as a result of globalization, it is as much for reasons of changing conceptions of the good life from within as it is from a helpless response to new circumstances from without.

Normative debate in IR theory has traditionally proceeded, as outlined above, on the basis of a categorical confrontation between community-based moral orders and universalist alternatives. This casts the state in an either/or moral position. Either it is, as the communitarians would have it, the custodian of community values, or—as decried by the cosmopolitans—it is the obstacle to the realization of a universal order. Theoretically, the state is either guardian angel or villain. In practice, the historical record attests to its performance of roles across the spectrum in between. A theory that is so far divorced from reality might have been tolerable in a more innocent age but needs to be discarded in the face of current complexities. Normatively speaking, globalization raises important questions about the creation, sustenance, and spread of values and is resistant to simple categorizations of the universal and the particular. The stability of fixed categories is ill-suited to conditions of fluidity and transformation. Moreover, if 'particular' identities are now developed with reference to the 'universal', then the relationship between these two ceases to be one of opposition and becomes instead one of mutual adaptation. Through this process the state comes to re-identify itself and, in turn, new terms of globalization are set.

Precisely the same is true of other aspects of state performance. The Great Divide encourages us to see the transformation of state roles—in sovereignty, economy, security, and rights of citizenship—as the necessary response of belea-guered states in the face of overwhelming external forces. In fact, the much more subtle reality is that these supposedly external conditions have, in part, been brought about by new conceptions of the state, of which the new policy agendas are symptomatic. The Great Divide encourages us to believe that the retreat of the state is a consequence of globalization and is thereby insufficiently sensitive to the extent to which globalization is also, and simultaneously, a consequence of the retreat of the state. Armstrong is therefore correct to point out that 'Globalization merely influences a particular conceptualization of what it means to be a state; it does not promote an alternative to statehood as such' (1998: 477). IR theory requires a form of thinking which goes beyond the Great Divide, and is able to give us purchase on these subtleties.

How is such rethinking to be carried forward, and with what implications for the agenda of IR theory? The book now turns to an overview of the globalization debates. Thus far, little attempt has been made to set out the essentials of global-ization. From a review of the literature, it will be shown that there is substantial disagreement about the evidence for, and the theoretical implications of, the generic developments that are covered by this term. Moreover, just as the Great Divide has a normative as well as a 'positivist' agenda, equally it will be seen that this is replicated in the discussions about globalization. From this survey will emerge a particular argument about the political dynamic of globalization. This provides the basic framework within which other central issues of IR theory can subsequently be addressed. Collectively, these are intended to serve as contribu-tions not only to an understanding of globalization, but also to overcoming the Great Divide in IR theory.

GLOBALIZATION

It is the function of this chapter to take stock of the literature about globalization as a basis for bringing about an engagement with theories of international relations. We need to know what claims are being made on behalf of globalization before the likely points of impact can be located. Such an exercise of review and synthesis would be inescapable in any project of this nature. But it is a particularly necessary task in this case, given the commitment to using globalization as a model for the understanding of other facets of international relations.

Reverting to the analogy employed in the Introduction, we must probe the claim that the 'industries' of international life now function under globalized conditions. How can we discern that this is so, and what might be the significance of the change? To develop the argument, we need to trace the effects that this has upon their modes of operation. To what extent is the manufacture of sovereignty no longer a state monopoly? Is it true that national economies are no longer state-run concerns but have been largely privatized instead? Are we moving away from concepts of national security because there are economies of scale to be gained in the global production of security? Is the state embarked on a process of conversion and diversification of its modes of normative production? To what extent is the production of contemporary democracy being restructured on a transnational basis? To probe such questions, we require an operational concept of globalization.

At first sight, any attempt to survey the impact on IR theory of the literature on globalization seems a distinctly futile task. Since there is no simple or agreed definition of what constitutes globalization, nor any consensus about how far the process has advanced, and in which areas, it is less than clear how such a vague and imprecise concept can be integrated into IR theory at all. About all that can be said with confidence about globalization is that it represents a major site of contestation. Paradoxically, however, the very intensity of this disagreement opens the topic up to investigation: the sources of controversy about globalization overlap with a number of core issues within International Relations.

The debate about globalization touches upon a range of such fundamentals. In its own way, it is another expression of deep-seated disagreements about the extent of change within the international system. As indicated in the Introduction, it is a point of entry for discussions concerning the 'actors' in the contemporary international system and about the 'structure' within which they operate. Just as the neo-institutionalists maintain that the modified anarchy at work is no longer uniformly hostile to co-operation by rational and self-interested states, so globalization is thought by many to create a new operating environment that demands new types of state behaviour. It provides, in short, a convenient yardstick with which to measure the degree of transformation that has taken place in international life.

As a result, different accounts of globalization impact on IR theory in different ways. However, the debate is not one confined to empirical matters alone—to measurement and quantification of globalization in the economic, political, and cultural spheres. Additionally, the entire subject of globalization is covered by a normative overlay. It is projected by the optimists as the rational endpoint of human development and, as such, as inevitable as it is to be welcomed. The antithetical viewpoint, according to the pessimists, is that globalization has unleashed a set of unplanned and anarchic forces that will precipitate new political and economic convulsions in the twenty-first century.

International Relations theorists have long posited the idea of an international order, characterized by the historical practices of sovereignty, war, the balance of power, international law, and the role of the Great Powers (Bull 1977). The task for contemporary IR theory is to discern the degree to which that order has changed, and whether its emerging attributes are best captured by the idea of globalization. In what sense then do we now live in a globalized *order* and what are its principal characteristics? Moreover, how deeply does this order penetrate? Is it best understood as an 'external' order that merely constrains and undermines the policies of states? Alternatively, is it itself reflective of fundamental changes in state practice that are already underway?

The globalization debates

The concept of globalization is as contested as it is popular: as it still bears the birthmarks of its multi-disciplinary paternity, it is virtually impossible, amongst the myriad accounts and interpretations, for the would-be synthesizer to discern a simple meaning or referent for the term. What is rendered complex by its very nature is further compounded by sheer volume: the torrent of literature on globalization shows no sign of abating. While there are differences of perspective that, as long as the reader is aware of them, can be rendered manageable, there are also conflicts of interpretation which are so fundamental as to destroy for the commentator any integrity that the processes of globalization might be thought to exhibit. In short, the quest for a globalization template, as heralded in the Introduction, is far from straightforward.

Not surprisingly, the consequence of all this disarray is that the utility of globalization as a theoretical concept has been much disputed. In typically robust fashion, Susan Strange dismisses a number of 'vague and woolly words' employed within the discipline, amongst which she rates globalization as the 'worst of them all', as it can refer to 'anything from the Internet to a hamburger' (1996: xii–xiii). Similarly, the term has been berated as 'a big idea resting on slim foundations' (Weiss 1998: 212). Equally, it has been disparaged for being nothing but an ideological project masquerading as a social-scientific concept. Some see it as the latest in a series of Enlightenment grand narratives purporting to outline a universal civilization and a common destiny for mankind: in this sense it simply incorporates and resurrects the belief in progress and becomes its current embodiment (Albrow 1996: 94–5). Others have denounced its 'economism; its economic reductionism; its technological determinism; its political cynicism, defeatism and immobilism' (Gills 1997b: 12). It is safe to say that the concept of globalization enjoys a status somewhat below that of motherhood and apple pie.

Nonetheless, the concept also has a strong body of support. Problems of definition, and disagreements about utility, have not resulted in diminished usage. Titles devoted to the subject continue to proliferate and to declare its centrality for contemporary social science. It has, for instance, been asserted that 'globalization may be *the* concept of the 1990s, a key idea by which we understand the transition of human society into the third millennium' (Waters 1995: 1). Others proclaim, with unalloyed enthusiasm, that it is 'the most significant development and theme in contemporary life and social theory' (Albrow 1996: 89). Yet others have conferred upon it the accolades of 'the word of the decade' (Axtmann 1998b: 1) or the 'buzzword' of the 1990s (Scholte 1996a: 44–5).

The high profile enjoyed by the concept, in turn, derives from the emerging conditions of global connectedness that appear to be prevalent in many facets of contemporary life. In commonly employed language, time and space are becoming compressed to unusual degrees and in unprecedented ways. In short, globalization is considered to be not merely a social theory, but a depiction of a new social reality with potentially momentous significance. According to one of the avowed champions of contemporary economic globalization, 'the basic fact of linkage to global flows is a—perhaps, *the*—central, distinguishing fact of our moment in history' (Ohmae 1995: 15). Why is it that well-informed observers can reach such bewilderingly divergent judgements about this topic?

Virtually all accounts of globalization recognize that it is multi-dimensional, even if some features are deemed more 'essential' to it than others (Sjolander 1996: 604). To that extent, we can sympathize with that pragmatic approach which accepts globalization as being necessarily a 'rubric for varied phenomena' (Mittelman 1996b: 2), and concedes that diversity is part of its intrinsic nature. There is not a single globalization, only globalizations. Even if globalization were to be regarded, for example, as predominantly an emanation of economic life, its theoretical interest would be considerably reduced if it could not be shown that it was also impacting upon other—social and political—domains. This inverts the point made by Hirst and Thompson, who justify their attack on the thesis of economic globalization on the grounds that, in its absence, the rest of the case becomes much less compelling: without economic globalization, there is little evidence to fall back upon (1996: 3). The mirror image of this reasoning is that, even if the strong case for economic globalization could indeed be validated, it would still remain much less interesting on its own, in isolation from the other spheres as well. While it is too much to say that the case for globalization stands on an 'all or nothing' basis, it nonetheless remains true that its significance for IR theory would be much diminished if it could be demonstrated that its impact was confined largely to aspects of economic life.

Given this multi-dimensionality, it is scarcely surprising that globalization is approached in diverse ways. To the extent that there is a unifying theme to these conceptions, it relates to the idea of decreasing territorialization, or to the diminishing political significance of traditional territorial divisions. As argued in one representative account, 'globalisation has challenged dominant conceptions of *political space* in International Relations' (Krause and Renwick 1996*b*: xii). It is, therefore, necessary to begin a review of the concept with some discussion of its significance for space and territoriality.

The impact on political space is a common point of emphasis in most of the globalization literature and bears witness to a 'significant shift in the spatial form of human social organization and activity' (McGrew 1997*b*: 8). There is emerging, we are told, 'a global social system in which there is no longer a frontier between internal and external' (Laidi 1998: 97). The repeated clarion cry is for social science 'to liberate itself from its own territorial assumptions' (Scott 1997*b*: 4), since these are deemed no longer accurately to reflect the social reality under investigation. How is such liberation to be achieved and what are its specific implications for theorizing about international relations?

Scholte has helpfully distinguished what he regards as three conceptions of globalization: the first denotes cross-border relations; the second, open-border relations; and the third, trans-border relations. As a result of the last, 'borders are not so much crossed or opened as *transcended*' (1997*a*: 430–1). Although he does not quite say so, Scholte seems happiest to identify globalization with that third category. At the very least, he believes that it is this third development which 'is the newest and offers the most distinctive and helpful insight into contemporary world affairs' (1997*a*: 430). This account is further elaborated when he associates globalization with the transcendence of borders: global relations 'are not links *at a distance* across territory but circumstances *without distance* and relatively disconnected from particular location' (Scholte 1996*a*: 49).

Clearly, the requirement that International Relations view its subject as 'relatively disconnected' from location would present a formidable, and presumably insurmountable, problem for the discipline. It would indeed undermine IR theory as it is currently understood since, even when not wholly state-centric, it has been reluctant to move much beyond notions of pluralism and transnationalism and, in either guise, remains firmly rooted in territory. Since standard definitions of transnationalism describe it as activity *across borders*, undertaken by non-governmental agents (Keohane and Nye 1977), it is evident that IR's language of transnationalism falls far short of Scholte's notion of the transcendence of borders.

However, it is far from clear that a conception of 'distanceless' and 'location-less' globalization is itself analytically sustainable or that, even if it were, its presence would be sufficiently widespread to constitute anything but minor exceptions to the rule. Apart from a few isolated and oft-repeated examples—such as the Internet and financial networks—most other human activities and relations appear to be steadfastly grounded. There is then the opposite danger that globalization, if defined too narrowly instead of too broadly, will focus attention on a limited, and wholly atypical, range of relationships. In any case, the depiction of globalization as locationless is itself quite misleading, as it fails to capture that dimension of globalization which is best described as state transformation. As will be argued at length below, this is fundamental to any understanding of globalization but such a perspective is endangered by superficial appeals to the 'end of geography'. Such mantras reinforce the stereotype that globalization is something going on 'out there', above and beyond the terrestrial activities of states. To describe the key attribute of globalization as the transcendence of borders equally risks losing sight of this statist dimension. Accordingly, the more mystical accounts of globalization need to be grounded in appropriate theories of the state, and not presented simply as descriptions of spatial transcendence.

Persevering with a largely territorialized conception seems, in any event, more compatible with a range of findings emerging from within studies of globalization itself. While it became fashionable in the late 1980s to depict the great corporations, not as multi- or transnational, but as '*postnational, stateless,* or *global*' (Mair 1997: 65), some degree of reaction has set in against this kind of nomenclature. At the grassroots of economic globalization, so to speak, analysts are no longer so persuaded about the 'placeless' nature of transnational corporations (TNCs). The finding of one such group of specialists is that 'recent developments in the organization of production processes . . . have led to an emerging re-evaluation of the relationship between TNCs and local areas' (Dicken, Forsgren, and Malmberg 1994: 23–4) in ways which enhance the importance of the local. There is a tendency, then, to give renewed emphasis to the complex interaction between globalism and localism in the strategies of these enterprises, such as Honda (Mair 1997: 67). If such a re-evaluation is taking place at one of the acknowledged leading edges of globalization, how much more questionable must be the alleged redundancy of place in most other aspects of economic life. Indeed, revisionist claims about the TNCs have been broadly repeated in the context of economic processes of globalization more generally. 'We argue that globalization does not represent the end of territorial distinctions and distinctiveness', it has been said, 'but an added set of influences on local economic identities and development capabilities' (Amin and Thrift 1994*b*: 2). This view is reiterated in other claims that the notion of 'locational substitutability', which underpins much of the economic globalization literature, is itself 'highly overgeneralized' (K. Cox 1997*c*: 119). If such territorially based distinctions and distinctiveness remain, they enjoin the theorist of globalization to observe caution before proceeding to dismiss their significance.

Additionally, the realm of the economic itself needs to be broken down into discrete elements. For example, in John Gray's analysis, globalization is regarded as a long-term and technology-dependent historical process, onto which has been grafted an additional but separate project for the creation of a single global market. Central to Gray's argument is the conclusion that both of these spheres, even within the economic domain, may experience different trajectories: the former he sees as a constant, whereas the latter he dismisses as a destructive, but relatively short-lived, phase. 'For humankind at the close of the modern period globalization is a historical fate', he insists, while drawing the contrast that 'technology-driven modernization of the world's economic life will go ahead regardless of the fate of a worldwide free market' (1998: 23). Another example of an attempt to apply globalization selectively to one aspect of the economic framework, rather than to the totality, is the suggestion that what is distinctive about globalization is that it marks a phase of 'deepening, but not widening capitalist integration' (Hoogvelt 1997: 115–16). Any such notion is welcome as a useful exercise in discrimination, even if it seems counter-intuitive to envisage globalization as a vertical rather than a horizontal process.

At the same time, this directs attention to the linkage between definition and historical development, and to the contentious issue of whether or not globalization is to be regarded as a qualitatively novel stage. As a matter of definition, a number of analysts insist upon a precise understanding of globalization that marks it off sharply from other forms of interdependence and internationalization (Petrella 1996: 62–4; M. Williams 1996: 116; Scholte 1997b: 14). Some have referred to it as implying 'a quantum leap beyond previous internationalisation stages' (Ruigrok and van Tulder 1995: 119). Dicken appears to agree that globalization is 'qualitatively different' from internationalization, but then partly contradicts his own position by elaborating that it represents 'a more advanced and complex form of internationalization which implies a degree of functional integration between internationally dispersed economic activities' (1992: 1). The former position suggests a qualitative threshold, whereas the latter is content to imply incrementalism. This confusion is compounded when he cites globalization as one of the sources furthering 'the degree of interdependence and integration between national economies' (1992: 87). It is not clear from these various comments whether globalization differs from internationalization and interdependence only as a matter of degree, or whether there is a difference of kind. In contrast, Scholte is in no doubt about the categorical distinction that needs to be made. For him, what is both new about globalization as a process, and revolutionary about it as an analytical concept, is its core meaning about the transcendence of borders. This distinction then forms the basis of the claim that globalization is a new and transformational phase going beyond previous levels of interconnection (Scholte 1997a: 430). Similarly, Held argues for recognition of a 'fundamental difference' between the present situation and previous levels of interdependence (Held 1995b: 101).

These issues might appear to be merely semantic but they underpin substantive claims about the novelty of today's forms of globalization and, by historical contrast, about the inexorability of today's economic and political development. Indeed, in some accounts, the irresistibility of globalization derives precisely from its novelty—from the fact that it represents a 'new stage' of capitalism. Since, historically, previous periods of internationalization have been challenged and turned back, as in the 1930s, the asserted novelty of globalization is used to lend weight to the case for its irreversibility. If globalization is a new phenomenon, we cannot speculate about any future retreat by appeal to historical precedents. For this reason, the dispute about the historical novelty of globalization becomes of critical importance to understanding future trends. Accordingly, a body of commentary has challenged the novelty of globalization, either as social development or as analytical category (Hirst and Thompson 1996; Helleiner 1997: 95–6; Scott 1997*b*: 15).

While there can be no objection to a precise definition of globalization, definitions should not be permitted to resolve the underlying issues of substance and historical interpretation. Even if, as end-state, globalization can be distinguished from greater interdependence between national entities, it is legitimate to suggest that the two are not so readily separable as aspects of historical process and development. At the very least, degrees of internationalization and interdependence can be understood to have been causally related to the advance of globalization (Clark 1997): they may have created preconditions out of which qualitatively novel conditions of globalization have subsequently evolved. For this reason, the sharp distinctions that seem appropriate in the making of definitions prove misleading when applied to complex processes of historical evolution.

These subtleties tend, however, to become lost in those historical accounts which see globalization ascending in relatively discrete stages, regardless of how the timetable is set out in individual accounts. Of these, there is a wide spectrum. Typically, at one end, Hirst contends that globalization is a continuing process that can be traced back for 'well over a century' (1997: 410). At the other end, Scholte is adamant that in its 'fully fledged' version globalization appears from around 1960, even if he is prepared to concede that 'considerable groundwork' had previously been laid (1997*b*: 19). This latter view is echoed in Cox's claim that it is tied to specific historic conditions which emerged only in the last three decades of this century (R. Cox 1996*a*: 24). Others claim that there has been a 'qualitative difference' since 1945 or 1950 (Amin 1996: 244–5). The very suggestion of 'groundwork' implies that there is a family lineage between those forms that are defined as globalized, and those defined in some other (and lesser) way. At the same time, the definitional approach seeks to deny this heritage: interdependence is thought to bear only a passing family resemblance to globalization.

Semantically, it also seems that a view of globalization as transcending space/territory/state misrepresents the nature of the process, and neglects the role of the state within it. Indeed, an absolute distinction between internationalization and globalization itself rests upon a version of the Great Divide. It assumes that internationalization is about states and describes the reconfiguration of their external relations. In contrast, globalization is claimed to project us into a world beyond states and territoriality which is distinct from such state-authored activities. This reproduces an analytic separation that fails to admit of any role for states, and of state transformation, in the process of globalization. There are subtle but significant distinctions between interdependence and globalization (see Chapter 5), but this is not the way to present them.

In the meantime, another set of problems must be considered. More is at stake in the debate about globalization than definition, historical interpretation, and issues of measurement. The debate extends also to whether globalization is a benign or malign force, and to the associated political stance that should be developed in response to it. We need an appreciation of this normative dimension as well to understand fully the framework within which the production of international relations now takes place.

The normative agendas of globalization

It is bad enough that there is no single conception of globalization, and commentators are unable to agree on the empirical evidence for its extent. These divisions are, however, considerably less acrimonious than the essentially normative or ideological confrontations that surround it: belief in globalization is as much a matter of faith as of fact. This reveals itself in the schism between those who regard globalization, neutrally, as a set of 'really existing conditions' and those who, to the contrary, regard it as a none-too-covert political project. In turn, this polarity expresses itself further in optimistic and pessimistic diagnoses about the impact of globalization.

The detached view is that globalization is a set of social, economic, and political conditions that can be analysed objectively: there is no need to adopt any normative position in relation to it. However, analysis does not so readily stand apart from prescription, particularly when 'inescapability' is deemed to be one of the inherent characteristics of globalization: the one then slides easily into the other. Cox represents these as two separate meanings of globalization: one is simply the extant 'complex of forces', while the other denotes an ideology within which the 'forces and policies . . . came to be regarded as inevitable' (R. Cox 1996b: 23). It is precisely this second meaning which is widespread throughout the literature, regardless of whether the inevitability is seen to be leading in a positive or negative direction. Typically, Scott describes globalization as a 'political project' and asks rhetorically whether we, as social scientists, 'are assisting the process of globalization by providing people with persuasive arguments to the effect that little can be done in the face of these enormous economic, political and social developments' (1997b: 2).

The literature on globalization also adopts a number of distinct, and often partisan, normative perspectives. Rosenau is unusual in trying to maintain that globalization is a value-neutral development. His position is that 'neither globalizing nor localizing dynamics are innately desirable or noxious' and that 'normatively, there is a good deal to be said for and against both of them' (Rosenau 1997a: 85). But his is a minority position. It is more common to espouse open advocacy, either for or against. Thus Hurrell and Woods identify a powerful cluster of liberal assumptions often attached to the concept: that it fosters economic efficiency, encourages the development of international institutions, and supports problem-solving approaches. It is thus welcomed by its supporters for the effect that it has in promoting 'societal convergence built around common recognition of the benefits of markets and liberal democracy' (1995: 449). Scholte similarly records the liberal expectation that 'contemporary globalization offers the prospect of at last fully realizing the promise of modernity' (1996*a*: 50–1). There is a widespread view of globalization as highly beneficial in 'subjecting workers and state to a new discipline, eliminating waste, reducing the power of the state, and so opening up new vistas of individual freedom and opportunity' (K. Cox 1997*b*: 2). Survival of the fittest is the means by which the species as a whole becomes fitter.

Against this, the critics view globalization as simply another phase of exploitative capitalism, a pretext for socially regressive governmental economic policies, and the means by which both domestic and international inequalities are further entrenched (Marshall 1996: 206). Its hallmarks are taken to be its 'anarchic and competitive character' (M. Cox 1998: 452). In this respect, the historical parallels are thought instructive. With reference to the nineteenth-century experience of a liberal international economy, it has been suggested that 'profound social dislocations accompanied the process of globalization and would eventually contribute to its undoing' (Kapstein 1996: 19). Globalization today will, for similar reasons, evoke counter-globalist political movements and reactions on the part of the most disadvantaged (R. Cox 1996*a*; Gills 1997*b*). Even erstwhile champions of the market have denounced the 'false dawn' represented by the globalization of the free market. They hold out apocalyptic visions: 'Today's regime of global *laissez-faire* will be briefer than even the *belle époque* of 1870 to 1914', is Gray's prophecy, with the added and chilling reminder that the latter 'ended in the trenches of the Great War' (1998: 7).

This posing of the issue returns the debate to the perceived interrelationship between the economic and political domains. In a restatement of Polanyi's broad thesis, it has been contended that contemporary globalization is currently resisted by an opposing logic of politics. 'The globalizing logic of capital', Scott hypothesizes, 'is always and already engaged in a struggle to escape political regulation, while politics is constantly fighting to keep economic activity under its control' (1997*b*: 15). By the same token, opposition to the deterministic logic of globalization may often be evoked by its own hidden political agenda. The wish to open up space for effective political action contra globalization is no more politically neutral than is the endorsement of globalization itself. Thus Gray tellingly chides Hirst and Thompson for the nostalgic undertones of their argument. He suggests that their scepticism about the extent of contemporary globalization derives from nothing other than the wish 'to defend as still viable political responses to globalization—such as European social democracy—that belong in the past' (Gray 1998: 64).

This presents the disagreement as a simple opposition between determinism and voluntarism, each dressed up in its respective political garb. According to the former, globalization is a foreordained process beyond the reach of political agency; in the view of the latter, the tide can be stemmed simply by choice of appropriate policies. Both positions are unacceptably simplistic and ignore the synergism between the two realms. There can be no straightforward clash between determinism and voluntarism because both the 'external' force of globalization and the 'internal' forms of resistance are part of a single logic of politics. They operate within the same field of forces, and not in separation from each other. The one is no more compelled, nor voluntarily selected, than is the other.

Beyond these political squabbles, there remains a more deep-seated normative issue, already hinted at in the exchanges between the optimists and pessimists. This is whether, or in what sense, globalization may be thought to constitute a form of *order* or not. Must we speak of globalization as a process without end-state, or can we legitimately speak of a globalized world order as a distinctive political form? The latter view is clearly set forth, for instance, in the suggestion that the contemporary Western state conglomerate, collectively, constitutes an 'emergent *global state*' (Shaw 1997*b*: 503–4). Globalization, to this extent and with whatever qualifications, represents an incipient political order.

The question has been raised in a number of contexts but remains resistant to satisfactory answers. Latham poses the issue succinctly: 'Despite the growing salience of the single term, globalization, to characterize much of our "post-Cold War moment" ', he remarks, 'the term refers to seemingly contrary processes . . . [This] may indicate that it makes a lot less sense to talk now about any overarching international order' (1997*a*: 205–6). But in which particular respect is the current order deficient, or more fragmented, than its historical precursors?

The argument has been presented in various forms, each of which casts globalization in a subtly different light. The first might be described as the dystopic absence of order: negative qualities appear in abundance but without any seeming coherence. The clearest example is provided in Falk's description of globalization as 'a constellation of market, technological, ideological and civilizational developments that have nothing in common'. Moreover, he adds for good measure, 'there is little, or no, normative agency associated with this emergent world order: it is virtually designer-free, a partial dystopia that is being formed spontaneously' (1997*a*: 125). We now experience new sets of connections, many of them more intense than hitherto. But what they conspicuously lack is any coherence, let alone any common purpose. Even at the most basic level, globalization seems not to constitute a 'minimum' order of the kind that has traditionally underpinned international society (Bull 1977). It has no common institutions fulfilling minimally agreed societal functions. Thus Rosenau insists that, as regards governance, 'the world is too disaggregated for grand logics that postulate a measure of global coherence' (1998: 32). Elsewhere, the same point is effectively made in the claim that globalization 'is a state; it is not a meaning' (Laidi 1998: 6).

Secondly, the themes of spontaneity and lack of design find an echo in those diagnoses of the contemporary disorder that bemoan the absence of effective controls. This is the essence of Gray's concern for the future of the world economy: 'It is the combination of this increasing stream of new technologies, unfettered market competition and weak or fractured social institutions that produces the global economy of our times' (1998: 76). On this reading, diffusion of control equals disorder. Whatever globalization represents, it is certainly not an order, merely a set of random and often contradictory developments.

In yet a third analysis, the emphasis again falls upon diffusion. 'Globalization can just as well be seen as the harbinger not of a new world order but of a new world *disorder*, even a "new medievalism" of overlapping and competing authorities, multiple loyalties and identities' (Cerny 1996a: 619). And yet, it may be asked, why should a return to a new medievalism be thought *prima facie* evidence of disorder, except perhaps in comparison with the clearly demarcated chain of command of the Westphalian system?

A fourth interpretation similarly makes the case in the negative by attributing disorder to the overthrow of existing orders. Thus Gray's anxieties are compounded variously by the challenge presented by the world market to state authority and, elsewhere, to its subversion of the American model of capitalism by an anarchic world of many capitalisms. In his extension of the Hobbesian analysis, we now live in a new state of nature formed by multiple capitalisms, without any overarching authority over them, and in which life is likely to be nasty, brutish, and short. In a similar and related way, it is the subversion of the existing order that is laid at globalization's door: 'Globalization is, then,' it has been pointed out, 'a threat to the American idea of world order, which has to be an order of nation-states' (Albrow 1996: 74). More generally, it has been asserted of globalization that its capacity to destroy the old is more impressive than its capacity to replace the old with something new: 'globalization can weaken old political and economic structures', notes Held, 'without necessarily leading to the establishment of new systems of regulation' (1995a: 96).

In a fifth version, globalization's inducement of disorder is attributable to its open-ended nature. In part, and as described above, this is because globalization contains within it contradictory tendencies towards both integration and disintegration. It thus lacks the capacity to generate 'a more clearly defined and homogenous global order' for the simple reason that, by its nature, globalization is a 'heterogeneous and fuzzy phenomenon' (Cerny 1996b: 135). Others make the same general point. It has been insisted that globalization 'does not tell us what specific form of social order actually obtains' but only something about its context (Saurin 1997: 109). In summary, globalization is deemed unworthy of the appellation of an order because it is no more than a transitional phase. In Albrow's account, it is possible to view it as 'the transition to a new era rather than the apogee of the old' (1996: 101). For this reason, it lacks the settled and durable condition that we associate with an order. This is why, according to Albrow, writers like Giddens and Robertson get it wrong because their association of globalization with modernity is inherently teleological and 'treats an outcome as a necessary product of a process' (1996: 99).

These arguments collectively portray globalization as disorder rather than meaningful order. There are too many disparate elements within globalization to discern any coherent 'design' to it. The process is unquestionably indeterminate in outcome. It is as misleading to imagine that globalization is a structure imposing its universal logic as it is to believe that state actors can, at political whim, choose to resist all its manifestations. Much of this can be readily conceded. Nonetheless, a major qualification needs to be entered at this point against the unduly anarchic accounts of globalization summarized above. What they all leave out of account is the notion of a discernible order in the residual sense of a 'meaningful' relationship between political transformation at the state and system levels. Just as the cold war international order was not simply a set of relations among states, but also a distinct form within them, so globalization is an order to the extent that it posits a synchronic relationship among, within, and beyond states. This need not be politically stable in the longer term, and specific forms of accommodation will be eroded across time. Nonetheless, the central claim must be that globalization posits a necessary connection between the international order and the types of state of which it is composed. In that minimal sense there is more coherence to globalization than the above-cited critics are prepared to allow.

Unhappily, when IR theory turns to globalization, it fails to adopt such an integrated perspective. Rather than explore the dynamic symbiosis between the 'internal' and 'external' dimensions of globalization, IR theory has tended to restate the Great Divide: globalization, so it is claimed, is a change of external circumstance that impinges upon state capacity. It is to this aspect of the globalization debate that we must finally turn.

Globalization and state capacity

The debate closest to the concerns of IR theory is whether globalization is some kind of autonomous force—driven by technology, economic organization, communications, or cultural patterns—or whether it reflects actual conditions of international relations and distributions of international power (Clark 1997). Liberal versions of globalization adhere to the former point of view in so far as 'states and governments are bystanders to globalisation: the real driving forces are markets' (Hurrell and Woods 1995: 448). If the driving force is not markets, then in other accounts it lies in uncontrollable technological developments. This is the heart of Rosenau's argument: 'For globalization is not so much a product or extension of the interstate system as it is a wholly new set of processes, a separate form of world politics, initiated by technologies that have fostered new human needs and wants' (1997a: 221). Such views carry implications for the diminished role of political agency, and prompt speculation about the supposed irreversibility of globalization.

The alternative standpoint denies that globalization has 'its own inexorable logic' (Waters 1995: 46, describing Robertson's position) and thereby maintains that it may well be discontinuous and reversible. For example, globalization has been described as being 'as much a dependent as a driving force' and one of the things on which it depends is the strength of 'democratic forces' (Albrow 1996: 92–3). Armstrong, while aware of the powerful pressures of globalization, reminds us also that these come up against the equally potent force of international society. The latter serves to shore up the 'social state' (1998: 461–2, 468–9).

These perspectives have structured the debates into the proponents of globalization as an autonomous force (Cerny 1993c: 13) versus those who regard it as politically driven and sustained (Kapstein 1994: v, 1996: 16; Albrow 1996: 92–3; Milner and Keohane 1996a: 24; Parker 1996: 76). Although they hedge their arguments with significant qualifications, both James Rosenau and Phil Cerny lean towards the former position. Rosenau maintains that 'some globalizing dynamics are bound, at least in the long run, to prevail' (1997a: 82), and elsewhere is adamant that it is 'the processes of globalisation that are setting the terms and shaping the structures of the emergent global order' (1997b: 225–6). Cerny, although speaking more restrictively about financial globalization, deems it to be 'irreversible' (1994: 226). This contrasts with expressions of the other view, that the persistence of globalization is contingent upon political dynamics and frameworks. Thus Hirst insists upon the necessary role of 'appropriate public institutions' in sustaining a liberal trading order (1997: 414–15). The most cogent exponent of this second view has repeatedly argued that economic globalization is reversible (Helleiner 1997: 95–6), and that 'the contemporary open global financial order could never have emerged without the support and blessing of states' (Helleiner 1994a: vii). A similar analysis of the international monetary system notes that transnational processes, including the organization of credit, 'are always and everywhere mediated by specific state structures' (Germain 1997: 6). In all such formulations, there is deemed to be a causal connection between state action and the globalization that is produced as a consequence of it. Globalization is thereby separate from state action and, to the extent that it is fostered, is so as a result of conscious state policy choices. Left out of this analysis is the possibility that state action is a fundamental part of globalization, not an independent cause of it; and that globalization occurs as much because of the form of the state itself, as in consequence of the external environment that it seeks consciously to create.

This general issue of the degree of its autonomy slides quickly into the related matter that dominates much of the writing on globalization: its impact on the capacities of the state. If globalization is seen to be autonomous, its consequence is generally thought to be the erosion of state effectiveness. This conclusion is reversed when the state itself is understood to be the instrument of globalization. In this latter case, globalization is presented as being, in some essential respect, at the mercy of state capacity, and to be unsustainable without the supportive political frameworks created by it. In the final section of this chapter, this dichotomous posing of the issue—the state in retreat or globalization's dependency upon the state—will first be reviewed and then rejected.

It is precisely because globalization is perceived to be a threat to the state's continuing ability to function and to perform its traditional roles that it holds such interest for political theorists and students of international relations. The combined case for the state's loss of sovereignty in the face of globalization is the shorthand expression for this concern, and is prevalent in the multifarious suggestions that a new world order is thereby in the process of emergence. Were it not for the seeming fact of 'the state in retreat', globalization would not have its contemporary resonance.

The argument comes, however, with a variety of distinctive nuances and emphases. Three categories, distinguishable if overlapping, can be discerned. The first is the most general and points to the obsolescence of the state as manager of its own functional activities, especially in the economic realm. This is classically conveyed in the assertion that there 'will no longer be national economies' (Reich 1991: 3). There have been many variations on this same central theme. Rosenau echoes the argument that 'all states seem likely to become increasingly ineffective as managers of their own affairs' (1997a: 362). Hoogvelt comments that 'the integrity of the national territorial state as a more or less coherent political economy is eroded' (1997: 67). In a refinement of these claims, it has also been suggested that the situation is more complex in that the state remains territorially fixed for political purposes, but not for economic ones. Part of the problem for the state, accordingly, is the creation of a 'disjuncture . . . between the "economic nation" and the state as the territorial administrative unit' (Higgott 1996: 33).

A second, and slightly more modest, framing of the argument is that the state's powers are diminished, in the sense that it is now one actor competing with many others. In this version, the argument has, of course, been around since the 1960s, especially in the form that presents the state's powers as being usurped by the multinational corporations. Strange writes of the TNCs as encroaching on the state's claims to power, and 'exercising a parallel authority' alongside them (1996: 65). In a more general variant, going beyond the corporations, other writers see the diminution of the role of the state as accountable to the emergence of other actors, who compete with them in functional responsibility. Thus Falk locates his analysis of the subversion of the state's capacity 'to control and protect the internal life of society' in the context of the roles played by the multitudinous non-state actors on the scene (1997a: 124–5). But it is a moot, and possibly definitional, point whether the growth of non-state actors is really what globalization is about and whether, in this case, the retreat of the state can be laid at the door of globalization, or merely at that of transnationalism.

The third and final version, but by no means exclusive of the other two, is the widespread notion that the state has been impoverished by its loss of controls, not to other actors, but instead to the impersonal structure of the market itself. Indeed, this might be seen as the cause of the functional disability highlighted in the first category. In this vein, Strange speaks of the generic shift in the balance of power 'from states to markets' (1996: 29).

But those who deny the autonomy of globalization tend to deny with equal force the validity of such interpretations. For them, the idea of the state–globalization relationship as being zero-sum is basically misconceived, as it fails to take into account the degree to which the state itself is the architect of globalization. To the extent that this is so, globalization falls within the penumbra of the state's own structural power, and it is contradictory to imagine the state losing power to its own creation.

Accordingly, there are those who continue to insist, against the erosionists, upon undiminished state capacity: some even go so far as to suggest that states are more potent now than ever. 'So-called "globalization" is not likely to displace state power', is one such confident judgement; 'If anything, it will make it more salient' (Weiss 1998: 13). This side of the argument is expressed once again in three principal versions: that all economic and market structures reflect political frameworks and choices; that the state remains potent in the development of the process of globalization itself; and that the state remains decisive, notwithstanding the effects and constraints of globalization.

The first of these is a recurrent notion and virtually the hallmark of realist views of international political economy. Its authoritative statement can be found in Gilpin (1987). It is endorsed, perhaps surprisingly, by prominent historical sociologists who have pronounced, unequivocally, that 'economic factors habitually reflect rather than cause geopolitical conditions' (Hall 1996: 165). Elsewhere, anti-erosionists base their case on continuing state efficacy, and on the assumption that 'markets and companies cannot exist without a public power to protect them' (Hirst and Thompson 1996: 188).

If that is true of markets in general, it has been contended that it is true of so-called 'free' markets in particular. This is the point which Gray has strenuously developed in his most recent work—the idea that free markets are not a natural condition but reflect political choice and action: 'free markets are creatures of state power' (1998: 17). From this initial assumption, the argument can readily be developed that globalization itself has been fostered by cumulative state choices and actions. In his analysis of the evolution of global finance, Helleiner constantly reiterates this message: 'financial globalization has also been heavily dependent on state support and encouragement' (1996: 193). In this sense, there can be no long-term subversion of states by globalization, as the future of globalization is itself dependent upon the continuing viability of these very states. 'The evidence of the past is that design can only become reality when effective geopolitical structures are put in place', one observer has written. Given the contingent and incomplete nature of the process of globalization, the conclusion can be drawn that 'the presence or absence of these remains the critical factor in determining whether globalization as scheme can be given the stability of an order' (Parker 1996: 76). Evidently, the demise of state-designed geopolitical structures would prevent any such completion.

Finally, what can be said of the fate of the state? The second school of thought likewise insists upon the efficacy and relative autonomy of state action in conditions of globalization. Although writing from a critical perspective, Mittelman is at the very least adamant that states and the state system should not be reduced to 'mere epiphenomena' of the global division of labour (Mittelman 1996*b*: 6). As against those who have debunked the continuing relevance of a national economy, some revisionists have entered the fray with studies of the dynamics of technological innovation. It is their finding that this depends upon national differences, and that 'nation-states, national economies and national systems of innovation are still essential domains of economic and political analysis'

(Freeman 1997: 45). Yet others shift their gaze to the political dimensions and still find hope for national political action, even if the hope is expressed in contingent form. Hirst challenges the conventional wisdom when he contends that 'public policy still has a measure of autonomy', but to this he attaches the qualification that this is so only 'provided electorates are willing to pay the price in taxation' (1997: 422). All such arguments, however, remain couched in the language of the relative strengths of the state versus globalization: the state is incapacitated by globalization, or globalization needs to be sustained by the state. In the next section, this opposition will be overturned.

IR theory and globalization

This chapter has reviewed the bewildering variety of debates about globalization: about its definitions and meanings; its historical novelty; its beneficial and detrimental qualities; the extent to which it reveals a single (and coherent) logic, or multiple (and dissonant) tendencies; and its impact on the viability of the state itself. It would be a work of supreme artifice to reduce this boisterous and wideranging discussion to a tidy core of issues, but some order needs to be imposed to make intelligible the connections with what is to follow in the remainder of the book.

What this requires as a first step is to recognize that, underlying the many specific areas of debate already considered, globalization is also contested along some more general fault-lines. These, by their very nature, touch upon issues that have a marked resonance throughout IR theory. One of these is that between the ideational and the material. This relates particularly to whether globalization is driven by material forces (technology, communications, or economic systems) and is significant in that realm alone. Alternatively, equally important might be its impact on human understanding of those changes. Waters combines the two in his frequently noted definition: globalization is 'A social process in which the constraints of geography on social and cultural arrangements recede and in which people become increasingly aware that they are receding' (1995: 3). Such an approach accepts that globalization impinges both on the material and the cognitive worlds, and that any theoretical account of it must address both. This is, of course, exactly what some constructivist approaches seek to do by giving due weight to ideational factors, while by no means discounting their material setting (Ruggie 1998; cf. Armstrong 1998: 473–5).

Another generic IR concern that emerges in discussions of globalization is that of the relationship between the economic and the political spheres. This manifests itself in the double sense that economics and politics may be *causally* related, the one following from the other or vice versa. As already noted, economic globalization is thought by some to pull political transformation in its wake, whereas others insist that political architecture must precede economic process. Alternatively, the two may be related *oppositionally*, in so far as politics is thought to serve as a check to the globalizing potential of economics. Virtually all theories of international relations are concerned with the dynamic interaction between the two fields. However, as things now stand, there is an impasse in the debate about globalization, and existing analytical preferences are simply reproduced. The apostles of economic or of political primacy do little more than interpret globalization within their respectively preferred paradigms, rather than using the test case of globalization as a means to develop a more integrated, and interesting, statement of the relationship. But unless the understanding of globalization can fashion some association between the economic and the political, it will be less than useful for incorporation into a theory of international relations.

The IR theorist needs to be sensitive to these general issues. But there are also profound divergences of opinion about the relevance of globalization to key developments within international relations itself. The contested nature of globalization can be illustrated, for example, in the competing understandings of its relationship to the end of the cold war. While in some accounts, globalization is regarded as a consequence of the end of the cold war, in others it is the progress of globalization that is thought to have destroyed the cold war's salience, and its *raison d'être*. It is appealing to imagine that it has been the termination of the cold war that has allowed the territorial extension of globalizing forces, since they now have purchase upon sectors of the globe from which they had hitherto been substantially, if not entirely, excluded. Thus viewed, the latest phase of globalization can be dated from the crumbling of the cold war in the 1980s, and interpreted as a consequence of it.

But the causal relationship can also be reversed with equal plausibility, resulting in the argument that it was precisely the encroachment of globalizing forces which eroded the basis of cold war competition, not to mention the economic viability of one of its protagonists. Viewed from this perspective, the utility of globalization lies in drawing attention to the continuities between the cold war and post-cold war periods (Ikenberry 1996).

So is globalization cause or effect? In truth, it is both. It depicts the extent to which the state has become disembedded from the post-war international order. In turn, the demise of the cold war increased the potential expanse of the new order within which it operated. The confusion about whether globalization precipitated the end of the cold war, or resulted from it, disappears when we remember that globalization was simultaneously taking place both at the level of the state and of the international system. If the focus on the latter tends to emphasize post-cold war discontinuity, the focus on the former reminds us of the continuities as well. Both are part of the reality of the post-cold war world, and globalization can accommodate the continuity as well as the change, provided that its location in both state and system is borne in mind.

But if globalization survived as analytical concept, it did so in part because of the flexibility and very diversity of reference entailed by it (Amin 1996: 231). This fuzziness is both its strength and its weakness. Moreover, it is precisely because of the contested nature of its core meanings that a host of other cognate disputes have proved recalcitrant to resolution.

This is evidently the case with regard to the normative debate. It is easy to dismiss this as a straightforward case of 'where you stand depends upon where you sit'. In economic terms, and with respect to access to global networks (travel, communications, cultural artefacts), globalization manifestly produces winners and losers. That the assessment of globalization should then take such a polarized form is no less than one might expect. However, there is also reason for believing that the issue runs deeper than this. Judgements about globalization reflect more than one's personal relationship to it: they also reveal differing assessments of what is intellectually at stake in confronting globalization.

This is true at two distinct levels. In the first instance, judgement varies in accordance with the scope of globalization. Narrowly conceived, globalization can be presented as little more than the current phase of the global market, and assessments made accordingly. In these terms, personal positions and stakes can readily be understood. However, when presented, as above, as a widespread process of social, political, and cultural change, the self-interested perspective is less pertinent, and less revealing. The very multidimensionality of globalization renders it unlikely that there will be winners across the board. Some who benefit in economic terms may yet feel threatened by cultural change.

At the second level, globalization is resistant to uniform judgement precisely because of a lack of consensus as to its nature. From this perspective, the debate is coloured by elements of determinism and voluntarism. Those who gravitate to the deterministic end of the spectrum (albeit for diverse reasons—technology, teleology, progress, libertarianism, or whatever) respond to globalization with celebration, or with resignation. At the voluntaristic end, there is either the fear that globalization, as historical contrivance, will suffer a new setback, or a determination to ensure that it does: either way the emphasis is upon political agency to sustain, or subvert, what has thus far been put in place.

There has been little attempt in all this to articulate the middle position, and for this reason the discussion of globalization has itself become analytically polarized. Deterministic approaches emphasize the notion of globalization happening beyond our reach, while we stand by as passive beneficiaries or victims. Voluntaristic approaches succumb to the appeal that we can slay the dragon of globalization only by a return to the good old political days. Both fail to give due recognition to the twin reality of globalization, as something that creates new constraints while at the same time itself reflecting changes in state forms already under way.

This is especially so in attempts to unravel the relationship between state and globalization. On the issue of state capacity, the cheerleaders whip up support for their respective teams. The globalists pronounce the end of national economies, of geography, and of the state itself. The statists denounce the misunderstandings on which such judgements have been reached. We are cautioned to beware 'the more enthusiastic of the globalists':

With little sense of history, they exaggerate the former strength of nation-states; with little sense of global variety, they exaggerate their current decline; with little sense of their plurality, they downplay international relations. (Mann 1997: 494)

Throughout these exchanges, we have been repeatedly confronted with simple choices that revolve around the state as the subject or the object of globalization. Substantively, we are invited to choose between the state as the indispensable political framework for the maintenance of globalization, and the state as the hapless victim of the globalizing forces that threaten it from outside. Either way, both sets of claims miss the point. What is presented as the erosion of state capacity is less the consequence of globalization (as some force independent from it), and more a depiction of that very state transformation that lies at its heart. IR theory at the moment operates with a duality of state *and* globalization when, more accurately, there is only a single process at work.

We are therefore faced with a debate about globalization that has adopted a closely integrated and highly structured form. The core issues, whatever the specific variation, are presented as pairs of opposed choices: determinism or voluntarism; economics or politics; order or disorder; progress or polarization; and so on. Above all, the key question for IR theory is rendered as follows: has globalization weakened the state, or is globalization itself a creature of the state?

But what if these are false antinomies and pose completely the wrong series of questions? As a first stage in the effort to overcome the Great Divide, the next chapter will challenge this presentation of the issue. If we are to develop a historically aware and politically sensitive understanding of globalization, the Great Divide is not the most promising point of departure: we must start elsewhere.

GLOBALIZATION AND THE STATE

This chapter will further refine the globalization template, and establish the framework within which the remainder of the book can address the state's ability to produce a range of goods and services in globalized conditions. As against the recurrent tendency of the Great Divide to make a sharp distinction between the internal (the state's domestic aspect) and the external (the exogenous environment in which the state finds itself), a scheme will be developed which seeks to integrate the two. It thereby also becomes possible to overcome the implied opposition between globalization and the state. The core of the unfolding argument is that globalization needs also to be understood as a number of changes within the state, and not simply as a range of external forces set against it. This echoes the similar claim that it is 'wholly erroneous to counterpoise globalization to the state' (Shaw 1997*b*: 498). We need, however, to move beyond such generalized critiques and articulate how it is that globalization represents a *state form*, rather than some zero-sum threat to existing state powers.

The first point that needs to be established is that, historically, transnational forces and the separate state have developed in tandem. In the past, the two have not been antagonistic and have, indeed, depended upon each other. This emerges clearly in the works of historical sociologists who point to the conjoint evolution of capitalism, transnational cultural forms, and the individualized nation-state. These, we are told, 'have always possessed a complex combination of relative autonomy and symbiotic interdependence' (Mann 1997: 477). If this is the case in general, there is no reason why the onset of globalization should mark some radical historical disjuncture between the state and other non-territorial transactions. The challenge for theory is to specify, historically, the admixture of 'autonomy and symbiosis' in the national and the transnational, and to identify the political dynamic which shifts the relative balance of power between the two across time. Shaw depicts recent political globalization as the emergence of an embryonic 'global state'. Whether that specific formulation is altogether persuasive or not, his more generally applicable analytical point is that contemporary forms of the state can properly be understood only within the context of this wider global formation. He perceives a 'continuing interdependence and mutual constitutiveness of these two major forms' (Shaw 1997*b*: 512). In similar spirit, this chapter seeks to elaborate a framework that makes sense of globalization and the state by showing what they have in common, instead of insisting upon what it is that brings them into inexorable opposition and collision.

It may seem contrary to common sense to devote so much attention to the state in a work on globalization. If any generalization can be made about globalization then it surely must be that economic, political, and social processes are no longer meaningfully contained within state borders. In this sense, all versions of the term 'global' stand as an implicit challenge to the term 'international' with its resonances of state-based and inter-state activities. Is it not the case then that globalization marks a departure from traditional IR theory exactly in so far as it seeks to escape the confines of its state-centric frameworks of analysis? And what is the point of a globalization frame of reference if the discussion leads to the state being reintroduced by the back door?

Such objections might seem reasonable but are essentially misplaced. It is not the objective in what follows to reduce all manifestations of globalization to a series of footnotes to the traditional IR agenda. Nonetheless, if the goal is to understand the unsettling effect that globalization has upon IR theory, then it is against the traditionalist conceptions that globalization must be set: only by measuring the extent to which conventional frameworks are now deficient can the impact of globalization be comprehended. Additionally, however, as this exercise is undertaken, it will also emerge that we must be circumspect in assuming an inherent antagonism between globalization and the state. If IR theory is to be reworked in the light of ideas about globalization, this reworking needs to admit the role of state transformation in the production of globalization, and cannot be confined to the assumed duality between the state and the forces of globalization. Such a reified antagonism helps neither in the comprehension of globalization nor in the development of IR theory.

The stages of the unfolding argument will be as follows. First, and in general terms, there will be a restatement of the artificiality of the separation of state form from international structure. This leads to a more explicit engagement with aspects of state theory, focused particularly on the issues of state autonomy and state strength. The question will be posed of what happens to such discussions once a globalization perspective is injected into them. The chapter then sets out a concept of the 'broker' state as an explicit refutation of neo-realist styles of argument. Finally, there is an attempt to explicate the significance of such an analysis for our understanding of globalization and its possible future trajectories.

Globalization: state or system?

In order to assess the nature of globalization, we need to have a clearer idea about the areas on which its supposed impact is being felt. For instance, conventional approaches to the topic enquire whether globalization is transforming the nature of the state, or of the state system, or of the global system more broadly conceived. To pose the question in this form is already to see the fallacy on which it is based.

Such a formulation of the issue assumes a readier separation between these categories than may easily be achievable in practice. This is especially so if it can be established that there is an intimate connection between the form of the state and the wider system of which it is a part.

Collectively, what this demonstrates is that the consequences of globalization cannot be studied by a methodology of disaggregation. It is not helpful to ask distinct questions about the extent to which globalization erodes the state, or transforms the international system, for the very reason that both of these are inextricably linked. Globalization impinges not only on states and the system of which they are a part, but also upon those specific political trade-offs between them that have done so much to shape the identities of both during the recent historical period. To present globalization as a threat to the state, in isolation, is then to miss the central point: what it destabilizes is not the state, but that particular accommodation between the domestic and international components of order.

An analogy might serve to illustrate the argument to be developed in what follows. The analogy is between globalization and the concept of 'anarchy' that has traditionally played such a major role in IR theorizing, especially within its realist variants. Definitions of the nature of anarchy are themselves deeply contested, and its precise characteristics lie at the core of the disagreements between neo-realist and neo-liberal writers (Baldwin 1993). What is this anarchy? Is it cause or effect? Is it an attribute of a self-help system of (any) states, or is it merely the creation of (specific) states whose intrinsic qualities are already assumed (Milner 1991; Wendt 1992)? Some initial clarification of these issues will set the scene for the ensuing discussion of the way globalization relates to IR theory.

Within the existing IR literature, there are typically two approaches to thinking about anarchy. The one operates from the inside out, and the other from the outside in. Neither provides an adequate or convincing account on its own. Nor can the two be simply aggregated. A better solution requires that the nature of the problem be redefined so that such an oppositional framework is avoided altogether.

Generally, anarchy (in contradistinction to hierarchical polities) is thought to refer to the absence of a central and authoritative body of rule-making and is, to this extent, defined in the negative, as a condition lacking the appurtenances of 'domestic' political systems. Whether or not this is a fully accurate conception of the 'international' (and this is precisely the issue that divides neo-realists from neo-liberals), the question is why this characteristic should have emerged at all. Is it a product of the state system itself? Or is it an artefact of the particular nature of the states that compose it? Or can no such theoretical separation be made?

Is it a product of the state system? This is indeed the claim of those who argue from the outside in. Such an interpretation is very closely associated with neo-realism. Indeed, the very notion of structural realism—in which anarchy is an attribute of the structure and structure is a component of the system—provides an interlocking set of definitions which explicitly and exclusively makes the connection. For anarchy to be an attribute of the individual states would represent an internal contradiction in the theory, and render the notion of structure itself theoretically redundant. On the face of it, then, anarchy is an outside-in formation, part of the structural circumstance that makes states do what they do. Should globalization, by analogy, be thought of in the same way?

The standard critiques of the Waltzian account, of course, do not accept much of this at face value (Keohane 1986; Devetak 1995). According to the inside-outers, the self-help system of anarchy develops, not as an inevitable structure between any sovereign states, but only as a consequence of the specific character-istics with which these states have already been endowed—primordially, and certainly before they 'enter' the structure. They are already egotistical, self-interested, rational maximizers of certain kinds of utilities before they encounter any other states. From this perspective, anarchy arises not out of a disembodied structure, but as a natural consequence of the genetic coding implanted in these particular types of body politic. It is this assumed 'naturalism' that gives rise to the apparently 'social', and not vice versa. Is globalization likewise a property of the individual states that is creating a global system in its own image?

The one-sidedness of both sets of argument soon reveals itself when we return to the substantive content of this anarchy and discover that it simultaneously— and necessarily—derives from both the agent and the structure. The notion of anarchy, as well as the associated image of the state of nature, posits a negative condition of absence of authority only when set against the positive condition of hierarchy wherein such rule exists. Otherwise expressed, anarchy describes those residual spaces left over when the pockets of domestic order were first carved out. Anarchy, to change the metaphor, is the disordered desert surrounding the oases of order within states.

Beyond this, however, confusion reigns supreme. As noted, the one strand of writing assumes such anarchy to be artificial because it has been created by the constitution of states and is, in that sense, *post hoc.* The other sees anarchy as being the original position, an atavism not yet eliminated 'out there', as it has been within the states themselves. In reality, the relationship is more reciprocal than this posing of the issue would seem to imply. We can have no concept of anarchy without hierarchy, and vice versa: without the desert, we would not recognize the oases for what they are. By extrapolation, without anarchy we would have no con-cept of the state as a unit of political action, and without the ordered state it would be impossible to define the condition of anarchy. There is a profound mutuality at work here that prevents any simple either/or rendition of the constitution of anarchy. And if this holds for anarchy, then it may be submitted that it holds equally for the condition of globalization. Globalization shapes the state and is, at the same time, what states make of it.

But not all states are equal in the 'making' of globalization. Most of the discus-sion in this book is primarily applicable to state forms, and state transformations, to be found largely in the industrialized North. This most certainly does not mean that globalization has no effect on the South, or that the South may not be criti-cal in the long-term trajectory of globalization. It is a simple recognition that globalization is not divorced from the power structures associated with inter-state relations and, as such, the strong states of the North have thus far imposed the heavier imprint upon it.

Nor is this 'making' of globalization an outcome of pure voluntarism on the part of states. Such a description is little more than convenient shorthand for a complex, and often punishing, political process. This returns the discussion to the conception of the state and its political dynamics. The strategy must now be to construct a framework which moves beyond crude separations between the internal and the external, but which does not do so by simply reducing the one to the other. How might such a theoretical perspective be developed in the context of globalization?

The strength of the state

The problem with existing IR approaches to the state is precisely that the fault-line of the Great Divide cuts through its internal and external dimensions. It is the presence of the state that defines domesticity, and its absence that denotes internationality. In fact, the domestic and the international cannot be so separated: they are essential parts of each other and it is the state that, politically, brings them together. In other words, if we are to develop a working concept of globalization, we must begin with an adequate theory of the state. In particular, we must recognize that the state itself is not simply an outgrowth of the internal, but already reflects the presence of the external as well. Traditional IR theory puts *all* of the state on one side of the Great Divide (for domestic purposes) and equally places *all* of it on the other side (for international purposes). Such a sleight of hand creates an illusion of two separate states, acting within separate fields of forces, when actually there is only one state acting within a single field. How then might the state be theorized in such a way as to make sense of globalization?

Much of the theoretical discussion about the nature of the state is concerned with the issue of autonomy. That idea emerged as a counter to those social theories, such as Marxism, that posited the state as the 'prisoner' of social or class forces. As Fred Halliday observes, 'once the state is seen as institutionally distinct from society, the question arises of the degree to which it can act autonomously, and represent values separate from that society' (1994: 79). The claim deriving from such notions is that, if the state is 'free' from domestic social forces, it can act 'strategically', making independent decisions about what constitutes its interests. This autonomy has been described as either 'infrastructural'—deriving from the state's capacity to penetrate the rest of society—or 'despotic'—a measure of the independent power exercised by state managers (Mann 1986, 1993; Jessop 1990: 279). Both accounts regard autonomy as an aspect of the relationship between the state and 'its' society. In other variants, autonomy is generated by the acquisition of special interests for the state 'by virtue of its insertion into an international order' (Jessop 1990: 92).

Of course, there are varying degrees to which such autonomy might be thought to exist. Some hold to the view that, in conditions of globalization, it is precisely the state's capacity to act strategically that has been eroded (Cerny 1996*a*: 635).

Others insist that the state retains this capacity because of its location at the inter-face between the international and the national. The state, it has been contended, 'looks both inward and outward, and in the process derives considerable power and autonomy, often by playing each spatial dimension off against the other' (Hobson 1997: 253–4).

This latter conception is fully suited to the development of a globalization tem-plate. Nonetheless, it is apparent that, for an analysis of globalization, there are serious shortcomings in the way that the issue of state autonomy has traditionally been presented. In so far as autonomy is an attribute of state–society relations, it slides over the critical issue of *which* society is pertinent to the discussion. As long as the sociology of the state proceeded on the tidy assumption of a demarcated national society, coterminous with the political institutions of the state, this was relatively unproblematic. However, it is precisely any such correspondence that globalization seeks to destabilize. What are we to make of state autonomy in the context of a relationship with a society that is no longer caged by the state? And if some state theorists (Jessop 1990: 288) wish to reject what they see as a false dichotomy between state and society—since neither is 'distinct' or 'self-determining'—how is the (bounded) state to be identified with (unbounded) society?

There is a great deal at stake in these issues, and this is just as true within a con-structivist framework. Clearly, the idea of a fully autonomous state is as prob-lematic for constructivism as for the varieties of neo-utilitarianism, in the sense that state interests and identity would appear as an unproblematic given. If such an assumption is unwarranted, and to be avoided, then we must make space for the suggestion that those interests are constructed through social interaction. Accordingly, we need to move towards a recognition that 'the state-as-actor is not fully formed or complete prior to interaction; it only takes on the appearance of completion in interaction' (Devetak 1995: 28). But interaction with what?

At this stage, it is conventional to respond that the interaction is with other states, resulting in the social creation of the state system or, for that matter, of some of its supposed characteristics, such as anarchy (Wendt 1992). However, if the idea of the simultaneously inward- and outward-looking state is taken seri-ously, it immediately becomes evident that there is a twofold process of interac-tion at work: 'internally' with regard to society and 'externally' with regard to other states and other actors. The formation of state identity is, by its very nature, bimodal and constitution takes place with respect to both. While arguably this pulling in two directions does create some leverage for the state, it must under-mine the suggestion that the state is fully autonomous: while the state is not a prisoner of either national or international forces, neither can it be viewed as being detached from both. Again, however, the problem is evident. How can we sensibly speak about the 'internal' constitution of the state if the pertinent soci-ety with which it engages—or at least much of it—is no longer 'in' there?

Similar issues arise in the context of discussions of state 'strength' (see Weiss 1998: 14–40). What creates a strong state? Two answers are conventionally pro-vided, and there is no reason to think that they are mutually exclusive. Once more they point, respectively, inwards to civil society and outwards to the society of states. Moreover, there is assumed to be a complex interplay between the two. External sources of strength can buttress states that are weak internally, but may also encourage them to pursue coercive policies that actually weaken them further. This has been dubbed the 'state-strength dilemma' (Holsti 1996: 117). What becomes equally apparent is that state strength is, paradoxically and confusingly, used simultaneously as a measure of state *separateness* from society and of state *closeness* to society. These confusions need to be addressed before globalization is inserted as a further complicating factor in the assessment of state strength.

The first measure overlaps with parts of the above discussion of autonomy, and locates strength as a particular form of state–society relationship. State strength (despotic) can be derived from the state's separateness from society. Alternatively, its strength (infrastructural) lies in its ability to penetrate its own civil society and to mobilize its skills and resources. The terminology of 'hard' and 'soft' states has been employed to designate similar sets of relationships (Mastanduno, Lake, and Ikenberry 1989: 467–8).

In this sense, an authoritarian state, whatever its 'despotic control' over civil society, might not be very effective in its mobilization. In short, state strength is not inversely proportional to the weakness of civil society, but correlates positively with its resilience. As others have explained, 'strong states . . . are not built on weak or poorly organized civil societies' (Ikenberry 1995: 119). The extension of Ikenberry's argument is telling in this context, as he urges that 'the great struggles to build citizenship, civil society, and states actually reinforced each other' (1995: 119). Already it can be seen that one element of the constitution of state identity is the engagement—internally—with civil society. If that is true of the state's identity in general, it is true of its strength in particular.

How does globalization affect our thinking about the constitution of state identity from within? In this first context, the idea of globalization might be thought to destabilize such reinforcement. This is the thrust of many observations. Typically, we find the following analysis: 'The state's roots are no longer in the nation; its extent is worldwide . . . The state in the Global Age has been uprooted' (Albrow 1996: 64). Leaving aside the specific sense in which this might be true, the import of the comment is to undermine the extent to which the state, and its social identity, is constructed from below by engagement with a distinctive social base. If societies are interpenetrating, the state is less likely to reflect the distinctive characteristics of *its* society. At the very least, globalization problematizes the notion of state strength as deriving from the singularities of its own social mobilization.

The other area in which the state finds its strength is within the social institutions of the state system itself (Armstrong 1998). As generally noted, the state is shored up from the outside by the panoplies of sovereignty, equality, and non-intervention. In the case of some of the weakest states of the South, strength is mainly derived from this quarter in the absence of effective domestic sources of sustenance (Jackson 1990a). But all states derive some measure of succour from a system that they have created: in a fundamental sense, they have an identity as part of such a system. 'The modern state as we know it', Skocpol avers, 'has always been . . . part of a system of competing and mutually involved states' (1985: 8).

It is, of course, also in this second domain that globalization is claimed to be exercising its corrosive effects. The system that hitherto has given the state pride of place, and privileged its exclusive prerogatives in the face of all other challengers, may no longer be as protective and nurturing of the state. To the extent that the state has been formed by a 'demand pull' from the outside, rather than by a 'supply push' from the inside, this external constitution may now be thought to be detrimental to the capacities and roles hitherto enjoyed by states. If this is so, states will be that much the less able to derive strength from the outside. They will become 'weaker', as their external bulwarks become less protective of them. In the worst-case analysis, the state is viewed as being under assault by a pincer movement from both directions simultaneously—eroded from within and less protected from without.

As will be argued below, the imagery of this kind of analysis is substantially misleading. To the extent that state strength is being diminished, this is not as a result of two separate processes but rather of one. Globalization does not manifest itself in two separate appearances. It is precisely the reconstitution of the system that has implications for the degree to which the state remains 'connected' to civil society, while, at the same time, the lesser protection afforded the state from the outside is itself driven by domestic restructuring. Any temptation to conceive of these as two distinct developments is to be resisted.

In short, there are several interconnected tendencies in the analysis of state strength. Some emphasize the externalist perspective, within which state strength results from the social institutions of the state system itself. Others prefer an internalist account, which subdivides into two principal variants. Within this internalist category, the first posits strength as a measure of the state's ability to act autonomously with respect to society: it is a benchmark of separateness. The second sees strength as proportional to the proximity of the state's identity to that of society. In this version, strength is largely a function of the legitimacy of state institutions in the eyes of its own (domestic) constituency. It is this argument that is advanced by Holsti, who specifies strength as deriving from vertical and horizontal legitimacy—the former centred on ideas of authority, consent, and loyalty, and the latter on definitions of the political community itself (1996: 84). The problem is that all these categories become highly unsettled in conditions of globalization. If international society is changing because of domestic transformation in states, and if society is no longer caged within separate states, on what meaningful basis can we distinguish between 'internal' and 'external' sources of state strength?

This discussion also has important implications for the analysis of democracy in conditions of globalization (as will be explored further in Chapter 8). The issue of state strength is seldom explicitly introduced as part of the literature about the democratic peace. And yet, implicitly, there is substantial overlap between the two concerns. Holsti offers the following conclusion:

The relationship of state strength to war, however, is emerging: since 1945 most wars of all types have originated within and between weak states. Strong states have warred against the weak, but not against each other. (1996: 91)

In so far as Holsti equates strength with degrees of legitimacy, it is evident that strength is indirectly a measure of democracy. By extension, it should come as no surprise that he posits a relationship between strength and peace: on this account-ing, theories of state strength offer a back-door version of the democratic peace. The link can then be made to globalization. To the extent that political globaliza-tion manifests itself, in Shaw's terminology, as the construction of a 'western state conglomerate', then globalization also becomes an element within the democra-tic peace. 'The western state can be defined as a single state conglomerate', he maintains, 'because borders of violence have been largely abolished within, and have shifted to the edges of, this bloc' (1997b: 501). Thus we can see in these for-mulations the significant extent to which theories of state strength, democratic legitimacy, and globalization have become enmeshed in the analysis of the prospects for future international peace and stability.

Many of these points can be illustrated in more tangible form by some recent contributions to the globalization literature and, in particular, by some of the observations in the highly dystopic work of John Gray (1998). This commentary is not intended to engage with the substance of Gray's claims, but merely to indi-cate the logical structure from which the argument derives. In his analysis of the economic future of Russia, Gray raises fundamental issues relevant to the forego-ing commentary on state strength, and its sources. His general contention is that in an age of globalization, the main danger comes from the weakness of states: 'Today human and social well-being', he maintains, 'is being threatened chiefly by collapsed or enfeebled states' (1998: 200–1). Nowhere is this more so than in the case of Russia, which now has a form of government best described as 'criminal syndicalism' (1998: 165). Given the nature of this problem, Gray's inescapable solution is to make an appeal for a strong Russian state. 'Until it has a strong, effective state,' he concludes, 'Russia will not have a genuine market economy' (1998: 165).

There are two problems with this mode of analysis, and they illustrate more general deficiencies in the way globalization is often understood and presented. The first is whether his description does not undercut his prescription: if states are weak for the reasons given, it is hard to see how they might be strengthened. The second, more specifically relevant to the present argument, is whence this strong state might be expected to derive. Is it to be created by spontaneous inter-nal generation?

As for the first problem, there seems to be an inconsistency in Gray's argument neatly captured in his throwaway line that until such time as 'Russia has solved its Hobbesian problem it cannot be a modern state' (1998: 165). This, of course, implies that an effective state will be the consequence of solving the Hobbesian problem, whilst it might be objected that a strong state is a necessary part of such a solution in the first place.

The second difficulty is the tension that pervades Gray's commentary on the state in conditions of globalization. At present, global markets work to fracture societies and weaken states. Countries with highly competent governments or strong, resilient cultures have a margin of freedom within which they can act to maintain social cohesion. Where these resources are lacking, however, states have collapsed or ceased to be effective. As a result, societies have been desolated by market forces over which they have no control (1998: 196).

What is problematic about Gray's account, as in his Hobbesian comment, is from whence the Leviathan is to come, and whether as cause or effect. Evidently, a strong state will not be generated by external forces, since the impact of globalization is said to be entirely one of weakening, even in those cases where strong societies are in existence. And so presumably, in the case of Russia and other weak states, strong states will need to be generated entirely from the inside in the face of uniformly hostile external pressures. But if the strong Russian state can be constituted as a product of Russian civil society, in spite of globalization, why is the strong state needed at all—since it is said to be needed to tame that society? And if not from its source in indigenous civil society, from whence might the strong state derive? In short, there are complex circularities in this argument and, to make sense of them, a more highly developed framework is required in which the dual constitution of the state is explicitly acknowledged, and its implications recognized.

The scope for the state to act autonomously and strategically is intimately linked to these analytical issues and this now requires further commentary before proceeding to an attempt to deal with the matters raised within the specific context of a discussion of globalization. The tendency of the argument so far has been that states are not detached from the internal or the external, but neither is their behaviour determined wholly by the constraints of one or other of the two domains. There is therefore some scope for 'strategic action' along the lines suggested by state theorists. The following remarks are instructive in this context. 'Adjustment strategy may be directed outward at international regimes, or inward at transforming domestic structures', Ikenberry suggests. He moves on to conclude that 'Which strategy is chosen will depend on the gross structural circumstances within which the state finds itself—defined in terms of state–society relations on the one hand, and position within the international system on the other' (1986: 57). At this point, it emerges that different forms of language are being used to describe essentially the same relationship. In substance, if not in form, there is little to distinguish Ikenberry's account—couched as it is in terms of state strategic action—from a constructivist interpretation—albeit framed in terms of dual constitution at both national and international levels. Despite the linguistic differences, the theoretical claim appears remarkably similar.

This becomes even clearer when Ikenberry's analysis is placed alongside, for example, the interpretation offered by Hobson. The latter's argument, presented as a critique of neo-realism, leads to the following conclusion. He suggests that 'by downgrading the state as the supreme actor domestically, in favour of an embedded state–society relationship, we can reinstate the state as a conceptual variable externally; and the state becomes non-reducible to the exigencies of the inter-state system (as well as the mode of production)' (1997: 274). In either case, the state acts or is constituted in such a way that its behaviour cannot be attributed to either domain in isolation. It is only within a field of forces that encompasses both that we can understand the identity of the state, and why it might choose to act in certain (constrained) ways.

Moreover, this notion of reflexive change seems to be corroborated in various empirical studies that are important to the study of globalization. Sassen's work on economic regulatory and legal change is a good case in point. A recurrent theme of her writing is that 'the state is involved in this emerging transnational governance system. But it is a state that has itself undergone transformation' and 'has emerged quite altered by this participation' (1996a: 22, 28).

A related image, although its authors do not directly employ it in the context of globalization, is that of the 'nesting' of polities. Although Ferguson and Mansbach (1996) develop this concept in ways more limited than the idea of the 'nesting' of states within a particular international order, it might be possible to extend the spirit, if not the letter, of their analysis in this way. The argument runs that some such concept is valid because 'polities share space and can claim the loyalties of all or some of the same constituents', and hence the image of nesting denotes a situation wherein 'some polities are encapsulated by others and embedded within them' (1996: 48). The direct relevance of this becomes clear in a further elaboration of the authors' position. 'It is as though one political form were superimposed on another', they write. In consequence, 'the latter may lose some of its separate identity, but in the process, the dominant polity may assume some of the trappings and features of the nested polity' (1996: 395). This is another linguistic variant, but, once again, there is little in this exposition to which the constructivist could take major exception. In the context of this discussion, the implication would be that domestic orders are nested in international orders. In particular, we should conceive of globalization as the nesting of a particular kind of state in a particular kind of international order, in which both take on similar characteristics. Crucial to this idea of 'nesting' is the mutuality that it implies.

The broker state and globalization

In short, there is a powerful case for attempting to move the analysis of the state in this general direction, as the most appropriate framework for an understanding of the phenomenon of globalization. As will now be demonstrated, the present analysis is in fundamental agreement with Hobson's critique of neo-realism. By emphasizing the external determinants of state behaviour, neo-realism fails to recognize of the national and the international that 'neither dimension is self-constituting'. Hence, there is no reason to accord primacy to the international since 'both realms are mutually constituted' (Hobson 1997: 9). State capacity cannot be viewed simply as the (negative) function of globalization since global-ization, in turn, is what states have made of it.

The suggested way forward has been latent for a number of years and arises as a by-product of historical analyses of the post-1945 international and eco-nomic orders. The intensification of the study of globalization in the last ten years now makes explicit the potential linkage between IR theory and these historical interpretations. Histories of the genesis of the post-1945 international system have long drawn attention to its unique quality in forging an inter-national order along with supportive types of domestic order. As a result, the two became mutually reinforcing and stabilizing, so much so that they became *necessary* parts of each other. The classic rendition, as noted earlier, was that provided by J. G. Ruggie:

This was the essence of the embedded liberalism compromise: unlike the economic nationalism of the thirties, it would be multilateral in character; unlike the liberalism of the gold standard and free trade, its multilateralism would be predicated upon domestic interventionism. (1982: 393)

In short, this suggested that no understanding of the international order was possible without an appreciation of the domestic orders on which it was based: the two were functionally integrated in a way that defied analytical separation. Welfarist states were, to that degree, nested in the international order and essen-tial to its viability. In turn, the international order developed qualities of those polities nested within it. More recently, the same theme has been developed further:

what the post-Second World War settlement did was to reconstitute nations, national identities, and national political systems within a new set of international constraints. To speak, then, of a postwar world order, or international system, without attending to the transformation of national realities, is to miss what was really at stake in the turbulent pol-itics of the early Cold War era. (Cronin 1996: 33–4)

This much is relatively uncontentious. The problem arises in understanding how changes in the nature of 'nesting' or 'embedding' occur across time, and with what consequences. If we are to explain the historical dynamic that underlies globalization, we need to understand how such evolution can take place. Otherwise, any notion of 'mutual constitution' becomes theoretically as static, and uninteresting, as the neo-realist structuralism that it seeks to displace. The basic model set out below claims that nesting generates its own political prob-lems, as the balance shifts in the imposition of costs internally and externally. A perfect equilibrium, such as Ruggie posits for the period 1945–70, is unlikely to be sustained in the long term. Once this equilibrium begins to be disturbed, polit-ical tensions spill across, and are absorbed, into either the domestic or the inter-national domain. What is crucial in this regard, however, is the relative distribution of these political costs.

The historical evidence then points to oscillations between domestic and inter-national upheaval. The following schematic presentation is much simplified but offers a rudimentary explanatory framework. It derives from, and develops, the embryonic exposition to be found in Gilpin (1987: 132–3). Gilpin suggests that in the nineteenth century, international norms (such as the gold standard and laissez-faire) enjoyed precedence over domestic stability. During the inter-war period, this was reversed, and multilateralist norms were abandoned wholesale to meet, unilaterally, domestic needs: 'all major states', Cerny notes of this period, 'tried to recapture hierarchical control over their economic processes' (1995: 606). They were driven to do so by domestic imperatives, and the price was exacted on all forms of internationalism. After 1945, a new balance was struck between the two, and international and domestic arrangements were readjusted to meet each other's needs. This explanatory model is revealing and can be extended. It might then be suggested that, since the 1970s, this equilibrium has progressively lost its stability. There has, once again, been a tendency for states to submit to international norms—in the specific sense of the disciplines of a highly competitive international market. It is upon this evidence that the new structuralist accounts, examined earlier, have been based.

The claim that international norms have asserted their priority over domestic needs refers to the brokerage role played by the state, and to the resulting distribution of political costs. Since 1970, the political costs of sustaining neo-liberal international norms have once more tended to be transferred to the state level, as unemployment, deregulation, and challenges to the welfare state have all been imposed as necessary adjuncts of the drive for international comparative advantage. What this suggests is not necessarily that globalization is about to be reversed, but that the domestic political costs of its continuation are now much more apparent (Zurn 1995: 150). In the 1950s and 1960s, when growth was universal and seemingly permanent, globalization was relatively cost-free. This is no longer the case.

What is the implication of such a framework? At the very least, it calls into question assumptions about a remorselessly progressing globalization. The stark political reality, as Kapstein notes, is that 'the fate of the global economy ultimately rests on domestic politics in its constituent states' (1996: 17). This holds out the possibility of growing instability (Strange 1994: 27) and of 'revolts against an open international economy' (Hirst 1997: 425). Indeed, some go so far as to see such a dialectical tension as an inescapable part of globalization, and therefore define the process to incorporate its 'politico-economic and socio-cultural counter-tendencies' (Gill 1997b: 5).

One might then anticipate symptomatic increases in levels of domestic dissatisfaction, signalling the erosion of the international–domestic compacts within which post-war globalization had been nurtured. If embedded liberalism represented the bargain struck, then neo-liberalism marks a tendency towards 'disembedding' (Bernard 1997: 87). In this case, and if one were to assume the irreversible erosion of state powers, there is no prospect of the post-war bargain being resurrected. However, if it is also the case that domestic tensions can no longer be resolved by 'renationalization', then this may rebound upon globalization itself: the contradiction here is that if the social compact 'unravels altogether, so too will international liberalisation' (Ruggie 1995: 523).

What this reinforces is the need for a more fluid, dynamic, and interactive conception of politics than is captured by a solely structural or systemic account. With Panitch, we can register reservations about overly ' "top-down" interpretations of the power relations between the "national" and the "international" ' (1994: 71). The process of globalization is more contested than this implies and gives rise to its own 'counterforces' (Albrow 1996: 82).

Theory and the embedded state

If such a tendency has been latent in historical studies of the post-1945 period, its implications have now been brought to the forefront by the study of globalization. It too emphasizes the necessity for exactly the same kind of integrated approach to the internal and external: globalization must not be seen narrowly as a shift in relations between states, but must at the same time be recognized as a transformation in the nature of the state itself.

A number of disparate writings point towards this same general conclusion. Developing a historical-sociological account of economic development and change, Hobson makes a complaint about IR theories generally, and neo-realism specifically, deriving from this same concern. 'I argue', he affirms, 'that the international and national realms are not discrete'. He further elaborates: 'The central claim is that the national and international economy are embedded not only in the inter-state political system, but also in the domestic political realm' (Hobson 1997: 2–3; see also Shaw and Quadir 1997: 40). This at least requires us to redefine the subject in such a way that the troublesome distinction between the domestic and the international, as separate political realms, disappears.

To note the problem is not, of course, to offer a solution to it. Others, seeking for a similar reconciliation, accept that its achievement will be elusive and concede the 'extraordinarily ambitious' nature of any such project (H. Williams 1996: 152). And yet Hobson's approach is instructive. Lambasting what he sees as the failure of *all* IR theory 'to take the state seriously' (1997: 1), he outlines his own conception in the following terms:

The key to my theory of state power is the notion that states are both domestic and international actors . . . They are situated centrally within national society, but are also embedded within an external decentralised inter-state system and a global capitalist economy . . . I depict states as residing within an international/national vortex. Indeed, there are actually no such things as the international and national systems understood in pure terms . . . Neither is self-constituting, but each 'dimension' is constantly structured by interaction with the other. (1997: 11–12)

This is about as close as one can get to an adequate rendition: it pushes us to devise a framework in which the two come to be analytically subsumed within each other. Others have made not dissimilar suggestions. In one reworking of neo-realism, the virtue of such an alternative scheme is that 'it does neatly incorporate the mutually constitutive relationship between unit and system . . . [It] does not assume that states are constructed entirely by forces generated from within' (Buzan, Jones, and Little 1993: 50). What follows is similar in spirit, if different in its detailed execution.

The essential feature of this alternative model is its acceptance of a unified field of political action, within which a significant range of processes is filtered through the complex of states: states are the nodal points within this field (Clark 1998: fig. 3, p. 496). When thus conceived, as something occurring simultaneously within states and also at the interstices where they encounter each other, globalization can be accounted for neither by a reductionist nor a systemic theory, nor by any sequential combination of the two. Reductionism would have to claim that globalization is something occurring at the unit level. And yet, following Waltz, we might suggest that in the past two decades there has been sufficient uniformity of outcome in the adoption of neo-liberal policies to warrant some assumption about a structural constant. Accordingly, systemic theory demands that we interpret globalization as a structural formation. But such a reversion to unmodified structuralism also fails to convince, because it holds out the prospect of a timeless reproduction of globalization, contrary to any historical sense. Only by a direct political engagement between the domestic and the international—bringing them into the same field of forces where the outcome depends upon the pressures both bring to bear on the state—can this basic tension be demonstrated. The analytical scheme for the process of globalization must encompass the area where both domestic and international forces are present, and act upon each other.

Such a framework reiterates what Ikenberry (1986), following Nettl (1968), has dubbed the 'Janus-faced' state (see generally Evans, Rueschmeyer, and Skocpol 1985; Hall and Ikenberry 1989; Banks and Shaw 1991; Navari 1991*a*; Halliday 1994). Much of this state theory, as we have seen, is concerned with the issue of autonomy, in the twin senses that the state should not be reduced to the agent of national social forces, nor thought of as the mere expression of international capital. The state operates between the two and is fully the prisoner of neither. States indeed derive their strength from a complex field of forces, within which they act both as 'units of an international order, structured from the top down and expressions of "societies" from the bottom up' (Cerny 1993a: 33). Indeed, with some licence, we might describe the state as the (shifting) accommodation between these counter-pressures.

The import of this framework is that, while as in the traditional model the state appears to generate the separation between the domestic and the international, as a political broker it is the state that conjoins them. It is the medium through which costs are transferred either inwards or outwards. Once this essential point is grasped, it becomes impossible to sustain any separation between systemic and reductionist analyses, because the fundamental process is how political costs are distributed between the two realms, through the state which operates in both.

As indicated, there has been a strong tendency for the issue to be presented in zero-sum terms so as to suggest that there is an inherently antithetical relationship between state and globalization. At the very least, some are predisposed to the idea of cycles in the balance of power between states and corporations. This balance shifts across time, such that business has been depicted as an instrument of state policy in the early part of this century, and again in the period 1945–70. In contrast, since the 1980s, 'these firms have freed themselves from the powers of states', and it is an open question whether or not this will now remain a long-term condition (Amin 1996: 248).

More commonly, however, the position is adopted that there is a two-way flow in the formation of the global economy, and this brings us closer to the essentials of the present argument. This much is implied in the claim that 'the recent trans-formation of the global economic system creates a new form of transnational structure in which the state is constantly engaged in sharing its decision-making power with the global forces of production and finance' (Shaw and Quadir 1997: 39). If this seems to indicate that all the concessions are being made by the state, there are also many counter-suggestions that this 'transnational structure' is itself in large measure formed and reinforced by states, such that the image of 'sharing' necessarily implies a degree of mutuality. The following illustrations may be briefly noted. Sassen insists that a corrective to some readings of economic glob-alization is the realization that many of 'the strategic places where global processes materialize are embedded in national territories and hence fall, at least partly, under various state-centered regulatory umbrellas' (1996*b*: 33). Similarly, other writers focus attention on the 'huge role' the state plays in maintaining market relationships (Wilkin 1997: 28), so much so that they have been described by one critic as the 'authors of a regime that defines and guarantees . . . the global and domestic rights of capital' (Panitch 1996: 85).

These writings seek to edge beyond the Great Divide. Regardless of the specific language employed, they rely upon an analytical method that is generically con-structivist. The case is well illustrated by Cerny's comment on the role of finance. His considered judgement is that 'It has always constituted both a cross-cutting, transnational structure *and* a crucial element of state building and state power' (Cerny 1994: 237). Thus conceived, financial globalization can scarcely impact upon the one sphere alone, when it is manifestly a constitutive element within both.

The focus on globalization, and the role of the state in globalization, illustrates this general claim. The state has been the broker of globalization, a key player in determining whether the costs of international disciplines should be borne domestically, or whether domestic disturbance will be allowed to overthrow international regulation. Metaphorically, one might think of the state as a bi-directional valve, responding to whichever pressure is greater, sometimes releas-ing pressure from the domestic into the international, at other times releasing it from the international into the domestic (Ikenberry 1986: 76). This echoes the finding that 'states are not mirrors of external processes, nor are they merely fil-ter mechanisms' but instead 'states actively process and channel international influences to bolster their domestic position' (Hobson 1997: 247).

Any such analysis requires a collapsing of the distinction between the systemic and the reductionist: only by a consideration of the state caught between the competing pressures emanating from both fields can the impact of globalization, and its likely future development, be understood. To make sense of the international structure, one must look at the identities of the states that help to create it. To comprehend the behaviour of states we need to see them as repositories of distinctive international orders. Compartmentalized analytical schemes prevent precisely the kind of insight that such an approach alone can offer.

The globalized state

Globalization, as concept, remains deeply contested along a number of dimensions: even the extent of the empirical reality that it purports to describe is a matter of substantial controversy. These reservations notwithstanding, the concept is now raising fundamental issues which mainstream theory can no longer choose to ignore, not least as it reinforces doubts about the Great Divide as an adequate foundation for the discipline. Globalization has not invented this scepticism, but it has powerfully accentuated it.

The deficiencies encapsulated by the Great Divide are an impediment to innovative thinking on a whole range of issues within contemporary IR theory, as will be demonstrated in the remaining chapters of this book. The Great Divide remains rooted in a belief that, *for analytical purposes*, we can pretend that there are two separate spheres of political action, the domestic and the international. Transcribed into neo-realist theory, this manifests itself as a faith in two forms of theory, reductionist and systemic, each developed around a separate domain with its own organizing logic.

The historical evidence about the oscillating development of globalization, as well as the critical debate about whether or not globalization is reversible, renders such a separation both artificial and misleading: neither a systemic nor a reductionist account, individually or sequentially, can provide an adequate interpretation of these issues.

In their stead, there must be an integrated approach that captures globalization as a process, uncertain in its outcome, but whose trajectory will be plotted by the counter-pressures emanating simultaneously from the international structure and from the state units themselves. The Waltzian image distorts because it assumes distinct fields of forces, operating at different levels, which do not seem to intersect. In reality, they do so through the medium of the state. Unless the imagery and terminology of the Great Divide is abandoned, International Relations may seem to embrace globalization but it will not be able to offer a meaningful engagement with it. If part of the reason for this failure may be put down to the elusiveness of globalization itself, a substantial share of the responsibility will nonetheless lie with the theoretical apparatus which International Relations brings to the encounter.

A prominent example of the existing weakness can be found in treatments of the relationship between the state and globalization. These are generally treated as distinct phenomena, the one impacting on the other. The notion that the two are mutually constitutive and transformational is as yet a subdued theme within the literature. What this chapter has sought to demonstrate is that such an interpretation can readily, and profitably, be grafted onto extant accounts of state autonomy and strength, explorations of state–society relations, and analyses of the strategic brokerage role of the state. Placed in these various contexts, the assumed opposition between state and globalization begins to dissipate.

This is not to assert that there has been no change in the role of the state, nor to deny important shifts in the range of its powers. It serves as a reminder, however, that it is superficial to attribute all such changes to the impositions of a globalization thought to be working entirely from the outside. The state's identity is undergoing continuous transformation and for a variety of reasons. It is helpful to conceive these as reflecting the shifting terms of political brokerage, as the state navigates between powerful cross-cutting currents emanating from a diversity of internal and external sources, all of which threaten its progress. But in response, the ship of state can be trimmed, in addition to the option of changing course.

With this framework in place, the book will now explore the impact of globalization upon IR theory in the context of its specific substantive concerns. These relate to the state's role as a provider of sovereignty, economic management, security, normative order, and democratic government. Within each of these areas, the literature about globalization poses fundamental questions. However, the hope is that by employing the above framework of analysis, some of the pitfalls can be avoided, and a more balanced verdict on globalization achieved. At the very least, the employment of this template, measured against the traditional functions of states, should provide some index of the ways in which IR theory needs to develop to meet the challenge from globalization.

4

THE SOVEREIGN STATE

According to the conventional wisdom, it is sovereignty that is most at risk from globalization: the diminution of sovereignty—generically, the quantum of state capacity—indicates the intensification of globalization since the one, of necessity, is inversely proportional to the other. What globalization principally signifies for International Relations is the reduced ability of the state to monitor and control a wide range of global flows and activities that impinge upon its territory, while not falling within its jurisdiction, or competence to exercise its jurisdiction. Before we move on to consider state resources in individual functional and policy areas, we must begin with that aggregate capacity—sovereignty—that has been regarded as the hallmark of the state itself.

If globalization is believed to be eroding the effectiveness of state performance, it follows that this will inevitably show up in any discussion of sovereignty. In these interpretations, the state is passive in the face of globalization. In this chapter, that conventional wisdom will be rejected. In its stead, the argument will be presented that we must envisage the encounter between globalization and sovereignty as identifying the contemporary condition of statehood. Against the notion that sovereignty is the victim of globalization, we need to explore the extent to which globalization occurs in tandem with modulated developments in the formalities of sovereignty. The sovereignty regime is predicated on the practices that states recognize. In this case, the state is an active instrument in the forging of globalization and, at the same time, in the redefinition of sovereignty. In short, the need for an analysis of sovereignty in a context of globalization is compelling. Any theory of international relations must be able to make sense of sovereignty. Above all, it must be able to convey, in historical terms, how a globalized practice of sovereignty is distinct from its previous incarnations.

One might initially broach the issue by asking whether sovereignty denotes a specific function or capacity of statehood, or is simply a shorthand expression for what it is that makes states in the first place. Do states produce sovereignty in the same sense that they produce security or manage the economy? Indeed, do they produce sovereignty at all? Is sovereignty something that states 'do', or something they 'are'? This is to raise the question whether sovereignty is more fundamental to state identity than its activities in other areas: it is sovereignty that identifies them as states, regardless of other regional and historical differences. Thus conceived, states are what they are because of their panoplies of formal sovereignty. If so, the erosion of 'immutable' sovereignty would indeed have portentous effects upon the personality of states. In order to address the impact that globalization is having upon the sovereignty industry, we need first to consider what the business was like before the onset of globalization. Sovereignty penetrates to the very essence of the state. If we wish to trace the impact of globalization, then it is within the realm of sovereignty that the search must properly begin.

Traditionally, the analysis of sovereignty has depicted it as a legal or constitutional entitlement to undertake, unimpeded, a range of activities. Thus regarded, sovereignty is an enabling precondition rather than a function in its own right. The state can, for instance, generate security for its citizens because that is what, on their behalf, it has a sovereign entitlement to do. Sovereignty can thus be considered an instance of a 'constitutive' rule, within whose ambit its 'regulative' functions can be performed. In sum, sovereignty seems to produce the state rather than the state producing sovereignty.

Such an approach, however, slides over a number of difficulties. Two caveats are immediately in order. First, this seems to imply an 'essentialist' concept of sovereignty, immune to historical change: the attributes of sovereignty exist in perpetuity and produce a single form of state. This is an unnecessarily constricting point of view. It is perfectly possible to regard sovereignty as a constant element of state identity, while allowing that the substance of that sovereignty might change. Secondly, the apparently absolute distinction between the constitutive and the regulative does not hold fully in this context. Indeed, as we will see in subsequent chapters, change at the regulative level within the state is a potent source of changing state identity and hence of the 'constitution' of sovereignty itself. What the state performs is as much a source of its sovereignty as the other way round.

But how are we to articulate this notion that state and sovereignty reshape each other across time? In particular, what is the significance for globalization of introducing a measure of fluidity into the concept of sovereignty? The following analysis asserts that sovereignty both traces, but also in turn shapes, the contours of globalization because both are rooted in changing state practice. To make such a claim is to adopt a broadly constructivist position, and it is within such a framework that much of the following discussion will be conducted.

For neo-realism, state identity is both constant in time and uniform in content: it is sovereignty that makes it so (Hopf 1998: 175). As against this, constructivist approaches argue for the adaptability of state identity. Any such account has critical implications for theories of sovereignty, since sovereignty is itself a key element of that identity. Typically, a recent exposition of constructivism insists that the exploration of identity is its key feature. 'The constructivist research program has its own puzzles', it is asserted, 'that concentrate on issues of identity in world politics' (Hopf 1998: 172). Oddly, however, in setting out the scope of his research programme, Hopf does not include within it the topic of sovereignty. And yet surely this is an element of state identity that is central to IR theory in conditions of globalization? Accordingly, if constructivism is to contribute substantially to the body of IR theory, the engagement between globalization and sovereignty is the perfect location for it to do so.

Amongst the many attributes of the state, sovereignty has traditionally been regarded as foremost, so much so that the two terms are often deemed to be inseparable, only states being endowed with sovereignty and sovereignty being the defining quality of statehood. Thus there is often a conflation of the two terms into a single unified idea, as in James (1986). According to Onuf's summation of standard conceptions, 'Sovereignty unproblematically defines the state' (1991: 426).

However, this position has been challenged from various directions. Some question the notion of sovereignty as an *attribute* of statehood, arguing instead that the element of *recognition* shifts the emphasis away from an innate state condition, to the manner in which 'it is attributed to the state by other states or state rulers' (Thomson 1995: 219). In this view, sovereignty is deemed to be a social, rather than a natural, creature: it inhabits the world of intersubjective meaning rather than the dense primordial forests of the state of nature. Others, by extension of the same logic, seek to break the exclusive link between sovereignty and the state by questioning the proposition that it is a 'concept which only applies to the state' (Brace and Hoffman 1997*b*: 1). Other bodies, such as the European Union or intergovernmental regimes, might be accorded sovereignty in particular functional areas. If sovereignty depends upon recognition, then both its bearers and its forms might be thought susceptible to change in accordance with prevailing historical conditions. Some such approach seems essential to comprehending the encounter between sovereignty and globalization, if the superficialities of 'the end of sovereignty' and 'the demise of the state' are to be avoided.

Sovereignty and the Great Divide

If, as argued up to this point, the Great Divide inhibits analysis of globalization, then it does likewise with sovereignty. In short, we cannot get a sensible purchase on globalization without unpacking the mysteries of sovereignty, and we can do neither within the analytical framework of the Great Divide. That stark separation, of course, itself derives from traditional reflections on the nature of sovereignty, since it is sovereignty that has provided its intellectual underpinnings. If the tyranny of the Great Divide is to be overthrown, the conventional approach to sovereignty must itself first be challenged. Sovereignty is presented as demarcating the internal from the external and does so by locating supreme authority within the state, but only contested power claims without. In this fundamental, and absolutist, sense, sovereignty *is* the Great Divide. It follows that a conception of globalization as set out in earlier chapters must have equally troublesome consequences for prevailing concepts of sovereignty. If the Great Divide is to be made to yield ground, it can do so only in so far as the concept of sovereignty is made to shift with it.

Despite its importance to them, International Relations scholars have long felt uneasy with sovereignty, regarding it as conceptually daunting terrain. For this reason, they have been deterred from making overly arduous forays into it, thinking them likely to yield too formalistic or legalistic an understanding of the subject. There have been, of course, some notable exceptions to this general rule (Hinsley 1986; James 1986). While conceding its importance as a political symbol, IR scholars have nonetheless been intimidated by its conceptual recalcitrance, frequently dismissing the effort to understand it as 'an arid exercise' (Miller 1981:16). And yet the concept cannot be ignored. So central is it that it is the principal embodiment of the Great Divide: this delineates the separation between the realms of the sovereign and the non-sovereign. Theories of international relations have traditionally started from this assumption, but it is precisely the viability of such a point of departure that globalization throws open to question.

For purposes of IR theory, sovereignty has customarily been treated as dualistic in nature, having both an internal and an external aspect (Hinsley 1986). This expresses itself in supremacy within, and independence outside, the confines of the state (Bull 1977: 8; M. Williams 1996: 112). There may be an unintended paradox here, it has been suggested caustically: the pervasive claim to the essential indivisibility of sovereignty is also invariably accompanied by an analysis that 'divides sovereignty along internal and external dimensions' (Onuf 1991: 432). The very unity of sovereignty thus seems to find expression in its bifurcation. In fact, it has been remarked that it was the very potency of this separation that salvaged sovereignty as concept when its validity was otherwise increasingly called into question. Political scientists, unimpressed by the incoherence of the concept as a referent for internal political organization, were nonetheless stymied in their efforts to banish it altogether by the seemingly undiminished appeal of its external facet to scholars of international relations: 'a concept which is highly contestable within societies seems perfectly straightforward when sandwiched between them', is one such rueful comment (Hoffman 1997: 12).

The implication of this dualism, as far as International Relations is concerned, is that the 'external' materializes as a by-product of the 'internal'. As far as most traditionalist theories have been concerned, it was unquestionably the latter that came first: domestic supremacy, as it were, enjoyed ontological precedence over external independence. The claim staked to inward sovereignty was, in that sense, the progenitor of international relations. The absence of sovereignty outside resulted, in turn, from the constitution of sovereignty from within. Such a sequence seemed to accord well with the analysis provided in the history of political thought. At the hands of writers such as Bodin, sovereignty was asserted as a principle of *domestic* political organization and, as one subsequent commentator was to remark, 'he would have been surprised if he could have foreseen that later writers would distort it into a principle of international disorder' (Brierly 1963: 10). As will be demonstrated below, IR theory is now much more sceptical of this rendition, preferring to see the state, and its 'domestic' sovereignty, as themselves partially created by an international system of social recognition, of which they are an integral part.

In terms of its practical effects, this theme of sovereignty as the source of disorder in the international system has since been at the core of much theory of international relations. In the eyes of generations of would-be reformers and 'idealists', a more peaceful world could be crafted only by the circumscription of sovereignty. And yet, in another paradoxical twist, those very twentieth-century international organizations designed to herald a reformed international order themselves became agents for the universalization of sovereignty, being unrelentingly committed to its observance and to its imposition as the essential test for membership.

More recently, writers on international relations have tended to focus on the external aspect of sovereignty, but by way of presenting it as a principle of order rather than of disorder. It has come to be regarded as one of the constitutive norms of international society, and hence fittingly enshrined in documents such as the UN Charter. In particular, there has developed a powerful strand of analysis of how sovereignty contributes to international order by legitimizing other cognate practices, such as those of non-intervention. Non-intervention is believed to mitigate the international state of nature and yet evidently, as a principle of order, is itself derived from sovereignty. 'For intervention to be meaningful', Weber contends, ' sovereignty must exist . . . To speak of intervention, then, is to suggest that sovereignty does exist' (1995: 128). Sovereignty, thus presented, and by analogy with the rules of property, stabilizes possession and hence provides one of the foundations of an effective international society (Vincent 1974). In short, sovereignty not only stands Janus-like, facing both inwards and outwards, like the state itself: it occupies the symbolic battleground over which writers and practitioners have fought for the very soul of International Relations. It both describes the theoretical field, and prescribes how its practical inconveniences might best be mitigated.

The debate about sovereignty does not, however, exhaust itself in the internal/external divide. As an overlay of complexity, it is also caught up in opposing claims between formalistic and substantive views, or what another writer has phrased the distinction between 'state authority' and 'state control' (Thomson 1995: 214). The former depicts sovereignty as a status bestowed by recognition, makes no assumption about the capacity of the 'sovereign' to act in an independent or autonomous fashion, and regards sovereignty as essentially constant in time. The latter tends to emphasize substantive capacity, to draw a sharp distinction between political potency and legal formality, and to think of capacities as historically variable. 'It is important to note', one survey of globalization suggests, 'that the concept of sovereignty does not carry with it the clear expectation that sovereign actors have the capacities to carry out these functions of rule, but affirms that they are recognized as having the right so to do without undue let or hindrance from other state actors' (Axford 1995: 136–7). This summary draws our attention to both usages.

The discussion of sovereignty thus proceeds at two levels, often with resultant confusion. For example, there is a widespread perception that interdependence has progressively undermined sovereignty. However, some of the arguments about the erosion of sovereignty as a result of interdependence have been rebutted on definitional grounds. Interdependence may circumscribe autonomy, but cannot question the legal entitlement of sovereignty—that is to say it may limit effective control, but not the authority on which it is based (M. Williams 1996: 113–14). This is also Thomson's point, that interdependence theorists have in mind the diminution of state control, but treat it as tantamount to the undermining of sovereignty in both its aspects:

The bottom line is not whether or not states can pursue autonomous economic, human rights or environmental policies in an interdependent world, but if and how interdependence (or anything else) is affecting the states' recognized claim to monopolize the coercive and policing function upon which their meta-political authority rests. (1995: 230)

This distinction holds that individual areas of capacity may diminish, whilst the overall form remains constant: control is variable but the state's identity is rooted in authority, and this is unchanging. Also implicit in this distinction is the claim that sovereignty, as formal condition, is an absolute: there can be no degrees of sovereignty, and it cannot be progressively eroded. It either exists or it does not. And since anarchy is created by sovereignty, the same must be said of anarchy: it is not a condition that can be partially mitigated. By contrast, those approaches to sovereignty which take it to mean 'effective political control' can readily accommodate notions of an erosion of capacity across time, or varying degrees of capacity across functional sector. For the same reason, anarchy—viewed as the side-effect of effective national control—is a condition that can be progressively modified. Whether or not anarchy is a condition that can be mitigated is, of course, the very stuff of the debates between the neo-realists and the neo-liberals, and the distinction between these two usages is familiar in that particular debate. But such shades of meaning are equally important in the present context: they are critical to the conduct of a sensible discussion of the relationship between sovereignty and globalization. Unfortunately, fine distinctions of this kind are not always respected. When some globalization theorists claim, without further elaboration, that 'Definitions of sovereignty must increasingly take account of questions of political economy' (Youngs 1997: 128), one is left to surmise that this refers to the substance, and not to the formality, of sovereignty. But one can only guess.

Sovereignty, in conventional understanding, creates not simply the division between the internal and the external, but also endows each with its own distinctive characteristics. But why should it be said that sovereignty creates the divide, rather than merely marking it? The reason is that by attributing a particular quality to a demarcated political space, sovereignty then creates a residual category— that which does not enjoy those properties of sovereignty. The distinction between the two thus becomes the fundamental dichotomy of political analysis. 'Sovereignty signifies a homogenous and well-bounded rational order of politics finding its focus in a hierarchical centre of decision,' writes Ashley, 'and anarchy is then defined residually' (1988: 238). Anarchy is thus the absence of sovereignty—a negative quality. In Ashley's terms, it is 'a problematic domain yet to be brought under the controlling influence of a sovereign centre' (1988: 230).

It is thus not international relations that establish the condition of anarchy, but instead it is anarchy that gives birth to international relations: this is what results from the prior existence of carved-out islands of sovereignty. The assumption herein is that sovereignty precedes the international, and gives rise to it. Again, this is the thrust of Ashley's argument when he notes that 'international relations finds its meaning precisely as a correlate of the recognition of domestic society as a prior, well-bounded presence' (1988: 253). Ashley is right to question this intellectual procedure. In what sense can sovereignty precede the international in this way? What meaning can it have in the absence of an international context? If sovereignty requires recognition, we obviously need to bring in the social context which the international alone can provide. This was Martin Wight's telling observation: 'It would be impossible to have a society of sovereign states', he insisted, 'unless each state, while claiming sovereignty for itself, recognized that every other state had the right to claim and enjoy its own sovereignty as well' (Wight 1977: 135). Within such a framework, the claim that sovereignty precedes, and gives rise to, the international becomes increasingly suspect.

It is for this reason that the stark oppositional categories assumed by such dualistic conceptions of sovereignty, and their resonances in theories of globalization, need to be questioned. Others have voiced a similar unease. Camilleri and Falk express misgivings about the 'national–international divide' on various grounds, including its tendency to overstate 'the importance of internal social, cultural and economic conditions in the shaping of politics and the state' (1992: 37). By extension, sovereignty is not merely a domestic characteristic, something that is wholly generated from within. It equally has an 'outside' dimension that derives from its recognition by others.

A number of revisionist positions have, accordingly, been developed, but from a variety of directions. Their combined logic, shared by the present discussion, is not simply that 'international' phenomena undermine the efficacy of the state's sovereignty over 'domestic' arrangements, but that this separation is itself questionable from the outset. Three versions of the claim, each somewhat different in derivation and import, will be set out at this stage as a framework for addressing the issues. Collectively, they present important ways of thinking about sovereignty in the context of globalization.

The first is another attempt to deal with the complex interrelationship between the political and economic. It questions the notion that sovereignty, as a supposedly distinctive political logic, can be separate in the context of the wider economic system. Conventionally, sovereignty and globalization are regarded as inherently conflictual: the one divides and pushes apart, whereas the other unites and connects. But however convenient this might be as a mode of analysis, the reality is that the two are not separable logics in practice. Accordingly, it has been claimed, 'sovereignty and the division of labour are not merely opposed principles but also are elements of a singular political and economic order, an international society of "embedded liberalism" ' (Inayatullah and Blaney 1995: 14). In this way the posited antagonism between the political and the economic is weakened, exactly in so far as the line between the international and the domestic is itself eroded. Political logic, as much as the economic, can cross, and transcend, borders. If this is indeed the case, there is greater potential for the co-existence of globalization and sovereignty than is normally allowed.

Ashley's is the second tack, and emphasizes instead the exclusionary effects of certain kinds of discourse. His complaint is that there are areas of uncertainty and difference in all facets of political life, but that some of these are ignored in order to bolster the major fault-line between the realm of sovereignty and the realm of anarchy. Thus any number of elisions occur in order to perpetuate the Great Divide itself. 'In effect, differences, discontinuities, and conflicts that might be found *within* all places and times', he writes, 'must be converted into an absolute difference *between* a domain of domestic society, understood as an identity, and a domain of anarchy, understood as at once ambiguous, indeterminate, and dangerous' (Ashley 1988: 256–7). This is a dispute about mental categories and the use of language. Above all, it is an attempt to deny any absoluteness to the distinction between the domestic and international spheres, and hence to the political characteristics of each (Walker 1990, 1993). Such an approach is, in principle, able to accommodate the grey areas where globalization and sovereignty overlap, whether or not it succeeds in doing so in practice.

The third assault takes an explicitly constitutive form. Denying the logic that sovereignty is in some sense the property of the 'pre-social' state, and hence something which antedated the 'Big Bang' when the universe of international relations was created, this viewpoint draws our attention instead to the mutuality of the internal and external aspects of sovereignty. From this perspective, sovereignty is employed as a device to illustrate the wider theme of the constructed nature of both domains. Thus rather than assign sovereignty as the exclusive property of the (pre-social) state, or entirely to the international system wherein sovereignty is recognized and thus socially bestowed, it is asserted that 'the two are in fact mutually constitutive but irreducible usages' (Wendt and Friedheim 1996: 247). In this third form, there is the opportunity to regard sovereignty as a constant source of state identity, while allowing that it is malleable as to its precise content. Globalization can then be regarded as a current phase of that identity, rather than as some exogenous threat to it.

Despite their differences, all three variants represent arguments for softening or overcoming the Great Divide. They challenge, respectively, these notions: that the state can be defined politically in separation from wider economic currents; that the only significant line of difference is between the international and the domestic; and that sovereignty can be understood as an attribute of state or system in isolation. Collectively, these observations point towards alternative, and more sophisticated, ways of thinking about sovereignty. The import of these arguments will assist in the following attempt to clarify the nature of the engagement between sovereignty and globalization.

Sovereignty and globalization

What is the relationship between globalization and sovereignty? Is globalization by its very nature the negation of sovereignty, or can the two peacefully co-exist? As already noted, the two are normally depicted as locked in zero-sum battle. This, however, affords no more than a shallow interpretation. It fails to take account of both the theoretical and historical nuances in this relationship.

Odd as it might initially seem, there is force to the suggestion that globalization requires sovereignty, not only as a real-life political infrastructure to sustain it, but also conceptually. Were not sovereignty still a meaningful part of the way we describe the world, we would have no need for a concept such as globalization. Globalization holds our interest in so far as sovereignty still registers its intellectual presence. From this perspective, even if less visibly, the very idea of globalization is inherently dependent upon that of sovereignty.

The argument that globalization and sovereignty are linked in a zero-sum contest is also deeply misleading when the historical record is borne in mind. The reason for this is that, if any one political practice has become globalized during the past century, then it is assuredly that of sovereignty itself. As has been claimed elsewhere, 'one of the most remarkable features of the twentieth century is the globalization of independent—or sovereign—statehood' (Jackson and James 1993*b*: 3). Not only has sovereignty expanded in the numerical sense—there are now approximately two hundred 'sovereigns'—but it has also proliferated geographically. The surface area enveloped in sovereignty, in consequence of imperial expansion and retreat, now represents the vast majority of territory on the globe. Evidently, there is also a 'positive-sum' aspect to the advance of sovereignty and globalization.

A moment's reflection reminds us then how subtle and interactive is the dialogue between sovereignty and globalization. Nonetheless, whilst sovereignty has become more extensively entrenched as a result of globalization, elements of the former have also been called into question by the latter. The recurrent claim of the literature on globalization is that the forms of sovereignty are at the very least changing, and at worst are being wholly undermined, by its progressive spread. Indeed, in some accounts, it is precisely on the basis of changing conceptions of sovereignty that the notion of globalization is itself to be understood: we know that globalization is happening because of the changing practices of sovereignty. As a result of this, it has been argued, 'the territorial state will for the foreseeable future continue to operate as an influential institution, but the presence or absence of sovereignty will be much less the defining characteristic of its structure or mode of action' (Camilleri and Falk 1992: 254). In similar vein, other writers record the widespread impression that 'the idea and practice of sovereignty are said to be increasingly undermined' by globalization, especially in so far as 'given political boundaries seem unable to account for or define the dynamics of social life' (Inayatullah and Blaney 1995: 3). So what are we to make of this paradox that sovereignty is more widespread than ever because of globalization but, at the same time, is thought to be in danger of succumbing to its potent charms?

Initially, it might seem that it is sovereignty—in the sense of substantive capacity or control alone—that is impaired by globalization, as the encroachments of the global economy curtail the ability of the state to delineate and manage a separate national economy. To an extent, of course, such constraints on autonomy have always been the case, as writers who give prominence to the global capitalist system have been at pains to insist. This has repeatedly raised the question of 'what sovereignty can mean when intertwined with the global division of labour' (Inayatullah and Blaney 1995: 16). Put bluntly, the point that has normally been made about 'weak' states in the world economy might now be applied to all states in the age of globalization. The idea that some states are, in Jackson's term, 'quasi-states' (1990*a*) could be considered the universal norm. 'For states of the Third World, in particular,' it has been claimed, 'the formal recognition of sovereignty conjoined with a peripheral role in the capitalist global division of labour results in a failure to achieve sovereignty substantively' (Inayatullah and Blaney 1995: 17). But is this comment now applicable to the Third World state alone?

As part of the answer, it will be demonstrated that globalization has implications for the 'formal' or 'authority' notion of sovereignty as well. Indeed, in most respects, it is in this area that its impact is the greater. Globalization is not simply about the diminution of sovereignty in the sense of the state's ability to manage its own affairs. More fundamentally, it is about the reconstitution of sovereignty *pari passu* with the reshaping of the state itself. What is happening to sovereignty is the shadow-play of the transformations that the state is currently undergoing. We might then suggest that there is not only a twofold linkage—between the concepts of sovereignty and statehood—but a triangular interrelationship—between state, sovereignty, and globalization. All three, of necessity, are synchronized in their movements.

What then is globalization believed to be doing to sovereignty? It is best to begin with an attempt to distinguish between the effects of globalization and the impact of interdependence. Williams is certainly correct to maintain that the consequences of globalization must be recognizably different from those resulting from interdependence. Indeed, it might be hypothesized that the difference resides largely in the fact that, whereas interdependence impinges solely upon sovereignty as autonomy, globalization additionally unsettles the conception of sovereignty as formal authority. To the extent that it does so, it encroaches more visibly on the terrain of state identity: 'not only is globalization distinct from interdependence,' Williams argues, 'but it poses a challenge to sovereignty which cannot be met through a restatement of the distinction between sovereignty and autonomy, a reassertion of the necessity to identify an ultimate source of authority in the conflict between state and community, or a return to the claim that sovereignty signifies constitutional independence' (M. Williams 1996: 119). Thus it would seem that globalization represents a much more fundamental assault on the traditional conceptual barricades of sovereignty. It does so because it entails a shift in both the domestic and international manifestations of sovereignty, and produces a new realignment between its elements of authority and control.

For these reasons, the rebuttal of the claim that globalization affects sovereignty cannot take the same form as that used in connection with interdependence. Hence, arguments deployed to demonstrate that interdependence has not damaged sovereignty cannot simply be extended to encompass the effects of globalization as well. There have been a number of objections to the argument from interdependence, most notably that offered by Thomson and Krasner (1989). They dispute the claim made for interdependence by turning the argument upon its head, and contending instead that interdependence requires sovereignty rather than threatening it. It is states, girded by sovereignty, that have stabilized property rights and this is the *sine qua non* of the international flow of goods and capital. According to this reasoning, 'the consolidation of sovereignty . . . was a necessary condition for more international economic transactions' (1989: 197–8). On this basis, they deny the possibility of major structural change—to the regime of sovereignty—occurring from below (1989: 216), as interdependence continues to require the regime of sovereignty to sustain it. Elsewhere, Krasner reiterates the same central argument at greater length. 'The historical record is far more mixed than would be suggested by the conventional notion that interdependence is threatening effective State control,' he maintains; 'if anything, State control has actually increased over the long term: *de facto* sovereignty has been strengthened rather than weakened' (1993: 314, 318).

If the ongoing argument of this chapter is valid—namely that globalization impacts upon both formalistic and substantive concepts of sovereignty—then the investigation of it must proceed along lines different from those set out by Krasner, who concludes that 'The basic question posed by interdependence, therefore, is not whether juridical sovereignty has been supplanted by something else, but whether it has become an empty shell' (1993: 301–2). This entails that only the 'control' dimension of sovereignty can change, not the fundamental identity associated with 'authority'. The latter may become hollow but, otherwise, has no potential for development. Even were this the case with interdependence, the challenge represented by globalization is different, and more fundamental. It requires us to look more closely at the interrelationship between the substantive and formalistic aspects of sovereignty than Krasner's analysis seems to allow.

So what is the case relating to globalization? The arguments centre upon the confluence of three sets of analyses concerned with authority, territoriality, and identity. Williams regards globalization as being distinct in its effects from those of interdependence or integration, in that 'increased transactions will not in themselves pose a problem to sovereignty unless it can be demonstrated that new authority patterns have emerged or are nascent in this process' (M. Williams 1996: 115). This formulation at least allows the possibility that changing forms of capacity can yield new networks of authority, both tied to the emergence of new state identities. Globalization might thus be thought important to sovereignty because, unlike increased transactions alone, it has the potential to touch upon issues of authority as well.

Elsewhere, the pervasive theme of commentary is that globalization problematizes sovereignty because it raises important issues about territoriality. For instance, the unsettling effect of globalization has been described as a new situation in which 'decisions and outcomes do not correspond with the choices of sovereign wills and are not contained by the boundaries within which they operate' (Camilleri and Falk 1992: 77). The point is echoed in similar claims that 'globalisation has undermined the state's capacities to maintain boundaries and exercise sovereignty' (Scholte 1996b: 61) and the suggestion that 'Globalization presents a different articulation of time and space. Authority structures need no longer be fixed to territorial actors' (M. Williams 1996: 117–18).

Finally, the connection is also made to issues of identity. According to Camilleri and Falk, there is a move from sovereignty to autonomy for groups and individuals and the 'redefinition of autonomy, hence of identity and community, points to a new concept of social contract, where no absolute authority is created and no rigid boundaries are erected in time or space' (1992: 232). In effect, what this amounts to is an attempt to think about sovereignty in separation from the state. 'If we are to define it coherently, we have to detach sovereignty from the state', is one plea (Hoffman 1997: 23). The means of such detachment must be changes in the identity of a whole range of social actors, including changes in state identity itself. Viewed thus, significant shifts in the identity of states (including those relating to sovereignty) must be considered as integral parts of the process of globalization, and not merely as some haphazard consequence of it. The force of these arguments, as well as their implications for theories of international relations, can now be examined in detail.

The constitution of sovereignty

It has been claimed of constructivism in general that it 'provides a promising approach for uncovering those features of domestic society, culture, and politics that should matter to state identity and state action in global politics' (Hopf 1998: 194–5). If this is so, how might it enable us to think afresh about issues of sovereignty? The central claim is that sovereignty is a 'constitutive principle' and, as such, reflects the co-constitution of state and state system (Onuf 1991: 430–1). The main implication of this ongoing process, in turn, is that states not only modify their behaviour but also their identity (Wendt 1996: 55). What does this mean for sovereignty?

The starting point for the analysis must be with the idea that sovereignty itself has been constructed and is adaptable. A shortcoming of IR theory's conventional approach has been its tendency 'to take sovereignty as a given . . . not as something that can vary over time' (Barkin 1998: 231). Once this move is made, globalization and sovereignty need not be presented in wholly antagonistic terms. What has been claimed with respect to shifts in human rights practices, in particular, has a wider theoretical import. The emergence of new norms of this kind, it has been said, 'need be neither a constraint on nor a signal of the decline of sovereignty, but rather represents an evolution of what sovereignty means' (Barkin 1998: 230). In terms of globalization, sovereignty is undergoing a process of readjustment reflecting the differing terms of engagement between its internal and external dimensions. Once again, the approach adopted here, rather than conceiving of globalization as eroding the capacity of states from the outside, investigates this readjustment with a view to understanding the substantive reconstitution of sovereignty that is now taking place. This occurs as much in response to redefinitions of the state from within as in consequence of its helpless abdication to irresistible forces from without. Such a view is at once a more modest set of claims than that entailed by 'the retreat of the state', and a more realistic appraisal of the historicity of sovereignty itself.

Claims about the social and historical construction of sovereignty are now relatively commonplace in the literature. 'The act of reciprocal recognition is necessary to create the condition in which states treat each other as discrete and disparate entities', is one such representative statement. It follows that 'as a-social as the outcome may seem, the creation of a society of sovereign states is inherently a social process, involving the mutual constitution of states' (Inayatullah and Blaney 1995: 12). While this quotation expresses the point in abstract terms, Weber gives it some substance. She takes the specific issue of intervention, and maintains that the interface between sovereignty and intervention provides an illustration of the changing parameters of statehood across time. 'Yet if we as theorists think about sovereign statehood in terms of authority relations which are worked out in practice . . .', she claims, 'then examining the intersection of discourses of sovereignty and intervention takes us a long way toward giving an account of how sovereign states are constituted in practice' (1995: 11).

If, in general, sovereignty has emerged and developed in this fashion, there can be no particular objection to the argument that sovereignty is now being reconstituted as part of its engagement with globalization. The focus instead shifts to the substantive form this reconstituted sovereignty might be taking. There is some willingness in the literature to admit that sovereignty might be undergoing transformation, rather than being undermined or becoming redundant. There is, however, little consensus on the extent of this transformation, or about its practical implications.

Camilleri and Falk seem to question the continuing relevance of sovereignty, at least in terms of formal conceptions of it. They are sceptical of attempts to maintain the integrity of sovereignty in the face of the more porous world of globalization. They dismiss any pretence that little has changed as a hollow victory of form over substance. 'The hypothetical absoluteness of sovereignty', they object, 'is thus preserved but only by effectively insulating it from the content, structure and history of the political process' (1992: 240). This seems to lead towards an abandonment of sovereignty as an analytical tool rather than towards any attempt at its reformulation. It does not allow for any adaptation in the formalities of sovereignty commensurate with changes in state capacity. For this reason, it presents a static image of sovereignty as authority.

The same can be said of Krasner's position, but for him this is evidence of the relevance of sovereignty, not a reason for its abandonment. Already unpersuaded by the evidence from interdependence, he rests his case on a combination of continuity and change—continuity in the *de jure*, along with change in the *de facto*, elements of sovereignty. This replicates the formal/substantive distinction already encountered. 'Yet the survival of *de jure* sovereignty for more than 400 years in an environment of radically changing technologies, military capabilities, actors, and power distribution could only have occurred if the specific components of *de facto* sovereignty were malleable' (Krasner 1993: 319). The robust persistence of one aspect of sovereignty is thus contingent upon the capacity for transformation of the other.

Others are more content to present the issue in terms of adaptation and variation. Sovereignty claims can, and do, change over time, as do the areas within which the claim is exercised. Thus against the neo-realist insistence upon the constancy of sovereignty, there is increasing acceptance of its variability. Some allow that 'the rules of sovereignty are neither fixed nor constant' (Barkin and Cronin 1994: 108) since they have occasionally been grounded on statist principles, but at other times have made appeal to nationalist forms of legitimation. Others draw attention to functional variability in the practice of sovereignty (Inayatullah and Blaney 1995: 20). Sassen makes the point directly: 'rather than sovereignty eroding as a consequence of globalization . . . it is being transformed. There is plenty of it around, but the sites for its concentration have changed over the last two decades' (1996*a*: 30).

What are the indications of such transformation? They are to be found mainly in the new identities and less territorialized practices mentioned above, but whether these as yet amount, in sum, to new patterns of authority remains seriously open to question. Nonetheless, the literature is confident that there are detectable changes in the nature of state identities, and that judgement is fully endorsed in these pages. Whereas for much of its historical development, the state forged a close link between its territoriality and its primary functions—economic, political, and security—this link is now more tenuous, and possibly no longer as necessary to the effective performance of these functions. Economically, as is generally argued, the main need for the territorial state was to provide a legal structure for property rights, without which economic activity would have been heavily circumscribed (Camilleri and Falk 1992: 25).

In the context of globalization, the maintenance of the connection between territoriality and these other functions becomes more problematic and possibly, in some cases, unnecessary. Thus it has been suggested that, while a substructure of national legal regimes continues to be essential for the development of the global economy, sovereignty may be experiencing redefinition to allow exceptions to its sway. One instance of this might be extraterritoriality. What is often portrayed in the globalization literature as the erosion of state competence may better be regarded, in fact, as the extension of a 'constituted' exception to sovereignty. In Sassen's version of the argument, new forms of economic regulation do not betoken the end of the state, but only a more widespread instantiation of the venerable practice of extraterritoriality (1996*a*: 13). Extraterritoriality was developed as a necessary part of a state system, and is fully compatible with sovereignty. It may simply be that the scope of this extraterritoriality has widened in recent years: a new system is emerging to meet the changing requirements of states in the performance of their various functions, and in response to the global networks and technologies which now surround them.

This is to imply the more general proposition that a state's identity, in terms of its ability to perform certain key functions, may no longer be so intimately connected to territory. Such a view is widely held. Scholte is not alone in his observation that 'globalisation refers to the introduction and spread of a fourth dimension of global space' in consequence of which ' "global" relations are placeless' (1996*b*: 43–4). As previously discussed, there are problems with any such formulation of the issue. However, its implication must be that either sovereignty is no longer relevant to this dimension, or it is being reconfigured to manage it in new and distinctive ways. The latter offers the more compelling account, and does not subscribe to any thesis of the end of sovereignty. It may then be preferable to conceive of this development as one in which 'sovereignty and territory . . . remain key features of the international system. But they have been reconstituted and partly displaced onto other institutional arenas outside the state and outside the framework of nationalized territory' (Sassen 1996*a*: 28). Such an interpretation seems to conform more closely to recent trends, and is more sensitive to the historical role of sovereignty.

This argument is similar in nature to the more general contention about the decreasing significance of territory as the basis of legitimacy for the post-cold war state. 'A state in the post-Cold War world is, thus, legitimated less by its relationship with a given piece of territory', writes Barkin, 'and more by its ability to ensure the political rights of its citizens' (1998: 249). This does not tell us how the rights of citizenship might themselves be shifting (see Chapter 7), but at least it anchors sovereign legitimacy in the changing terms of engagement between the hitherto supposedly discrete domestic and international realms, rather than in either in isolation.

These are faltering attempts to make theoretical sense of the profound—yet still largely mystifying—transformations that are taking place in world politics. It remains to try to tease from them some appreciable meaning for theories of international relations.

Sovereignty, globalization, and theories of international relations

Under the pervasive influence of the Great Divide, globalization has been routinely canvassed as a force that is separate from, and inherently in opposition to, sovereignty. The implicit theme of much IR writing at the end of the twentieth century is the portentous struggle that is taking place between these two irreconcilable forces and, depending upon personal preference, we support one force or the other. It is central to such an image that globalization, whatever its cause, represents an external threat to the state's internal capacity.

However, if globalization is conceived in the manner set out in these pages, then such an analysis does not withstand serious scrutiny. It becomes self-contradictory. Since sovereignty is constituted as much from without, and globalization equally reflects changes from within, any presentation of sovereignty as the internal guardian against the marauding hordes of globalization outside must be profoundly misleading. It follows from the alternative model advanced in this book that, rather than being contradictory forces, globalization and sovereignty are substantially interwoven developments. They depict processes of state transition arising out of the shifting parameters of the domestic and the international, and of the resulting balance of political pressures between them. And if they are essentially aspects of the same process, the one cannot sensibly be thought of as the negative effect of the other. Globalization is not some external presence standing apart from sovereignty, but is instead another way of describing the changes that sovereignty is undergoing. They are not subject and object, but two alternative formulations of the same set of transitions.

If this claim is accepted in general, what might be its significance for some specific issues in IR theory? The template can be applied to three dimensions of sovereignty: the type of 'good' that it is and how it is produced; its relationship to anarchy; and its role in the 'counter-forces' to globalization.

The argument of this chapter has revolved around the notion of the state's production of sovereignty, and whether or not, in conditions of globalization, it remains sufficiently competitive to stay in business. By way of clarification, it was earlier pointed out that sovereignty is often viewed as forming two types of good—one prescribing a formal competence, and the other describing an actual capacity. The literature on globalization has queried the state's ability to deliver one or other of these forms of sovereignty. But which kind of sovereignty is it that globalization is claimed to diminish?

More so than the provision of other goods and services, such as security or economic management, the state's production of sovereignty is about self-creation. This is the real significance of the distinction between the formal and the substantive. If the latter describes the hand that is dealt at poker, the former prescribes what the game of poker is actually about. Changes in sovereignty do not simply vary the strength of the hand that states are dealt by increasing or reducing their capacities, they also signify variations in the game of sovereignty itself. As sovereign, the state seeks to remake itself—in response to conflicting domestic and international pressures—by discarding traditional capacities and acquiring new ones. It also delegates functions to other international and transnational bodies. As has been clearly explained, 'the erosion of individual state sovereignty does not imply the erosion of the state. Sovereignty is not an intrinsic feature of state agency, but one social identity a state may have' (Wendt 1996: 61).

Transformation in the formal dimension of sovereignty thus gives the false appearance that the state's substantive capacities have diminished. However, and against the retreat-of-the-state argument, it needs to be understood that any reduction of this kind is frequently as much the result of a voluntary withdrawal as of an enforced retreat: 'nothing prevents the complex of other tasks for which the modern state has assumed primary responsibility to be discharged by organizations that have only a nominal relation to the state', is one suggestion (Onuf 1991: 441). For instance, the provision of the institutional structure required for capitalist production is one set of functions that is largely in the process of such transference (Wendt 1996: 60), even if the extent to which this has occurred is a matter of dispute. The state can exercise its sovereignty through delegation, and by lending legitimacy to such transfers of function (Hirst and Thompson 1996: 190). These movements reflect the state's self-image of what its functions should properly be, and indicate ways in which this image has changed over time. The state is performing less in certain areas and, when these are measured against previous high-water marks, there seems to have been an appreciable fall in the level of state competence. But this is driven as much from within as from without. The key question that then needs to be explored 'is the degree to which the decline of state authority and control in the economic realm may be contingent on an enhancement of its authority and control in other realms' (Thomson 1995: 224).

Changes in sovereignty as capacity do become enshrined in the changing formalities of sovereignty. If it is the case that 'states acquire new roles even as they cede power' (Hirst and Thompson 1996: 190), then there is a dynamic relationship between political control and political authority, or between capacity and formality. The shifting balance describes, at any one moment, the state of the state.

The same can be discerned in the relationship between sovereignty and anarchy. As already noted, these terms tend generally to be regarded as opposites, and to be defined by mutual negation. Instead, they should be understood to be broad and evolutionary categories, with a capacity to interact and refashion each other.

This is not the conventional image. Normally, sovereignty is considered to exist within the bounded space of states. Anarchy, by contrast, is thought to haunt the unclaimed space in between. Sovereignty constitutes the state and, by default, anarchy is its residue. In effect, sovereignty and anarchy are presented as spatially separate and distinct domains, with no place for them to meet. But this is misleading. In practice, most political situations reflect their mingling, with varying proportions of each. Sovereignty and anarchy intersect and the state is constituted, variably, by the degree of their overlap—as, indeed, is the international realm. The line between sovereignty and anarchy does not coincide with the territories of states. We must therefore beware of the danger, as one observer puts it, 'that we automatically treat whatever is external to territorial state actors as "non-state" and therefore anarchic' (Wendt 1996: 59). Instead, the state and the international system are both permeated by sovereignty and anarchy to varying degrees.

In turn, this denotes the extent to which the (inter-state) realm of anarchy can be diluted by degrees of international governance at the same time as the (domestic) realm of sovereignty can slide towards anarchy. It is in this context that Hirst and Thompson envisage the continuing vitality of state action as the 'crucial relay between the international level of governance and the articulate publics of the developed world' (1996: 191). However, it is a misconception to imagine that it is the growth of international governance that is causing the diminution of sovereignty. The two are instead part of a reworked bargain, whereby less control over domestic affairs is a constitutive element within the trade-off for more international governance. Concisely expressed, the erosion of the state is not a *consequence* of regimes or institutions or globalization, but a *precondition* for them. The 'weakening' of sovereignty occurs in tandem with the 'weakening' of anarchy as both dilute each other to some degree.

These sets of claims have significant implications for the third area of discussion: sovereignty and the counter-forces to globalization. If, as argued, sovereignty is not opposed to globalization but part of it, it follows that neither can it form a free-standing defence against globalization. Appeals for a reassertion of sovereignty to halt the advance of globalization are thus misplaced, as sovereignty is not some separate barrier that can be placed before it. The idea that sovereignty is the 'solution' for globalization is as confusing as the idea that globalization is the 'problem' for sovereignty. Such structures of argument serve only to reify an unworkable duality. Sovereignty can no more stop globalization than we can run away from our own shadows.

This is not to deny that a process of adjustment between the two can, and does, take place. But it is driven as much by new or reformulated state functions as by any redefinition of the international rules of the game alone. A new sovereignty regime cannot be imposed from the outside and in separation from the state activities of which it is a part. If, as argued in these pages, globalization is best regarded as a process of state transition, then the course it follows will largely be set by these new forms of state functionality. Appeals to sovereignty, as some kind of exogenous regulator, are simply restatements of the problem, rather than contributions to its solution. As mirror images of each other's transformations, sovereignty on its own can do little to alter the face of globalization.

The implications for IR theory are clear. In the production of sovereignty, the state is engaged in two levels of activity: the substantive, in which historically its performance varies both by category and by degree; and the formalistic, in which it recreates itself along with the system of which it is a part. In globalized conditions, both sovereign forms are affected. But that is tautology. It is not globalization that is the independent cause of these changes. What globalization offers us is a persuasive narrative of the changing face of sovereignty, and also of the changing face of the state. 'The convenient separation between domestic and international affairs is collapsing', we are told, and 'globalisation is the best word we have to describe that phenomenon' (Guehenno 1998/9: 6). If it conveys some sense of that collapse, it must necessarily tell us something important about the contemporary transitions in sovereignty.

In more concrete terms, this in turn measures the balance of political forces operating upon the state, both from within and from without. In accordance with the previously outlined template, shifts in sovereignty reflect this state of political play. Constituted sovereign authority prescribes what the state is entitled to do but, reflecting the practicalities, the state exercises its individual capacities variably. In turn, major shifts in the arrogation or delegation of these capacities can begin to transform the formal doctrine of sovereignty as well. But there is no linear process at work here. Wendt is assuredly correct to insist, with regard to what he describes as 'international state formation', that it may not continue indefinitely 'since it creates fundamental tensions between the national and trans-national functions of state actors' (1996: 61). This is exactly the point. The state operates in a single field of political forces and may tilt in either direction. Most recently, governments have experienced greater difficulty in exercising sufficient power 'relative to domestic and global forces' to maintain their legitimacy (Goldblatt *et al.* 1997: 284). Janus-faced sovereignty is no more immune to these pressures than is the state itself, and is a clear measurement both of current trends and of the political consequences attendant upon them.

Successive chapters will now review the shifting identities of states with respect to the provision of the various 'goods and services' in which they are engaged. These chapters will attempt to capture the essence of globalization by exploring the current state of the state, as it is exposed to new terms of engagement between internal and external forces. Much of the supposed erosion of state control is thought to be experienced, above all, in the economic sphere and it is within this realm that sovereignty is deemed to be considerably underproduced. It is to the evidence from this quarter that the enquiry will turn first.

5

THE COMPETITION STATE

The notion that developments in the international economy are the leading edges of substantial transformation in statecraft has been a recurrent motif in the history of IR theory. At least since the mid-nineteenth century, international commerce has been thought to have a potentially pacifying effect on international life. Succeeding generations of functionalists and integrationists have regarded economic interaction as the primary vehicle for developing a regional or world society, from which political restructuring would inescapably flow. Marxist theorists were wont to assume that it was from within the world capitalist system that the final crisis of the class-based, and imperialist, state would emerge. During the 1960s and 1970s, interdependence theorists made great play of the extent of economic and material interconnection, and concluded from this that there were radical changes under way, both in the categories of actors on the international stage and in the nature of their interests. Given this preceding intellectual history, it is scarcely surprising that it is from within the economic domain that globalization theorists have drawn attention to the most dramatic potential for change. Neither is it remarkable that, for the very same reason, some critics dismiss globalization as 'only a recycled version of a very old idea' (M. Cox 1998: 451).

The predominant implication associated with the concept of globalization is that of a decline in the capacity of the state: the obverse side of globalization is the state everywhere in retreat (Reich 1991; Muller and Wright 1994a; Ohmae 1995; Strange 1996). In the more extreme versions, the state all but disappears. In the new financial geography, 'the coherence of national financial spaces is dissolving' (Leyshon 1996: 79). Even the financial instability of the late 1990s, associated with marked economic downturns in East Asia, Russia, and elsewhere, has not diminished the ardour of the globalization enthusiasts. They take it to confirm their case—either by demonstrating the levels of financial enmeshment that have been instrumental in transmitting the instability, or by clamouring for new forms of global economic management. In turn, these arguments signify, for the globalists, the persisting reality of globalization even in the face of financial turmoil: the situation merely underlines the inability of individual governments to 'buck markets', as well as the absence of effective regulation at the national level.

This chapter will review the current state of the state as an economic actor and its implications for IR theory. To what extent does the state remain a significant producer of economic goods? Does it still make sense to speak of distinct *national* economies? The chapter will rehearse the debates about the demise of the state as a controlling element within the global economy, as a preliminary to advancing a more balanced interpretation. In conformity with the ongoing argument, it will be suggested that, while usually portrayed as the *source* of the state's economic redundancy, globalization is equally a *measure* of state transformation. If the state, since its inception, has always had an economic function as an extractor of revenue. its other tasks of economic management were grafted on much later in its historical development, and can scarcely be regarded as an inalienable part of its nature. That it may, in turn, have transferred or delegated some of these func-tions to other actors, or to the global market itself, does not by itself indicate the end of the state as we know it. States are not what they are simply because of what globalization has done to them; globalization is at least as much what it is because of what states have already become. It is this mutuality that is commonly obscured in many versions of the economic globalization thesis.

The case for globalization, and the consequent reduction of state capacity, is most insistently made in the economic sphere. Indeed, so prominent is the eco-nomic literature within the field that there is reason to question whether the eco-nomic case for globalization might not be the exception, instead of the basis on which to construct a more generalized account. Certainly, those writers who develop the argument from a political, or security, perspective generally reach more circumspect conclusions than do their economic counterparts.

The economic argument most frequently deployed has two principal elements. First, it is maintained that states no longer have policy autonomy as regards the management of their own economic arrangements and they are, to this extent, eroded from the outside by the forces of economic globalization. Secondly, in the face of this onslaught, all states have adapted uniformly and become similar kinds of economic actors. Whereas previously states attempted to engage in inter-national economic transactions for the benefit of domestic constituencies, they now mediate between internal and external demands at the behest of external economic forces. The rules of competition are imposed from the outside, and the economic state must conform to them if it is to succeed. While such engagement is purportedly for domestic economic benefits—by enhancing the economic effi-ciency of the state and its competitive edge—the criteria for measuring success nonetheless tend to be established from the outside, either directly by inter-national economic institutions or indirectly by shared international norms.

This chapter will subject to scrutiny the various elements of these arguments and, once again, reconstruct them in such a fashion that a sensible framework for IR theory can emerge. For this to be done, the supposition of a zero-sum rela-tionship between state and globalization will once more be challenged. In its place will be developed the notion of a competition state with different, but not neces-sarily reduced, capacities. As already noted in the preceding chapter, the state may reshape itself so that certain functions are given up, or delegated to other actors. At the same time, it may acquire responsibilities for new areas of social activity, such as consumer protection, environmental management, and the regulation of relationships hitherto deemed to fall within the private sphere. We should not simplify the real significance of such complex, and by no means unidirectional, developments.

In conformity with the ongoing theme of this book, the case will be made for viewing the economic engagement between state and globalization, not as antagonistic, but rather as one in which state and globalization are both reshaped through their mutual encounter. From this perspective, globalization becomes a phase in the continuing historical adaptation of the state, and not a qualitative endpoint that marks its irreversible transmutation, let alone its impending demise. If this is the core of the argument, how is it best transcribed in theoretical terms?

The state in retreat?

It is commonplace to depict the emerging relationship between state and globalization (which already, of course, begs the question by assuming that these are discrete and separable phenomena) as entailing some kind of antagonism or contradiction. Cerny (1995: 598) expresses it thus. 'In recent decades', he writes, 'an accelerating divergence has taken place between the structure of the state and the structure of industrial and financial markets in the complex, globalizing world of the third industrial revolution'. He further describes this as a 'new disjuncture'.

In what does the disjuncture reside? It is commonly conveyed in *policy control* terms, and this will be the focus of much of the following analysis. Alternatively, the disjuncture is depicted in aggregate terms as a sharp move towards structural inequality. As Wilkin (1997: 19) suggests, the 'revival of liberal conceptions of freedom has coincided with the restructuring of the global economy that has taken place since the mid-1970s and has led to a widening of inequality across a whole range of indices, from wealth and income to mortality and morbidity ratios'. Were these inequalities simply products of internationalization, they might be put down to traditionalist state-centred dominance/dependence types of analysis within which appeals to globalization are otiose. However, the fact that these inequalities occur both within and between states explicitly makes the link to globalization—and hence the focus on the territorial state alone does not capture the essence of what is happening. This engenders the view that globalization, by its very nature, is associated with inequality and a fragmentation of economic interests. 'The global economy divides every society into new camps of conflicting economic interest,' we are told. 'It undermines every nation's ability to maintain social cohesion' (Greider 1997: 18). The imagery of globalization as progressive inequality both within and across borders suggests that the disjuncture is not simply one between state and global economy, but more generally between the economically advantaged and disadvantaged wherever they might be, and of which state policy is as much a symptom as cause. At any rate, the connection between globalization and inequality is made, confirming one assessment that 'a universal state of equal integration in worldwide economic activity is precisely what globalization *is not*' (Gray 1998: 55).

This much at least is implicit in the language of economic 'disembedding' that is widely employed to analyse the transition to neo-liberalism. As against the notion of the state as guardian of domestic economic interest, stabilizing the international economy while protecting domestic corporatist bargains, neo-liberalism has entailed a relative demotion of the state's domestic priorities. However, the argument that the state is in terminal decline because of this transition is itself predicated on a belief, largely mistaken, that the state is thereby abdicating its historical tasks and losing its essential claim to legitimacy. In fact, of course, it is more accurate to regard the period of welfarism as the historical exception in the state's performance, rather than as the rule. As has been noted, the 'resurgence of free-market liberalism in the 1980s, the assault on the doctrine, and the partial curtailment of the practices, of welfare-liberalism, while apparently an aberration in relation to the post-war decades, was more a reassertion of the core liberal values and ideology' (Richardson 1995: 145). On this reasoning, the onset of the age of economic globalization, in so far as it is reflected in state policy, is not the inauguration of some brave new world but a step backwards towards 'normalcy', before the distractions of Keynesianism were pursued. Even such a generalization is, of course, superficial as it ignores the state-interventionist character of much neo-liberal policy. Nonetheless, its connotations of cycles and continuous historical change need to be more seriously addressed than is done by some of the more apocalyptic accounts to be found in the literature on economic globalization.

In this context, the previous chapter's discussion of sovereignty is much to the point, as there is deep-seated confusion about the impact which economic globalization has upon sovereignty. It is argued in some quarters that economic globalization erodes 'Certain aspects of national sovereignty, but not the institution of the nation-state itself' (Holton 1998: 101–2). Others go beyond claims about the undermining of the state's operational controls, and speak explicitly about the end of sovereignty (Scholte 1997b: 21) or, more modestly, about the need for a 'rethinking of sovereignty' (M. Williams 1996: 115–20).

The pervasive assumption of much of this writing is that the globalization–state capacity relationship is zero-sum, and a remorseless globalization now has the upper hand. This at least seems to be the import of Falk's suggestion that globalization 'has already won out in the sense that the language and imagery of a state-centric world have become anachronistic in crucial respects' (1997a: 126). In similar vein, it is contended that globalization erodes control over national economies such that 'states faced with a declining autonomy . . . grapple to articulate the modifications in behaviour required to claim back control over their policy agendas' (Higgott 1996: 34).

It would be churlish to deny the force of these comments: this is, after all, the way that the issue of globalization has tended to be addressed. Within those terms, there is an ongoing debate about whether geography and state territorial management still matter. Important distinctions are made between distance and space, on the one hand (thought to be of less importance), and place or location, on the other (thought to be of enhanced importance) (Daniels and Lever 1996: 3). But this is to pursue the discussion within the existing framework.

Instead, there are equally compelling reasons for putting an alternative analytical gloss on the issue. From a second perspective, the notion of a loss of state capacity to globalizing forces misses the essential point that states are not only the vehicles of globalization but are also themselves reconstituted by it. At the same time, globalization can the more readily encroach where the state has, for its own reasons, abrogated existing responsibilities. Such a proposition derives from the previous discussion of the Great Divide and conforms to Sassen's questioning (1996a: 6) of what she calls the 'global-national duality'. As these two domains are conceived as being separate and exclusive, 'Dualization has fed the proposition that the national state must decline in a globalized economy'. It is this duality which is artificial, and needs to be revised. In this sense, we can endorse the alternative view that the 'state is a key element within processes of globalization rather than something opposed to them' (R. Brown 1995: 56; see also Scholte 1997a: 441). Within this perspective, the focus shifts from state retreat to state adaptation (Weiss 1998: xi). The present argument therefore reaffirms the following critique:

there is a tendency to ignore the extent to which today's globalisation both is authored by states and is primarily about reorganising, rather than bypassing, states; it promotes, in this sense, a false dichotomy. (Panitch 1994: 63)

In saying this, however, we must equally avoid the danger of sliding from the view of the state as an agent of globalization to that of the state as the passive formation of global systems: the attempt to bridge the Great Divide must not end by simply refashioning another version of structuralism. However, there is such a tendency within some of the literature. It emphasizes the materialist and capitalist basis of the new post-cold war hegemonic order. From this viewpoint, the 1980s witnessed the removal of the final barriers to a genuinely worldwide system. Through the 1980s, the Third World was disciplined by the destruction of its vestigial 'national development' and 'revolutionary' projects, and became fully incorporated into the economic strategies set by the key capitalist institutions. Additionally, its final defeat in the cold war ensured that the separate world of socialist development was swept away, thus leaving a single international division of labour.

Furthermore, this line of argument continues, the main experience of states at the capitalist core during the 1980s and 1990s has been the neo-liberal revolution that they have undergone. In this, they were driven by the need to compete in a more adverse set of economic conditions, and in the face of emerging challengers (Wilkin 1997: 24). The neo-liberal state has become much less the instrument for national economic management, and more 'connected' to the needs of highly mobile capital and production. Above all, in this intensely competitive environment, the state can no longer afford to sustain the rising economic costs of national welfare programmes. The period has therefore been associated with the attack on existing forms of the welfare state (Helleiner 1994b: 173; Martin 1994:

69–70; and Teeple 1995). Deregulation and privatization have been extended into the sphere of provision of essential social services. According to such claims, 'national regimes of extensive labour rights and social protection are thus obsolete', as the state can 'only provide those social and public services international capital deems essential at the lowest possible overhead cost' (Hirst and Thompson 1995: 175–6). As part of this process, however, the operational powers of the national state are further eroded, since it was on the management of the national economy, and the provision of welfare services, that the state reached the apogee of its controls in the 1950s and 1960s.

Although differing nuances are to be found in such accounts, what unites them is a shared assessment that the state now functions from the top down, as a conduit whereby external demands are imposed upon national societies. States do not project national economic demands into the international domain, but instead impose international disciplines upon domestic constituencies. Thus regarded, the flow of democratic accountability is in a direction precisely the reverse of that imagined in its more orthodox formulations. Moreover, within a spectrum of writings, these demands are presented in such a way as to amount to a form of structuralism alternative to that found in neo-realism. States are constrained to behave in similar ways for structural reasons, but the pertinent structure in this case shifts from the anarchy/power features singled out by Waltz to the competition/neo-liberalism of the post-embedded-liberal global economy.

This outside-in interpretation of state behaviour can be found in a plethora of writings. It is very much present in Cerny's analysis of the 'competition' state which is constrained to 'act more and more like a market player' (1990: 229–30). This tends to induce uniformity of state policy as each minimizes welfare provision to make itself more internationally competitive. 'The functions of the state', it has been contended, 'become re-organized to adjust domestic economic and social policies to fit the exigencies of the global market and global capitalist accumulation' (Hoogvelt 1997: 67, 138; also Brodie 1996: 385–6; Gill 1997b: 14).

The idea that these external constraints reveal the workings of an international structure, at least on a par with that found in the Waltzian analysis, has accordingly been set out in a more self-conscious and systematic way. An early statement of this theme can be found in Webb's discussion of the effects of international capital mobility:

all of the governments included within the scope of this study . . . responded in a similar, though not identical, fashion to change in international capital mobility . . . This mobility has persisted over time . . . and is likely to continue to persist. We are therefore justified in considering it an element of the international economic structure and studying the effects of its structure on the policies of individual governments. (1991: 312–13)

This adaptation of neo-realist theory, which refashions the concept of structure to include aspects of the economic system, has been further elaborated by Andrews who, in turn, emphasizes the currently existing structural constraints which impede 'either unilateral or collaborative reversal of these trends' (1994: 214). This view has subsequently been endorsed by Milner and Keohane, who reach the conclusion that 'Like anarchy, exposure to the international capitalist economy has become a fact that individual states confront and can only ignore or seek to change by paying such high costs that no state can afford it' (1996: 257): capital mobility and deregulation may not determine, but they assuredly constrain, the range of choice. Another variant, if less fully developed, can be found in the appeal to the global market as a new international anarchy. In this version, states are 'constrained . . . by the risks and uncertainties that accompany an international market that tends to anarchy' (Gray 1998: 70). What the future holds, we are told, is a 'deepening international anarchy' of this kind (Gray 1998: 207). By implication, one is invited to imagine self-help, of a self-interested kind, as the behavioural norm in such a setting.

It is not the present intent to challenge the evidence that has led to such findings. However, in terms of an attempt to confront the division into systemic and reductionist approaches, it is unsatisfactory to elide it by simply opting for a restated systemic position, in which the state is 'reduced' to an outside-in artefact, albeit of the economic variety. This does not take us beyond the Great Divide but simply reinvents it in another guise. It gives too much weight to structure, and takes too little account of the resultant political impact upon the states. Indeed, there is even the suggestion that the sphere of politics is simply reconfigured in conformity with the external economic framework that now directs it. 'Politics does not disappear,' it has been remarked, 'but its rationality is synchronised with the economy' (Altvater and Mahnkopf 1997: 319). This wholly elides the state as meaningful political market, let alone as residual agent of domestic interests.

We need to recognize that those interpretations which are cast in terms of the 'retreat of the state'—as well as the extreme culmination of them which reduces the state to no more than a fabrication of the (economic) system—distort the significance of globalization (Weiss 1998: 11). Instead of regarding globalization and state power as a zero-sum relationship in which globalization erodes state capacity, it is more instructive to think of globalization and a reconstitution of the state occurring in tandem. Indeed, a shift of attention away from the decline of the state, toward a recasting of the state, is precisely the point made in criticism against Susan Strange (1996). Questioning why reconstitution should be conflated with retreat, Douglas comments: 'Why the historical transformation of a particular form of state (the Keynesian Welfare State) should be taken to be equivalent to the historical transcendence of the state itself is left unexplained' (1996: 21). This observation has considerable force, and the alternative perspective which it offers has a major potential advantage: by eschewing an outside-in determinism, it leaves open the possibility of this reconstituted state responding differently in future to the 'structural constraints' in which it presently finds itself. Instead of a mechanistic, timeless, and depoliticized account of globalization, in which recent trends are bound to reproduce themselves endlessly into the future, such an approach recaptures both politics and a sense of real history. There has been no linear, and painless, progression towards globalization in the past, nor is there any reason to believe that this is how it is destined to unfold into the future. The complex reflexivity between the state and the field of forces in which it finds itself is too unpredictable to allow of such simplistic projections into the future: the state may be driven to strike back in ways that are less supportive of globalization.

The limits of state economic autonomy

A wide range of commentators is agreed that the economic capacity of the state has been much reduced by globalization. These views share a common core whilst then proceeding to emphasize different points of detail. 'Where states were once the masters of markets,' Strange declaims, 'now it is the markets which, on many crucial issues, are the masters over the governments of states' (1996: 4). This sentiment is echoed by others who likewise point to 'the loss of autonomous regulatory power of states', and insist that 'their powers of shielding domestic economies from negative effects of globalization have diminished' (R. Cox 1996*b*: 26–7).

This diminution of state economic capacity is thought to manifest itself in a number of distinct ways, and to be driven by disparate causes. Generally, however, analysts claim to detect the impact of globalization in the seeming depoliticization of economic processes, and their subjection to forms of technical rationality. Such a development itself takes multiple forms, but typically is illustrated by the ceding of overt political control over the setting of domestic interest rates, via central banks or other similar devices (Teeple 1995: 70). Alternatively, control of economic policy, where it has not devolved 'downward' in such fashion, has devolved 'outwards', and now takes the form of international 'coordination efforts' concerning 'monetary and fiscal policies—policies that had traditionally been considered "internal" ' (Webb 1991: 310–11). Such transformations can be judged in various ways. The optimists believe that politics and society will adjust to these external imperatives, while pessimists fear that 'the conflict between the economic objectivity that is imposing itself and the autonomy of politics and society . . . can lead to societal sclerosis or, in certain cases, self-destruction' (Amin 1996: 218).

By what mechanisms is economic globalization deemed to sap the policy autonomy of states? Although individual authors develop their own specific lines of argument, there would appear to be three standard versions that generally recur. These pertain to the following aspects of globalization: the drive for international competitiveness; the constraints of financial soundness; and the consequences of capital mobility. Each of these operates individually, but contributes by mutual reinforcement to a combined, and powerful, effect. In the aggregate, this is thought to minimize the state's policy discretion with regard to its own national economy.

The arguments are all fairly conventional, and do not need to be rehearsed in great detail. According to the first, the range of policy options is narrowed by the imperative to remain internationally competitive. This, in turn, dictates prudent, and where necessary reduced, levels of governmental borrowing, as well as restraints on public expenditure. While this is virtually the hallmark of all writing on economic globalization, it is a theme particularly well exemplified by Phil Cerny. He maintains not only that the quest for competitiveness is the driving force of contemporary state policy but also that 'states are transforming— marketizing—*themselves* in the search for competitiveness' (1996*b*: 124–5). Implicit in this notion of 'marketizing' is, of course, the unwillingness or inability of states to put up any policy resistance to the economic environment in which they find themselves. To do so would invite economic harm by rendering key economic sectors less able to compete. The result is a 'race to the bottom: lower wages, lower taxes, less accountability' (Greider 1997: 101). States subject themselves to this competition because they see no choice: the fear is that production and investment might move elsewhere, in so far as globalization is predicated on assumptions of the complete 'substitutability of locations', itself a concomitant of decreasing economic territorialization (Storper 1997: 31–4). Accordingly, the policies consequent upon state marketization give the appearance that 'the state seems nothing more than the hand-maiden of the almighty global economy' (McCarthy and Jones 1995*b*: 8). Even those who deny the crude versions of this erosion of state economic capacity still accept that all states face challenges from new competitors where governments have higher levels of transformative capability. In this variant, the nature of the competitive challenge may differ, but competition remains nonetheless the principal dynamic of the contemporary international political economy (Weiss 1998: 143).

The second element operates closely in tandem with the first. A state that is unsuccessful in this international competition risks being burdened by higher levels of social expenditure. At the same time, and in a vicious circle, high social costs diminish the ability to compete. The dilemma facing the welfare state is that 'its continued legitimacy is dependent upon the satisfaction of expectations that it has itself sanctioned but which threaten to undermine economic competitiveness' (Hay 1996: 109). To break out of this cycle, governments must be seen to pursue policies that are considered sound by the international markets. The point is again set out tellingly by Cerny. 'Governments increasingly measure their performance according to criteria acceptable to the financial markets', is his considered judgement, and, accordingly, 'they must be seen as "strong" or "sound" if they are to retain the confidence of the international financial community' (1996*c*: 87). In one specific development of this type of argument, the point is made that states are now more dependent upon borrowing to fund their expenditure, and this in any event renders them more vulnerable to market pressures (Germain 1997: 163–4).

The resulting necessity to be mindful of the scale of deficits is, of course, driven by the third factor. When capital markets were largely national in character and operation, governments were less beholden to them. However, in conditions of high mobility, such as have characterized the period since at least the 1980s, budgetary excesses are now more exposed to punishment. Thus commentators speak of 'the disciplining power of global capital movements' which has resulted in governments 'curbing public expenditure, giving priority to the control of inflation and enhancing the strength of private power' (Wilkin 1997: 24). Typically, Milner and Keohane locate their discussion of the diminishing efficacy of national fiscal policy in this context of capital mobility (1996a: 17). Otherwise expressed, the contention put forward by neo-classical economics is that 'national governments neither can nor should control the flow of capital across borders, and hence cannot regulate interest rates, fix currency values, or pursue macroeconomic policies' that do not conform to market preferences (Schor 1992: 1).

This much is commonplace. In terms of the analysis of globalization, the major issue to emerge from it is whether or not these constraints are to be viewed, as discussed above, as some kind of new structural constant. Alternatively, and taking a wider historical perspective, the period since the 1980s may be thought no more than a specific phase and one that is itself subject to change. This is precisely the question that lies at the heart of much of the economic globalization debate. In the words of two contributors, the 'declining policy autonomy of states as they cede control to markets may only be a temporary phase, until new forms of intervention are demanded and discovered' (Milner and Keohane 1996b: 249). But even if this were to come to pass, would it signify that the states were 'winning back' the autonomy that they had lost? Or is there another, and preferable, way of conceiving of any such potential development? The discussion will revert to this point shortly. In the meantime, it must first review the related claim that economic globalization does not merely reduce the policy autonomy of states, but that the evidence for this resides in the increasing *uniformity* of state behaviour. Just as in the case of the Waltzian analysis, so we are told, we are entitled to infer the existence of structural constraints from the perceived regularity of agent behaviour.

The theme of similarity in state behaviour is striking in this context. In the case of Webb, it explicitly forms the basis of his claim to the existence of structural effects: 'all of the governments', he avers, 'responded in a similar, though not identical, fashion to change in international capital mobility' (1991: 312–13). Others have reached similar conclusions, even without such formalized neo-structural arguments. 'The new orthodoxy', it is claimed, 'suggests that the changing international political economy puts roughly the same demands on all governments' (Brodie 1996: 385–6).

Uniformity thereby becomes the clearest expression of state impotence. Even the seasoned observer can reach dramatic conclusions. 'It is nothing new or unusual that the nature of an individual state is subject to change,' writes Strange. 'What is new and unusual is that all—or nearly all—states should undergo substantial change of roughly the same kind within the same short period' (1996: 86–7). The most striking formulation of this analysis is provided by Richard Falk, who laments the passing of the humane and compassionate state in the face of the new economic orthodoxy. Such is the pressure for uniformity and conformity that 'Sweden can no longer be Sweden!' (1997a: 130; cf. Weiss 1998: 113). Distinct national policy identities are all thought to succumb to the universalizing imperatives of the global economy.

The material expression of this conformity is the striking similarity of economic and social programmes. In consequence of these external forces, the 'state is no longer in a position anywhere to pursue the general welfare as if it were mainly a domestic problem' (Cerny 1990: 230). Instead, there has been an attempt across the board to impose 'stringent monetary and fiscal policies' (Kapstein 1996: 21). These influences have penetrated deeply into the policy fabric of the state, eroding post-war practices and reshaping labour relations, with greater emphasis upon flexibility. 'Corporatist bargaining and employment policies are challenged everywhere', notes Cerny, 'by international pressures for wage restraint and flexible working practices' (1996b: 128). All the post-war bargains that shored up 'embedded liberalism' are thereby undermined (Teeple 1995: 142). Once again, we are in the world of structural determinism in which the economic system disposes from the outside, and reduces the individual state to a mere instrument of its grand design. 'Thus, with the globalization . . . of the world economy', Hoogvelt concludes, 'there is a tendency for states to become instruments for adjusting their economies to the pressures of the world market. Adjustment to global competitiveness is the new categorical imperative' (1997: 138).

What these outside-in interpretations fail to admit is that any validity they might have, in turn, depends on an 'inside' transformation in the viability of the democratic state (see Chapter 8). The determinism is operative only in proportion to the breakdown of democratic procedures, since this is what 'disconnects' the state from domestic preferences, and regenerates it as the instrument of the global economy. It is unelected and unaccountable economic power that renders 'adjustments to the international economy . . . a fixed point of orientation in economic policy' (Held 1998: 18). If this is so, we must explain how the economy exercises this structural power. The answer must assuredly be that it is underproduction of 'domestic' democracy that allows the global economic structure to dominate in this way. Accordingly, the fate of the competition state is inextricably bound up with the transformation of the democratic state. This, by itself, should make us wary of attributing all effects to the externally generated demands of the global economy alone.

That there has been a generalized tendency for states to adopt the policies mentioned can scarcely be denied, although details are, of course, disputed. Some research indicates that, whatever pressures there might be on the welfare state, they do not emanate from globalization alone. Nor, as a rule, are proportions of national budgets devoted to welfare spending actually experiencing reductions (cited in Holton 1998: 93). The significant analytical issue is then whether this trend is, as its critics surmise, driven by global economic pressures, or whether it might be explained by some other sets of factors. Indeed, the interest in economic globalization itself tends to rest upon the assumption that it is external economic forces that are driving changes in state policy. The very idea of an international economic structure gives expression to this presumption. That social policy is rooted in economic concerns is thus widely accepted. Many analysts likewise attribute to globalization the undermining of 'national forms of redistribution politics according to social need' (Holton 1998: 92). Were things otherwise, the scholarly interest in globalization would assuredly be much diminished.

But there *are* other ways of accounting for the recent uniformity of state social policy, beyond the constraints of a reified global economic system (Weiss 1998: 90–110). According to this kind of perspective, the scaling back of welfare provision since the 1980s is driven by the recognition of the policy mistakes of the past, or by the new realities of social costs in the future. Such assessments are predicated primarily on a fear of a return of inflation—itself the catalyst of new economic behaviour—rather than external constraints (Notermans 1997: 205–7). This reflects not simply a change in economic theory, but a necessary change driven by welfare policy itself: the Keynesian welfare state was failing in its own terms, and has not simply been the passive victim of the new global economic orthodoxy.

The role of globalization, then, is merely to offer a convenient pretext, an ideological rationale that lends plausibility to a set of changes dictated for other reasons. It is this latter analysis that is implicit in the following account:

> Globalization . . . appears as an *external* constraint—not a matter of political choice at all, but rather of economic necessity—so that nation-states can do little besides follow the dictates of footloose capital in a downward spiral of deregulation, lower social spending and lower taxes. (Mishra 1996: 316–17)

The attempt to offer a satisfactory explanation of this state policy convergence is yet further complicated by two additional considerations. The first is the extent to which a case can be made for the continuing robustness of state policy on the grounds of its having opted for globalization in the first place: we cannot adduce state impotence from globalization, since globalization is the policy choice of the state. This circularity is noted by Hoogvelt, who remarks upon the fact that 'the sceptics in the globalisation debate make rather much of the continuing, indeed in some cases apparently enhanced, exercise of sovereignty and regulation by national governments'. Her own conclusion is that 'much of this regulation amounts in effect to no more than a regulation *for* globalisation' (1997: 131). And so how much policy autonomy does this reveal? Secondly, perhaps the true measure of state robustness is not whether it can opt to enhance globalization further but whether, once set in motion, it can do much to reverse it. Here the sceptics probably have the louder voice (Andrews 1994: 214). But might not all such judgements be missing an important point?

The resilience of states

The case against the erosion of state capacities is frequently made by simple denial: globalization has not diminished the state, because it is the state that has fostered globalization and which continues to sustain it. According to this perspective, whatever antagonism there might be in the relationship, it is the state that is the determinant and globalization one of its consequences. These claims need to be reviewed as a preliminary to a more satisfactory theoretical resolution.

The argument that globalization is a condition initiated by state policies is regularly developed. One of its most vocal champions attributes the dynamic of globalization to various policy decisions taken since the late 1950s, amongst which the most important were: liberalization initiatives which favoured the market; abstention from controls on capital movements; and the prevention of major financial crises (Helleiner 1994a: 8). By these various decisions and non-decisions, states created an economic climate conducive to the intensification of international financial integration. A similar situation has been identified as regards the development of the international system of credit, within which, it is claimed, 'the actions of states have thus been an integral element' (Germain 1997: 161).

Such counter-arguments are designed to question the diminishing capacity of states and also, by implication, to hold out the prospect of the reversibility of globalization. As against the view of globalization as a structural given, Andrews concedes, some hold that 'the degree of capital mobility between states is simply a consequence of national policy decisions to liberalize national financial markets' (1994: 197). From this perspective, the notion of globalization as a condition separate from the policies of states is illusory. It is for this reason that the claim is made that 'capitalist globalisation is a process which also takes place in, through, and under the aegis of states; it is encoded by them and in important respects even authored by them' (Panitch 1994: 64). The conception of globalization as a process set against states, and constraining their behaviour, is, to that extent, entirely misleading.

Equally so is the suggestion that state regulatory capacity is in terminal decline. This has been challenged from a number of quarters, but the central proposition is that the market is not itself a self-regulating mechanism and is itself contingent upon political frameworks put in place by benign public institutions. Without these supports, the market is not self-sustaining. Thus it is argued that the policy innovations of the 1980s will, in due course, be politically tempered by the reassertion of new forms of state intervention, so that policies become once more embedded in national political preferences (Boyer 1996: 110–11). The pervasive theme is the redefinition of the state's functions rather than any notion of state retreat (Moran 1994: 176). 'What is observed in practice', one critic comments of changing state capacity, 'is a redrawing of the borders of the public sphere in a way that excludes certain fields better left to private activity, while at the same time strengthening and even expanding the state's regulatory capacity in other fields like competition or environmental and consumer protection' (Majone 1994: 80).

But to enter the argument on these terms is to perpetuate the Great Divide previously encountered. The construction of any dichotomy between globalization and state power is bound to deceive. In other words, the important realization to emerge from these debates is not that state powers endure, if redefined, under the impact of globalization but rather that globalization and the redefinition of the state are essentially transcriptions of each other. To speak of globalization is then, by this very act, to address the evidence for the reconstitution of the state.

What then are we to make of the quite inconsistent conclusions drawn by different analysts? For instance, there is Palan's judgement: 'The study of the relationship between the state and the global economy', he insists, 'must not be founded, therefore, on the premise of an inherent contradiction between them' (1994: 47). Yet elsewhere, others seem to take the opposite very much for granted. They highlight precisely the contradiction emerging from the new situation in which 'the space of production is becoming globalized while the spheres of political and social management remain limited by the political frontiers of states' (Amin 1996: 249–50). Palan's point is that the global economy itself requires political sustenance from states; Amin's is that their organizational bases are so different—territorial and non-territorial—that they pull in opposite directions. But this is exactly the nub of the issue. How is the requisite politico-institutional support for globalization to be sustained when it is itself seen to be undermining the state's principal claims to legitimacy? Globalization needs the legitimacy of the state but is simultaneously the greatest threat to it. However, such a formulation of the problem also points towards its resolution. Globalization cannot long take on its present disembedded form without destroying itself, and will in large measure be reconstituted as a result of the legitimacy deficits occurring at the national level. The state and globalization are caught up in a relationship that is at once both contradictory and not contradictory (see Bernard 1997: 87). Globalization throws into question the legitimacy of a territorially demarcated political structure while, at the same time, being fully dependent upon it for its own sustainability.

Economic globalization and IR theory

The preceding discussion has been framed in terms of a debate about the erosion of state economic capacity. As demonstrated, such a debate is based on a misleading conception of globalization. The reason for exploring in detail 'the retreat of the state' is that it compels us to face the deeper reality that is at stake in understanding globalization. If the foregoing account has merit, it not only offers an alternative framework within which to conduct the investigation of state economic capacity but also opens a window onto some other areas of concern to IR theory.

How then do these issues of economic globalization contribute to the wider agenda of the IR theorist? They do so in four main areas: by revealing a different way of distinguishing between globalization and interdependence; by broadly confirming the utility of the analytical scheme that constructivist theory brings to bear on the issues; by channelling the discussion into central questions concerning legitimacy and the changing nature of community; and by more effectively integrating IR theory with theories of the state.

Globalization, according to the economic accounts reviewed in this chapter, is not simply interdependence to a higher degree. Following the distinction made by writers such as Hirst and Thompson (1996) and Scholte (1997*a*), it is presumed that globalization refers to the submergence of distinct national economies and the emergence of forms of supraterritoriality in economic organization. In contrast, internationalization is taken to denote levels of interconnection between separate and still distinct national economic entities. As noted in Chapter 2, any suggestion of an absolute distinction of this kind is problematic. However, on the basis of the above analysis, we are now in a position to create a more tenable, albeit qualified, differentiation between the two.

What contributes to confusion on this issue is the flawed manner in which globalization is conventionally presented. Interdependence has all the appearance of being a natural outgrowth of state policies, something closely related to the pursuit of domestic goals. By way of contrast, globalization is something occurring 'out there', wholly at variance with national goals and ambitions. By extension, interdependence is presented as if it were a condition of the states' own making whereby they are better able to achieve their national interests, even if it imposes some constraints on the modalities of doing so. To that extent, it is an endogenous part of state activities. Globalization, on the other hand, tends to be understood as a condition imposed autonomously by technology, or by the dynamics of an economic system working to its own independent logic. To this extent, it is often deemed to be an exogenous obstacle to state interests. This is the subtext of attempts to distinguish between the two on the basis of degrees of territorialization, and in terms of which globalization is deemed to be the more radical condition.

In fact, once the foregoing account of globalization is embraced, the reality is closer to the reverse of this kind of analysis. Paradoxically, interdependence is a more 'purely external' condition than globalization. Interdependence, by most accounts, amounts to a change in the state's external relations with others *without any necessary change in itself.* Such a claim might initially seem perverse and, of course, needs to be qualified. It might be open to the obvious objection that much writing on interdependence is precisely 'transformationalist': it is on this basis that neo-liberals rest their case for prospects of greater co-operation between states. But even allowing that claim, it remains a limited one. It suggests no more than that state transformation is *behavioural* and is a *consequence* of interdependence.

In the case of globalization, and as suggested above, *domestic transformation* is an essential ingredient of globalization. State transformation in conditions of globalization entails a necessary change of state *identity* and is a *precondition*, or at the very least a *concomitant*, of wider systemic change, not something that occurs as an incidental by-product of it. It is in that sense that globalization is the more radical condition, and why there is less dispute that changes in state policies are wrought as part of it. Whereas many are sceptical about the impact of interdependence, most commentators seem to agree that the changes brought about by globalization have been extensive. But such a consensus is right for the wrong reasons. If anything, interdependence represents a more autonomous structure than globalization, for the very reason that state transformation is much more deeply implicated in the latter than in the former. State policies do change during globalization, but not as a contingent outcome. Conversely, interdependence can develop in the absence of an 'interdependence' state, whereas globalization depends upon the globalized state. This is the more convincing basis on which the distinction can be made.

Secondly, and more generally, the above analysis has important implications for the discussion about agents and structures. The issue is raised precisely because of the tendency within the literature to present economic globalization as an elaboration of, or alternative to, the Waltzian notion of structure, and to conclude on this basis that it is a major—external—constraint upon state behaviour. The uniformity of state policy, as much in the domestic realm as in foreign policy, can then be 'deduced' from the economic conditions in which states now find themselves. The structure of economic globalization becomes a given on the assumption that capital mobility and the free market necessarily define the relations between competition states.

However, for all of the reasons already set out, this conception is misleading. In part, this is because of the apparent contradiction between the two images of globalization to which appeal is simultaneously being made. On the one hand, it is argued that what is distinctive about globalization is that it incorporates its 'agents', so much so that they lose their separate identities. At the same time, it is maintained that it constrains their behaviour as independent actors. There is a tension between these claims. Globalization might cause national economies to disappear, or it might cause them to behave in uniform ways, but one surely cannot argue for both propositions at the same time.

At heart, confusion develops because this account fails to allow for the fact that structure (globalization) and agent (state), in this instance, are not wholly separable categories but essential constituents of each other. To posit economic globalization as merely a change of structural circumstance is thus to ignore the fundamental transformation that is wrought in the 'agent' as an inevitable accompaniment of the development of this new 'structure'. To take the latter as a given, which independently impacts upon the behaviour of states, is entirely to miss this essential point.

By the same token, the constraints of the global economy are not some autonomously existing set of constraints but themselves, in large measure, an extension of state activity, and reflections of new state identities and interests. It has been helpfully suggested, in making the same kind of point, that 'regulatory institutions are a constitutive part of the global economy rather than external constraints' (Holton 1998: 68). We might go further by insisting that regulatory institutions and the global economy are, conjointly, an indication of the extent of state transformation already undertaken.

Thirdly, the discussion points to important issues about legitimacy and community that do not always attract the attention they deserve in the debates about globalization. Here it might be said that the effects are paradoxical. Globalization is not immune to the requirements of legitimacy, but having no political constituency of its own it is dependent upon states for provision of this service. Thus globalization, as 'structure', is embedded in the state units, even as it simultaneously appears to delegitimize them. This already suggests that the core issue in tracing the future trajectory of globalization is likely to revolve around legitimacy. If legitimacy is traditionally constructed within a territorial space, then globalization is unable to generate it for itself. It requires the political and social processes of the individual state (Hirst and Thompson 1996: 190), which can also legitimize any transference of function to other bodies.

This, at any rate, is the situation at the moment. It is, of course, possible that if globalization dismantles existing communities, new forms of community might emerge to take their place. The articulation of community thus lies at the heart of contemporary IR theory (Archibugi, Held, and Kohler 1998; Linklater 1998) and is itself the pressing issue, both with regard to the durability of current forms of globalization, and in a theoretical understanding of their dynamics. On this basis, we might dissent from some of the gloomier prognoses. Despite his own argument against the assumed linearity of much globalization reasoning, Gray himself succumbs to a form of linearity in his image of the global economy spiralling out of control. At its root, his fear is that the free market has destroyed other protective social institutions, including the state: 'the free market has used the power of the state to achieve its end, but has weakened the institutions of the state in vital respects', he remarks dismally (1998: 24). For all his railing against the notion of globalization as an end-state, the resulting global capitalist anarchy is precisely the end-state to which he himself ends up subscribing. He makes no allowance for a reconstitution of state activities by the resurgence of 'national' communities, nor for the generation of new forms of community acting through other transnational forms of governance. Indeed, the latter he dismisses out of hand (1998: 207). But there is no more compelling reason to anticipate the collapse of all forms of community and social protection than there is to imagine the single global market as 'the Enlightenment's project of a universal civilization' (1998: 3)—a vision that Gray rightly dismisses. Both extremes seem to lack any sense of political dynamic, and both fail to comprehend the evolutionary potential of political identity and forms of community. In short, globalization's major potential contribution to IR theory is in its elucidation of ideas of community: this is the intersection where all three intellectual projects meet.

Finally, and persistently, the discussion of globalization leads back to theories of the state. The depiction of economic globalization, not as some exogenous process impinging upon states from the outside, but wrought by and through states while at the same time reshaping them, underscores the inescapable connections. Globalization does not simply hold incidental implications for state theory, but is itself a form of state theory. Until this integrated project is recognized for what it is, globalization will continue to befuddle the theorist of international relations.

In any event, and as already argued, it is important that globalization should not be considered as an economic phenomenon in isolation. The thrust of this chapter has been that much of what is presented as the demise of the economic state, in consequence of overwhelming changes within the structure of the global economy, can more readily be appreciated as a reflexive change in the nature of the competition state itself. To be sure, the state by no means monopolizes economic activity, nor is it the only source of economic restructuring: corporations, markets, and consumers all play their part. But their combined interactions do eventually filter through states at some point, thereby contributing to the construction of globalization. It is quite erroneous to imagine that there is only one-way traffic in the opposite direction.

To support this contention further, we need to cast our net more widely. What is happening to the state in functional spheres beyond the economic? Is the only story to be told one of declining state autonomy in the face of remorseless globalization? Or is there a more complex process that needs to be unravelled, whereby what the state now seeks to provide in the shape of 'goods and services' is as much a function of its changing self-image and identity as of any impotence in the face of deterministic global forces? We turn next to a discussion of the security state. Is the production of contemporary security to be understood only as some variant of post-cold war global structuralism? Or do we need to make some allowance also for the more deep-seated identity crisis that the security state is now undergoing?

6

THE SECURITY STATE

As in the other functional areas so far considered, there is a perceived link between globalization and both the substance and mode of attainment of security. In parallel with those other spheres, the most common depiction of this relationship is that of globalization impinging upon the state from the outside and transforming the security environment within which it operates. As a result, the state is portrayed as having a diminished capacity to produce security: globalization of security presents yet another policy challenge to the already embattled state. Such accounts are once again deeply flawed and misleading. They conjure an image of globalization as a disembodied process occurring over and beyond states, and simply impacting upon them as a new constraining influence from the outside.

As will be argued in this chapter, changes in the substance of security reflect deep-seated 'internal' transformations as well. The claim about globalization in general, that it is 'not just an "out there" phenomenon' but also an 'in here' development (Giddens 1998: 311), is thus specifically applicable to globalized security. This is symptomatic of revamped societal bargains under way within individual states, and not simply of a logic of state activity dictated by new systemic structures 'outside'. Let there be no mistaking, however, how critical these new societal bargains are. As has been pointed out, 'in the implicit contract between individuals and the state . . . the most fundamental service purchased . . . is security' (Holsti 1996: 108). How tenable are such contracts if it is true, as claimed of Northern states' pronounced reluctance to go to war, that the 'original backbone of the nation-state is turning to jelly' (Mann 1997: 492)? Hence, one astute commentator raises the essential issue that 'there would seem to be a close relationship between the relative decline of inter-state violence and the weakening of the role of states in the global process' (Laidi 1998: 94). The loss of the state's identity as the principal unit of war-making is symptomatic of what appears to be its more general decline elsewhere.

However, the new security order is as much a measure of state performance as of non-performance in this area. In conformity with the ongoing argument of this volume, the analysis in this chapter will seek to collapse the duality between state and globalized environment. The new security agenda is not entailed simply by the declining capacity of states to produce security of the traditional variety. It is instead revealing of the changing social contracts within states and these are, at the same time, part of the changing logic of state functionality in a globalized setting. Neither can be explained in separation from the other. Globalization, to echo one similar judgement, does not change merely 'the external context within which states operate', but reflects also change in 'the very nature of states' (Guehenno 1998/9: 7).

For the past decade at least, analysts have adumbrated a transformation in patterns of security. Premonitions of a new security agenda have largely been associated with the end of the Cold War, but are also understood to be symptomatic of wider tendencies in international relations, already in being before the onset of those tumultuous events. The object of this chapter is to trace the extent to which a substantive shift in security, and the seemingly reduced ability of the state to produce it, can be attributed to processes of globalization. It thus examines the claim that the 'clash of global economic forces with subnational, national, and regional political interests is likely to offer one of the more profound and vital challenges to security relations in the coming decades' (Dewitt 1993: 5). This contrasts with other interpretations which locate the crisis of state autonomy in nation-states' 'own projections of military power, rather than by economic or even cultural and social globalization' (Shaw 1997*b*: 500).

To the extent that globalization is a root cause of changing patterns of security, what is its significance for the state's role in sustaining it? More generally, how do recent attempts to theorize security fit into the analysis of globalization, and what are their implications for the Great Divide? Does it make sense to speak of a retreat of the security state, or is there an alternative framework within which these trends can be better explained?

Of all the potential manifestations of globalization, those in the security domain have been the least systematically explored. This in itself is perhaps surprising, since globalization 'does not seem so new to the world of strategy' (Guehenno 1998/9: 5). The bases of the claim to the impact of globalization on security will be set out in detail below. At the outset, we can make some attempt to distinguish its effects from those engendered by more modest moves towards internationalization. In general, even within traditionalist conceptions of 'military security', there has been widespread recognition of this tendency towards 'internationalization' of security (Held and McGrew 1993: 267). Obviously in this context, the meaning of 'internationalization' is not the same as that of globalization, and perhaps connotes little more than a suggestion of multilateralism. States are now less than ever inclined to pursue their security within a unilateralist framework. For this reason, analysts have developed a concept of 'world' as opposed to 'national' security, drawing attention to high levels of interdependence as the reason why security is no longer 'sustainable through unilateral means' (Klare and Thomas 1994: 3). In so far as this is the case, we are witnessing a diminution of the 'go-it-alone' mentality that has been the distinctive hallmark of national security in the recent historical epoch, and a corresponding shift towards what has been called 'the transnationalization of legitimate violence'

(Kaldor 1998: 103). Of course, there may be many explanations for this tendency—such as the sophistication of military technology and its consequent cost, the restructuring of the defence-industrial base, the inability of most states to deploy the whole range of military capabilities, and the drift towards collective legitimation of military action. Cumulatively, these trends suggest a decline in the role of the state as an independent producer of security, in favour of a shift towards its 'cartelization'. In the production of security, globalization denotes a move away from the age of laissez-faire to an era of oligopoly.

This does not mean that the selective recourse to collective security, by itself, is evidence for a globalization of security. The relevance of collective security to the discussion of globalization has been questioned on the basis that it is an overly state-centric concept and thus ill suited for embracing other social forces: 'the notion of an international collective as a single fabric of like units', it is asserted, 'becomes questionable' (Latham 1996: 91–2). On this account, collective security has been overtaken by the rise of non-state security actors. This point may well have force. But even were it possible to incorporate other actors within collective security structures, the substantive change in security mapped out by this tendency would still be of a lesser order than that assumed within the context of globalization. The fundamental reason for this is that globalization requires a change in the nature of the security state itself, not simply of the setting in which it finds itself. By contrast, and as argued previously, this is not a necessary condition of multilateralism or internationalism. States can opt into, or out of, collective defence and collective security arrangements without experiencing fundamental change to themselves. In sharp contrast, it is this focus on the simultaneous transformation of the state and its environment that sets globalization apart from those other trends.

Analysing contemporary security

However, the discussion of globalized security lacks a degree of focus precisely because it is part of a much wider set of claims about a broadening security agenda. To the extent that such tendencies are recognized, there is appeal to a diverse range of sources of change, going well beyond what can reasonably be accounted for by even the most expansive concept of globalization. Nonetheless, part of the broadening of the concept of security, which has been such a feature of the academic literature of the past decade, can be and has been attributed to the effects of globalization. Typically, Lipschutz (1995*b*: 14–15) locates the effort to redefine security in the material processes deriving from 'economic globalization'. Tellingly, and as will be developed further in this chapter, he insists that this impacts upon security, not just from the outside, but also 'internally' by way of transformations in the state itself. It is not that the state has a reduced security capacity, but that it has a different set of security tasks to perform, as well as altered priorities amongst them.

There are two separate issues that permeate this analysis. The first is, as noted, whether there is a detectable shift in the nature of security and, if so, to what extent it might be attributed to globalization. The second issue is whether any such impact is positive or negative. Have the prospects for security improved, or deteriorated, as a result of globalization? Arguments have been developed in both directions and have been neatly summarized elsewhere. On the positive side, it has been hypothesized that the 'intensification of global connectedness associated with economic globalization and ecological interdependence, for example, would indicate that cooperation between states is more than ever necessary' (Bretherton 1996: 100–1, also 150). Some are struck by the amelioration that will flow from this increased multilateralism, as it 'will no doubt facilitate dialogue at the elite level between states, providing significant gains for global security in a narrow sense' (Lawler 1995: 56–7). At the same time, the evidence for the claimed deterioration of security in the 1990s has itself been subjected to rigorous, and sceptical, review (Booth 1998*b*: 41–5). On the other hand, the gloomier prognosis holds a presumption of increased tension and conflict, since 'economic globalization may be associated with rapid social change and increased economic inequality, while the globalization of ideas presents significant challenges to cultural identity' (Bretherton 1996: 100–1). Images of a New World Disorder, partly attributable to globalization, have been conjured up on this kind of basis (Booth 1998*b*: 51). Other versions of the down side have been noted: global communications might aggravate rather than reduce tensions (Bell 1993: 173). At the very least, the ambivalent impact of globalization upon security has been adjudged a 'two-edged sword' (Booth 1998*c*: 340, 342).

This very uncertainty about whether security prospects are improving, or deteriorating, is itself compounded by an underlying debate about what security itself means in the post-cold war world. A range of concerns has questioned the dominant approach to security that developed within strategic studies during the cold war era. The need to move away from what has been seen in many quarters as an overly militarized conception of security, taken in conjunction with the appearance of 'new' security challenges (Booth 1991: 318), has contributed to the emergence of a distinctively critical approach to the field (Krause and Williams 1997). This is also associated with appeals to expand the security horizon, by incorporating within it 'resource, environmental, and demographic issues' (Mathews 1996: 274). Beyond this, as Booth has argued, what is problematic about traditional approaches is that for 'countless millions of people in the world it is their own state, and not "The Enemy", that is the primary security threat' (1991: 318). It follows that the study of security within a framework of state security alone is limiting, and has the potentiality to be fatally distorting. But in the absence of agreement about whose security is being discussed, and what form it might now take, it is unsurprising that there is little consensus on whether globalization makes matters better or worse.

Many such arguments do not significantly depend on globalization either for inspiration or validity. They simply claim that, during the cold war, the study of security was hijacked by an overly statist perspective and this now needs to be adjusted, if not discarded altogether. But there are some analyses of security that do directly raise the issues of direct concern to this volume. Threats to security, in the traditional representation of them, take the form of 'external actors penetrating the threatened state in some material fashion' (Lipschutz 1995b: 18–19). But this imagery can itself be queried. As Lipschutz goes on to observe, 'missiles, pollutants, and immigrants all come from the "outside" and menace the inside. The world of intermingled order and chaos, however, is already "inside", snatching bodies, as it were' (1995b: 18–19). What this comment perceptively challenges is the conception of two separate worlds, in which domestic security is set against the contrasting insecurity outside. This polarity has always been artificial, but is rendered even more so under conditions of globalization. This is why Kaldor cautions us that the 'binary oppositions that shaped our interpretation of violence, between private (criminal) and public (legitimate), or between external (international) and internal (civil), can only be applied with difficulty to the contemporary context' (1998: 108). It is, of course, precisely this blurring of the inside/outside line of separation that is suggestive of the logic of globalization, and which provides our analytical point of entry into an understanding of its relationship with security (Guehenno 1998/9: 6).

The focus upon states in the analysis of security raises, in turn, a number of interrelated issues previously encountered in other contexts: the internal–external divide; the roles of strong and weak states; and a focus upon state versus societal security. Buzan offers an interesting insight into the first two of these, and usefully combines them in a way that assists our thinking about the security dimensions of globalization. He draws attention to a twofold set of developments at the 'domestic' and 'systemic' levels. In the former, he points to 'the expanding, consolidating and deepening "strong" state', which is now more potent than ever. In dialectical opposition, there are systemic developments 'that seem to threaten the state as such with erosion or even dissolution' (Buzan 1995: 194). Of particular significance is the conclusion drawn from this. Since the systemic effects are felt universally, their impact is, by definition, more pronounced on the weak states. 'For weak states', he notes, 'the penetration effects of the international system have increased much more than the development of the state' (1995: 195).

What is problematic about this formulation is the divorce made by Buzan between these two developments. Precisely because he wishes to maintain a distinction between the strengthening of the (domestic) state and the variable weakening of the (external) state, he is led to conclude that the weak state has been penetrated more than the strong. However, in a context of globalization, it may well be that exactly the reverse is true: it is the strong states that are penetrated most. Indeed, it is their suffusion by the forces of globalization that is the source of their strength. And what this suggests is that we need to be more circumspect about our usage of the concepts of weak and strong states, and also about the extent to which we posit the separation between the internal and external. Any insistence upon a real separation between the inside and the outside encourages a belief that the measure of strength is the capacity to resist penetration from the outside. But is it not just as possible that, in an era of globalization, states are

strong precisely to the extent that they are 'penetrated'? Or by way of another formulation, they are strong to the extent that they have adapted to the new conditions, of which they are themselves the active progenitors, and in which the
distinction between inside and outside is much less pertinent than before. Only
the weakest states feel the need to insist upon that separation. Quasi-states are
merely the objects of globalization, whereas strong states are also its subjects.
Might this not account for the finding that 'anarchy within states rather than
between states is the fundamental condition that explains the prevalence of war
since 1945' (Holsti 1996: 82)?

This indirectly draws attention to the third issue as well—state versus societal
security. Without doubt, the former has tended to be the dominant conception,
if for no other reason than that 'Claims about national security have the decided
advantage of referring to a specific understanding of who is to be made secure—
citizens of states' (Walker 1995: 32), whereas other models of security lack preci-
sion on this issue. For all that, a significant cross-section of the literature has in
recent years insisted that consideration be given to security referents other than
the state. For example, Crawford (1995: 156) feels that the societal dimension was
already implicit in Polanyi's analysis, as he asked, 'can society be protected from
the most destabilizing consequences associated with the introduction of market
forces?' Such a framing of the issue requires us 'to distinguish between the security of the state and the security of society'. Although approaching the matter
from a different direction, Waever reaches the same conclusion. Positing a scheme
of state and societal security, he concludes that the former has sovereignty as its
ultimate criterion, whereas the latter is centred upon identity (1995: 67). The
weakening of the territorial state, he thinks, leaves identities ever more exposed
(1995: 67–8). It may even render societies more vulnerable in a tangible way, as in
situations of war, when they often become the only targets that otherwise mili-
tarily weak belligerents can hope to damage (Freedman 1998: 48).

Allowing that there might be significant changes taking place in the ways that
we think about security, it still does not follow automatically that these changes
are being brought about by globalization. On the face of it, there could be many
causes of such changes—ranging from military technology, at one end of the
spectrum, to broad shifts in social organization and identity, at the other. For purposes of initial presentation, the analysis will be framed around three factors: the
impacts of globalization itself; the consequences of the end of the cold war; and
transformations in the nature of the state. Unless we can distinguish the effects
that are specific to globalization, it is impossible accurately to assess its implications for security.

There is a case to be made that the new security agenda derives from the end of
the cold war and from changing functions of states, but has little to do with the
notion of globalization. A plausible argument might be mustered that the reori-
entation of security thinking simply traces the emergence of issues from the grip
of the cold war: identity, nationality, human rights, and democratization have all
been liberated by the end of the cold war. Alternatively, one might take the position that security is simply the barometer of state functions. The 'expansion' of

the security agenda has thus been driven by the new tasks that states now perform. The point is made by Buzan, citing the domestic sources of a 'more comprehensive' security agenda. 'States have now to worry not just about their military strength and the security of their ruling families,' he suggests, 'but also about the competitiveness of their economies, the reproduction of their cultures, the welfare, health and education of their citizens, the stability of their ecologies, and their command of knowledge and technology' (1995: 191).

It might thereby be thought that we can account for the changing substance of security without any direct appeal to globalization at all. However, such a summary dismissal of globalization is actually an evasion of central issues, notably the extent to which the end of the cold war and state transformation have themselves been driven by globalization. If this connection can be made, so can the connection between globalization and security. The basis of this more inclusive argument resides in the contention that the end of the cold war represented, at most, a *partial* revision of the post-war order but was, in most other respects, a continuation of it. This is the theme that Ikenberry has done much to develop. Distinguishing between the characteristic confrontational elements of the cold war—its bipolarity and containment—on the one hand, and the integrative trends within the liberal democratic camp, on the other, Ikenberry portrays the latter as very much alive and with us still. Indeed, it is 'stronger than ever' (1996: 79). From that perspective, the 'post-cold war order is really a continuation and extension of the Western order' (1996: 90), and thus elements of the same order endure but are now writ large. Similarly, albeit from a different direction, Shaw (1997a: 36) detects profound sociological changes, dating back to the onset of the nuclear age, in the relationship between the state and the military sector. If that is the case, changing frameworks of security can be attributed as much to the continuities as to the discontinuities of the post-cold war international system. Moreover, it is within the context of an integrative western system that the dynamics of globalization have unquestionably been located (Clark 1997). Thus viewed, the end of the cold war becomes itself more a symptom of other changes than an independent causal force effecting them. This much is implicitly conceded in the view that 'the multidimensionality of security is not a new discovery . . . but the substantive specifications of those dimensions that were appropriate during the cold war are likely to differ from those appropriate for the 1990s' (Baldwin 1997: 23).

The same can be said for transformations in the state. However seductive the appearance that changing state functions have been 'internally' driven, thereby resulting in novel security demands being made 'externally', such a separation is equally simplistic. At the very least, there is the force of emulation at work in the changes to the inner workings of the state. Just as the military-extractive state of the seventeenth and eighteenth centuries led to the transformation of most states by competitive emulation (Tilly 1975), so states have developed concerns about competitiveness, education, and command of knowledge because they are encouraged to do so by an external survival-of-the-fittest logic. Without doubt, processes of globalization are involved both in the shaping of this logic and in its effective dissemination. In short, it is untenable to pretend that contemporary security bears the imprint of the end of the cold war, and of radical state transformation, but has escaped the logic of globalization. The end of the cold war, and state transformation, are parts of this logic and security is unquestionably caught up in both.

We can now review the standard bodies of evidence appealed to in support of the claim that security is being reshaped by the impact of globalization. For purposes of presentation, this evidence will be divided into four interrelated sets of arguments. These are commonly presented as follows: the detachment of security from territoriality; the enmeshment of security in global networks; the creation by globalization of a new security agenda; and the diminished capacity of the state to provide security for its citizens. These are the principal ways in which security and globalization have been related to each other. It remains to assess the force of these respective arguments and to explore their implications for theories of international relations.

The globalization of security

Within the traditional literature of IR, there can be few topics that have been regarded as more territorialized than security itself. Security has normally been defined as the protection of vital interests within a sovereign space. It is thus territory that 'ties down' security, and supplies the traditional referent for its enjoyment. Without it, we have a conceptual difficulty in specifying the subject of security. And yet it is precisely this territorial dimension that globalization calls into question. By doing so, it poses a frontal challenge to existing frameworks for understanding security as well.

If this is the case, there is a compelling argument that the globalization of security be traced back to the introduction of nuclear weapons, as John Herz (1973) pointed out long ago and others have since reinforced. It was the capacity for territorial defence that was most directly challenged by the nuclear weapon, and indeed by other forms of aerial bombardment. As Harknett concedes in his reworking of Herz's argument, 'the pre-nuclear conceptualization of territoriality as a hard-shell of defence in which protection was achieved by planning to repulse an offensive attack has indeed been undermined by nuclear weapons' (Harknett 1996: 145–6). More generally, Ruggie has acutely drawn attention to what he terms the 'unbundling of territoriality'. For all that there has been a remorseless trend towards sovereign partition of territory, international society has itself required exceptions to it. Extraterritoriality is the prime example, but Ruggie characterizes the process more broadly: 'International regimes, common markets, political communities, and the like constitute additional institutional forms through which territoriality has become unbundled' (1998: 190–1). Without question, globalization helps explain this unbundling or, more accurately, globalization *is* this process of unbundling, even when authored by actors in addition to states. If Ruggie's unbundling is driven by states in quest of a working inter-state system, the wider unbundling has been encouraged by other social actors seeking viable non-territorial networks of activity and giving rise, even if inadvertently, to the rudiments of a global society.

The instances of this de-emphasis of territoriality are manifold and need not be described in detail. They include new military agendas in which military forces are now less exercised by the requirement for defence of national territory, narrowly construed. Sorensen locates this favoured motif of globalization—'the irrelevance of borders'—within the security debate: 'armed forces are increasingly assigned tasks which have nothing to do with national defence in the traditional sense', he comments, and illustrates the claim with reference to 'humanitarian intervention in domestic conflicts and the defence of basic human rights' (1997: 267). Others envisage the emergence of new security communities that are no longer territorially defined. These are described as *cognitive regions* within which the threat of war has been all but eliminated (Adler 1997: 254).

This is not to deny the qualifications that need to be entered against all such claims. The evidence for globalization of security is much more ambiguous than in other spheres, and we must guard against any temptation to present security in radically de-territorialized terms, no matter how significant some of the trends in that direction might be. Three caveats will be entered at this point, each of which touches on profound theoretical issues that pervade this discussion. The first follows Freedman. Although couched as part of a slightly different argument, his observations have relevance in the present context. He dissents from any belief that the revolution in military technology holds out a prospect of war reduced to the 'virtual', in which pain and inconvenience can be minimized. Freedman correctly reminds us that 'territory, prosperity, identity, order, values—they all still matter' (1998: 78). To this extent, traditionalist notions of security, and of the role of force within it, are far from irrelevant, even if they are now joined by additional concerns. Secondly, as a corrective to the impression of the end of territoriality, it must also be remembered that territoriality remains a powerful form of defence within the international system, and nowhere more so than amongst its weakest members. It is on this basis that Third World writers question the tendency within Western security literature to emphasize the new agenda, with its explicit shift in focus away from the state and towards the individual. Ayoob, for example, restates the common view that within the South, strong territorially organized states are the only available bulwark against penetrating forces from the North (1997: 139–40). Finally, there is ambivalence at the core of the security developments of the past decade. Cox provides a compelling account of this. He neatly suggests that 'The United States stands at the heart of the contradiction between these two principles: it is the champion of globalization, yet its role as military enforcer is territorially based' (R. Cox 1996c: 292). The relationship between globalization, territoriality, and security is thus more complex than some writers on the subject would have us believe.

The second category is really a set of arguments, rather than a single position, but is unified around the central claim that security is increasingly structured into global networks. The content of these networks varies from one account to another, but collectively they contribute to a new conception of security, given the state's reduced capacity to act autonomously in its pursuit. This is the security argument which most directly parallels those already encountered above, such as the general 'loss of sovereignty' thesis, or the inability of the state to sustain its own macro-economic policy given conditions of intense capital mobility. In the present context, globalizing networks are deemed to have hollowed out the security state.

What form do these networks take? They are, in fact, specific instances of the more general forms of globalization hitherto described. In that sense, they derive from those tendencies, already encountered, towards globalization of production and exchange, systems of global communications, and the restructuring of state responsibilities for its own citizenry.

The application of these developments to security can be undertaken most conveniently albeit somewhat narrowly, in the setting of defence hardware and technology. In this case, issues pertaining to security are subsumed under the more general discussion of globalization of production. Supply of military equipment is very much a part of this global system of production, as well as of exchange. Moreover, the individual state, as supplier and consumer, has less control over either of these systems. From this perspective, various ideas that were central to cold war concepts of national security have come to be challenged, such as the protection of the national-defence industrial base, of national industrial champions, and of technological skills required for military equipment. These imperatives no longer make the same kind of sense given the degree of privatization that has taken place, the escalating costs of military technology, and the relative internationalization of the defence industry.

Crawford usefully develops this line of analysis and draws attention to the 'encroachment of the market on the allocation of goods and services necessary to military strength, and the subsequent chipping away at the state's ability to control the allocation of those resources' (1995: 159). So significant is this transition that she sees it as marking a historical watershed. 'The trend in increasing state control over those resources, evident since the late nineteenth century,' she attests, 'would seem to have reversed itself in the late twentieth century' (1995: 159). The importance of this trend is further magnified by the interlocking of civilian and military technologies, with the balance shifting in favour of civilian technology, upon which the military is now increasingly dependent, rather than the military providing the spin-offs for the civilian sector (Crawford 1995: 155).

The impact of globalization upon security can also be conceived in a much wider framework, operative within a notion of systemic security whereby security itself is part of an interlinked network, the whole impacting upon the individual parts. Such a notion is appealed to in the viewpoint that 'the relative security of the inhabitants of the North is purchased at the price of chronic insecurity for the vast majority of the world population' (Wyn Jones 1996: 203). States consume security as best they can, but the system rations their varying degrees of access to it.

There are, as always, qualifications that need to be entered against all such claims. At the very least, there is the respectable interpretation that the world's security system has become less, not more, integrated since the end of the cold war. It was during the cold war that the two superpowers took the leading role in integrating the security perceptions and policies of their respective blocs. Also, because of its bipolar nature, the cold war ensured that the workings of a single balance of power would impinge upon all regional security structures around the globe. Set against this experience, the end of the cold war has amounted to an act of liberation, although not necessarily beneficent in its consequences. It represented the removal of the constraints of a global contest (Walker 1993: 7), as a result of which there has been some 'unbundling' of strategy itself (Guehenno 1998/9: 8). This has allowed the possible 'emergence of regional powers dominating regional sub-systems' (Hoffmann 1995/6: 32). Such notions of growth in regional autonomy call into question facile assumptions about the intensity of globalization of contemporary security. At the very least, they remind us that globalization may reveal itself in a variety of localized forms.

The third possible manifestation of globalization is in the setting of new security agendas and the creation of new security problems. These pertain, particularly if not exclusively, to issues of identity. In short, it may be thought that globalization is part of the complex of forces leading to the emergence of non-state-centric paradigms, and the reintroduction of societal dimensions of security. Generically, these are manifestations of the so-called twin assaults on the state from above and below—from globalization without and from fragmentation within. Such a stark opposition is again misleading but serves to introduce the general theme. In the words of one writer, 'secular changes in technology, economic relations, social epistemes, and institutions are causing globalising and localising pressures that are squeezing the nation-state from both above and below' (Adler 1997: 250). The consequence of these antagonistic tendencies is the destabilization of existing identities. In terms of globalization, they generate feelings of threat and encourage ' "local" resistance to homogenization which produces the exacerbation of a feeling of insecurity together with a fear of losing one's own national identity' (Guibernau 1996: 135). Bretherton likewise refers to the antagonism between globalization and cultural particularism, and depicts the latter as a defensive reaction to the former (1996: 105).

Under the heading of this new security agenda, three examples can be briefly described and linked to the globalization thesis, as illustrations of the process in general. These are the challenges represented by: ethnic identity; population movements; and the emergence of new forms of economic insecurity. The first of these has already been alluded to and is too familiar to require detailed elaboration. It depicts the most highly visible, if still somewhat contentious, aspect of international security in the 1990s. Through Eastern Europe and the Balkans, the former Soviet Union and parts of Africa, there has developed what has been described as the 'imperialism of parochialism' which has 'come to take centre stage in many theatres of military security' (Chipman 1993: 143). To the extent that this agenda of ethnic struggle has its roots in global pressures, the link to security can be made in a very direct, and disturbing, way.

Secondly, a prominent feature of the globalization landscape is the reality of, and even greater potential for, considerable movements of populations. There is, of course, much that needs to be said against this. There are more politico-legal restrictions on human movement today than at any time in the past hundred years, and so if there is a globalization of human mobility, its manifestations are deeply paradoxical indeed. And yet, for all that, there are significant movements, driven by both short-term emergencies leading to influxes of refugees (Rwanda's overspill into Zaire, Albania's drift across the Adriatic to Italy), and long-term structural factors concerning economic opportunity and encouraging quality-of-life migrations. Bretherton makes the general point when she refers to migration as a 'global phenomenon which has, itself, been identified as an important aspect of the globalization thesis with the potential, ultimately, for blurring national and ethnic differences' (1996: 123). This long-term potential notwithstanding, the pressure for population movement creates shorter-term tensions and insecurities, and itself exacerbates the politics of identity. In some cases, it does so by contributing to the (narrower) redefinition of citizenship.

Thirdly, globalization is linked to the emergence of new security issues by way of its economic agenda. While from the perspective of the global economy, the organization of production might seem 'placeless', from the point of view of individual states this is scarcely so. The very ease with which phases of production can be transferred globally, and the tenacity with which mobile capital searches out new theatres of investment, can induce economic insecurities. As has been said, there is now a 'heightened fear of *economic* competition among industrialized states as they search for ways to ensure that innovative activity takes place on *their* territory and not elsewhere' (Crawford 1995: 158). Systemically, globalized production may be relatively placeless, but in terms of its material consequences it remains firmly rooted. Indeed, the penalties at the national level for failure to compete are more severe than ever. This too is part of the insecurity syndrome of the present age.

Finally, the subject can be examined in the framework of the retreat of the state from the provision of security. Perhaps surprisingly, the globalization literature has paid much less attention to this aspect of state endeavour than to the other functional areas. While the perceived retreat of the state is widely noted in the literature on sovereignty, economy, and democracy, it is a relatively underdeveloped notion in the context of international security (Harknett 1996: 139). This is in itself a striking omission, given the widely recognized connection between the historical development of the state and its military functionality.

When the reduction of state capacity for security is alluded to, it is within a range of differing contexts. Thus the diminished security state can be construed narrowly to refer mainly to its loss of control over defence production and technology. This is the argument of Crawford, already encountered, that 'military resources—especially high-technology ones—are increasingly found in global commercial markets over which states have little control' (1995: 150). The most dramatic illustration of this kind is the demise of the Soviet Union. This event can be graphically portrayed as an instance of catastrophic defence failure engendered by globalization. 'The story of the Soviet demise', writes Crawford, 'is, thus, partly one of how the Soviet state first lost out on the capabilities acquired through the international diffusion of technology and, subsequently, how it became dependent on markets controlled by the West as its own defense industrial base became subject to the forces of globalization' (1995: 167). In this case, the inability to cope with profound changes in the production of defence technology was a contributing factor, not only in reduced security capacity, but also to the failure of the state itself.

Another dimension of state decline can be substantiated by the ongoing privatization of security provision: 'a dramatic growth in private security', one commentator remarks, 'could challenge this control and eventually may threaten global order with military force that is less accountable and controllable than state militarism' (Howe 1998: 1). In parallel with the retreat of the state from a range of social and welfare services, and the withdrawal of the state from what were once deemed to be its core industries, such as energy and transport, analysts also discern the privatization of security (Shearer 1998). 'The privatization of warfare' has been referred to as another example of the 'contracting-out of responsibilities and services traditionally identified with or provided by the state' (Kritsiotis 1998: 11). Of course, there are mundane and literal examples of this in the privatization of some state (domestic) security functions—such as custody and transport of prisoners—as well as privatization of key elements of defence or defence-related industries. However, the notion of privatization of security must extend beyond such cases if it is to be understood within a context of globalization. The role of mercenaries would be one case in point (Kritsiotis 1998). More generally, the argument perhaps finds expression in the suggestion that, in present circumstances, states 'have a monopoly on the ability to *legitimize* violence, but they do not have the ability to *monopolize* violence' (Deudney 1995: 97). The activities of private security companies—such as Military Professional Resources Incorporated, Executive Outcomes, and Sandline—loom large in any such discussion (Howe 1998: 2–6). What this suggests is both a security leakage to other bodies, and a degree of devolution of the security function to private companies. In this sense, it may be possible to conceptualize recent trends in international security as the counterpart to the deregulation that has taken place in the economic sphere.

However, there are more deep-seated arguments about state capabilities that go well beyond such market-centred analyses. These pertain to new bargains between state and civil society, and to the types of security that states are now required to produce. They also relate to the apparently reduced reliance of states upon the military mobilization of their own societies. It is within this context of fundamental state restructuring that appeals to the imagery of the incapacity of states appear at their most superficial. The relationship between globalization and security is much more complex than any such simplistic account would have us believe.

According to the school of sociological realists (Giddens 1985; Tilly 1985; Hall 1986; Mann 1986, 1993), the military is one of the institutional clusters that have left their distinctive imprint on the formation of the modern state. Indeed, some would go so far as to define the modern state in terms of its great success in extracting resources for war-making activities (Tilly 1985). It is but a small step from such historical accounts to the classical conceptions of the state as the institution which has monopolized the legitimate resort to violence, both internally and externally. Thus conceived, the relationship between the state and its security function is an essentialist one, and any change in the latter can be assumed to have dramatic consequences for the former. As has been suggested, a 'security materialist' approach to the subject holds that 'states and state systems emerge, persist, and are replaced according to whether they are, in the long term, viable or functional as providers of security' (Deudney 1995: 89). If this were the case, the globalization of security would reach to the very centres of state power and legitimacy. Thus it is that legitimacy has become a key site for detecting the presence of globalization.

It is precisely on the basis of the state's inability to perform its traditional security functions that a number of analysts have claimed to discern a growing legitimacy deficit. 'Legitimacy deficits and crises can also be expected', writes Deudney, 'in situations where a significant gap exists between the state apparatus' obligated promise and its potential performance in meeting the security needs . . . of the members of civil society' (1995: 101–2). Such a deficit was first diagnosed as a consequence of nuclear weapons: these were deemed to have undercut the state's capacity to protect its own territory and citizens since 'defence', in the classical understanding of it, was no longer possible against them. In the nuclear age, the 'state apparatus can no longer relate to civil society as the effective protector of civil society from destruction' (Deudney 1995: 99). Others, writing in similar vein, insist that the consequent 'level of vulnerability produced by the threat of nuclear attack is such that territoriality must be rethought' (Harknett 1996: 148). Such diagnoses are, in terms of strategic theory, largely uncontroversial and accord with the standard distinction about the nuclear-age move from defence to postures of deterrence. States, on this reckoning, could no longer prevent damage to themselves by physical means but could at best dissuade, by threats of retaliation, those who might seek to inflict it.

There is, however, a more subtle implication for security in the nuclear age that has been less noticed. This is the claim, particularly developed by Martin Shaw, that nuclear technology makes states less dependent on society as the instrument of security. 'From the mid-1950s onwards', he contends, 'nuclear weaponry has had an accelerating influence on war-preparation. Its primary effect has been to demobilize societies' (1994a: 146). This is in the sense that the human and industrial potential of society may now have much less relevance for the outcome of wars than was the case in the world wars earlier in this century. As with other forms of technological innovation, nuclear weapons have created structural unemployment in the security industry, and society has been increasingly 'laid off'.

Such a claim is contentious on a number of counts, not least in so far as nuclear weapons are now less salient elements of post-cold war security. It might then be thought to follow that the state once more has to fall back upon increased reliance on societal resources. However, there is also much historical evidence against this proposition, even as an interpretation of the cold war period itself. Simply because of the demands of the cold war, which overlapped with the formative years of the nuclear age, the major nuclear protagonists arguably did much more, not less, by way of mobilizing their societies than had hitherto been the case. Such a development can hardly be denied as regards the Soviet Union, but is also widely recognized as a portrayal of the 'national security state' in the United States.

But even if Shaw's point is questionable as a specific account of the consequences of nuclear weapons, at least in the short term, it might yet have force as a more general interpretation of the changing framework of security in an age of globalization. Even if societies were not immediately stood down from the mid-1950s as a result of the nuclear revolution, is there not persuasive evidence that they have increasingly come to be so from the 1990s onwards? The logic to which this responds is not that of nuclear redundancy alone, but the more general futility of attempting to fight total wars by mobilizing all the resources of a *national* society, when resources can no longer be harnessed on any such recognizable basis. If the great wars of this century were fought and won as clashes of resources and production, how are total wars to be fought in conditions of globalized production? And what are the implications for state capacity of any such reduced dependence on national society for the production of security?

The point can be pursued by highlighting two trends that have become conspicuous in recent years, at least in the context of the military policies of the developed democratic states. The first is a package of tendencies associated with the promise of military high technology, and often run together under the general rubric of the revolution in military affairs (RMA). Freedman has tellingly investigated this topic, and provides a succinct summary of its rationale. 'The series of developments that are brought together in the RMA', he concludes, 'have the connecting theme of the separation of the military from the civilian, of combatants from non-combatants, of fire from society, of organised violence from everyday life' (1998: 17). One is necessarily led to ponder whether it is just a military logic, and the potential of smart technology, which lies behind such tendencies, or whether there might also be a more deep-seated socio-political and economic transformation under way. If total wars are no longer possible—as societies can make less contribution to them—it makes sense to redefine warfare as the sphere of military activity, segregated as much as possible from the life of society.

At the same time, there is a second, and equally conspicuous, tendency. This is the widely remarked sensitivity to incurring any appreciable level of military casualties, as clearly demonstrated at the time of the Gulf War. This reluctance is most visible in the United States, but is a common feature in the majority of contemporary developed states. States, then, are increasingly reluctant to put not only the lives of their civilians on the line, but also those of their soldiers. Is this a contradictory development, or does a consistent logic make sense of both trends? One writer neatly poses the issue in his comment that it is 'perhaps ironic that in the nuclear age concern about the safety of the individual soldier has reached new heights' (Spybey 1996: 127). Is it ironic that such a principle of 'combatant immunity' should be under development? And is it paradoxical that there should be a trend towards the separation of the military from society, at the same time as there is also a trend to minimize for the soldier what might hitherto have been deemed the inescapable hazards of the profession? If security is being re-professionalized, and society demobilized, is it not inconsistent at the same time to seek to evade the professional responsibilities that the military are supposed to accept?

Alternatively, we are forced to consider whether there is not a single logic that can account for both movements simultaneously. What seems to be questioned by these developments is where the security buck stops. Accordingly, it can be suggested that the reason for the trend towards the segregation of the military from society is, in fact, the very same reason pushing for a lessening of the risks incurred by the military as well. Any such analysis must focus upon the notion of a changing societal bargain or compact. If it is broadly true, as Shaw suggests, that in the historical development of the state, the 'incorporation of the workers into parliamentary democracy was itself largely a trade-off for universal military service' (1994: 145), then it would follow that the abandonment of universal military service betokens a new trade-off. This, in turn, might entail a growing divergence within Shaw's implicit association of 'political rights with military duty'. Political rights, and by extension social and economic rights, thereby become further separated from the citizen's obligation to bear arms. At the same time, it might also be thought that the soldier's obligation to make the ultimate sacrifice is also reduced. Precisely because the state now provides less—security, welfare, economic benefits, sovereignty—it is led to make fewer demands on both its civilians *and* its soldiers.

The same conclusion might be reached from an 'externalist' perspective. What traditionally legitimized the demands the state could make of its own society was the bargain whereby, in return, the state would provide a range of social goods, above all the security of their enjoyment. Symptomatically, the altered terms of these domestic compacts call into question the basis on which the resort to violence can be legitimized. Revealingly, analysts do claim to detect a shift of this nature, especially since the end of the cold war. The drift from security unilateralism to multilateralism itself draws attention to the extent to which 'the use of force is subject to greater collective legitimation' (Ruggie 1998: 197). This is not to suggest that, *in extremis*, a state can no longer act individually, but the emerging norm is evidently to act as part of a coalition, both as a matter of practicality and also as the policy of preference. If states still have the monopoly on legitimation of violence, they now express this multilaterally if at all. Ruggie locates these developments in the context of his argument about 'territorial unbundling' which, as suggested above, seems to be a fair description of the very nature of globalization. What this then implies is that legitimation of violence is indeed ceasing to be monopolized by individual states, at the very same time as the provision of social goods is thought to derive increasingly from globalized processes.

This seems like a compelling case of form following function. Since the state can no longer take all the credit for this provision, the social compacts are being reconfigured on a multilateral or transnational basis, and the state is less entitled to legitimize violence on its own account. It follows also that it cannot require its citizens to make undue sacrifice for its cause. To this extent, security is becoming disembedded from the specific national compacts that have been so characteristic of the history of the previous century. If this is now true of strong states, it has in a sense always been the case for weak states and this, in turn, might imply a greater uniformity in future of state underproduction of security.

Security, globalization, and IR theory

It remains to pull together briefly the elements of this discussion with regard to their more general implications for theories of international relations, since the objective of this chapter is not merely to clarify thinking about the nature of security itself. The commentary will dwell on three key points: how the foregoing analysis affects our thinking about the Great Divide; the contribution which it makes to theorizing the state; and the manner in which it provides a framework for addressing the 'actor question' in International Relations.

It should come as no surprise to discover that when security is placed in the context of globalization, it provides compelling additional evidence for the artificiality of the Great Divide. As discussed extensively above, the analytical division of labour between the domestic and the external is constructed around the core concept of anarchy, which both defines the pockets of security within states and results in the lack of security in their mutual relations. At heart, the subject matter of International Relations, as traditionally conceived, is a security problématique, as the supposedly different conditions within and without the state render inapplicable the logic of the domestic analogy to inter-state practice.

How does any such framework stand up to the implications of globalized security? What hopefully emerges from the preceding examination is, once again, the illusory basis of any claim that the state's quest for security is driven by an externally structured condition, constraining it to act in uniform ways. What security is taken to be, and how and by whom it is to be pursued, are subjective factors that in some measure are generated from within states, and in relation to prevalent social compacts. As the latter change, so do conceptions of what values most deserve to be protected, by whom, and at what cost. Any image of a structure existing independently of the norms that constitute it is thereby bound to deceive.

Secondly, such an approach to security moves us towards a more sophisticated conception of the state in international relations. The reified and timeless state, abstracted from all meaningful historical context and yet endowed with certain primordial interests, is perhaps more the caricature of the neo-realist depiction than the working model of most classical realist portrayals, as even Ashley (1984) was happy to concede. But even the historical state has often been presented in unduly skeletal form. Thus standard attempts to define the state in terms of certain essential and timeless qualities, such as its monopolization of legitimate resorts to violence, can now be seen to be historically delimiting. If the earlier arguments have validity, then it becomes apparent that this attribute of the state is not an essential condition of its being, in all historical circumstances, but rather a quality developed in a specific set of conditions. The redefinition of this function, entailing both a delegation of security roles to, and a usurpation of security functions by, other actors does not then signify the end or the retreat of the state, but its transition from one historical phase to another. Monopolization of the sources of military security is no more essential to the functioning of the state than is its intervention in the economy, or its provision of specific levels of social welfare.

Finally, and running through both preceding points, it follows also that discussions of globalized security articulate the general complexity of the actor question in International Relations. No functional area more pointedly reveals the paradoxes of trying to define the 'actors' than that of security. This much is amply highlighted by the preoccupation in much of the critical security literature with the 'referents' of security. In this context, three principal images are in open competition—the security of states, the security of societies, and the security of individuals. Of these, it has been claimed that the first continues to function along the lines of 'national self-help', but that this is now detached from the other two where 'the threats to community and individual security are becoming increasingly transnational' (S. Brown 1994: 15).

The first is, in any case, often regarded as *sui generis* on two counts. First, it should be regarded as mere instrumentality—a means to an end rather than an end in itself. Secondly, the state is commonly regarded as a distinctive security referent since it simultaneously has the capacity to be both a provider of security and also the main threat to it. The principal alternatives are to depict security with reference to societal needs or to focus on the individual. The focus on identity in much recent literature leans towards the former, as its main concern is with collective interests in preserving certain cultural forms and practices. In the latter, the concentration on the individual tends to work towards the notion of security as the defence of certain individual rights or values. There is no simple way in which this complex framework can be reduced to a single point of focus, nor is there any compelling reason for making the effort to do so.

Contrary to the implicit suggestion in some globalization literature that homogenization reduces the importance of intervening social and political structures, we need to remind ourselves that globalization is not some form of backdoor cosmopolitanism which reduces the complexity of international action. Within a globalized security framework, just as in a globalized world more generally, there continues to be the same proliferation of actors as before: if anything, the spectrum is widened and not narrowed. The oft-repeated observation that globalization takes heterogeneous forms should be borne in mind in this context.

In short, there is no reason to expect that globalization will simplify the diversity of security actors, and every reason to expect precisely the reverse.

Conclusion

Contemporary security studies appears to be in some kind of schizophrenic condition, pulled in two opposing directions and leaving its personality torn down the middle. To the one side, there has been consistent pressure to expand the horizons of security by colonizing other functional areas, such as the environment, economy, culture/civilization, and human migration. All these have been thought amenable to securitization, both as disciplinary construct and also as policy prescription. At the same time, security studies has been engaged in a war of national liberation against the perceived tyranny of the military preoccupations of its erstwhile traditional agenda. The focus on military security, it is thought, has both narrowed the range of security studies and delimited the sphere of International Relations itself. We are thus enjoined to cast the security net wider into other functional areas but, at the same time, to liberate other social spheres from militarization.

The field of security studies began to show signs of discomfiture well before the end of the cold war. The tumultuous events of that epoch aggravated dissatisfaction with the orthodoxies of the discipline, and enlivened the debate about whether security should continue to be constricted by the framework of militarized inter-state relations. As an alternative, some urged that it should get into the business of human emancipation as a more extensive project. In these early post-cold war encounters, mention of globalization by name was conspicuously absent, and it remains at a fairly subdued level. Nonetheless, it is apparent to the reader who is familiar with the general literature on globalization that there are themes found elsewhere which are shared by the concerns of the security analyst. What globalization can bring to bear on the topic of security is an awareness of widespread systemic developments without any resulting need to downplay the role of the state, or assume its obsolescence. The question that has to be addressed by the student of contemporary security is not whether security should be reconceptualized around individuals or societies as alternatives to the state, but how the practice of states is being reconfigured to take account of new concerns with human rights and societal identity. This is not intended as some kind of normative judgement that states are more important than individuals or society, but simply an acknowledgement that the best evidence of these changes is etched on the face of the state itself. Because the model of globalization developed in this book seeks to move beyond the limited frameworks constructed around divisions between internal and external developments, it copes well with an integrated theory of contemporary security.

New social compacts reveal changes in the trajectory of state functions. States have less need to mobilize their citizens, and consequently make fewer military demands upon them. At the same time, they are now pursuing political strategies that commit them to make less social provision. Placing these two trends in juxtaposition necessarily invites examination of any connection and, in particular, of the direction in which any causal links might flow. Is the reduced military imposition upon society 'demand-led' in the sense that it is less needed, given the attempt to re-segregate the military function from wider aspects of society? Alternatively, is it 'supply-led' in the sense that states are less willing and able to pay the 'social wage' for military sacrifice? Either way, these issues demand that we view the new conceptions of security other than in terms of state retreat alone, as this is much too simplistic. The apparently diminished role of the state is as much a reflection of its changing subjective character as it is of changes in the objective conditions of security in which it finds itself. We need to be mindful that security is a construct not of a 'historically frozen realm of power-hungry states' but of a 'dynamic process of interaction among individuals, groups, states, and international institutions, all of which are capable of adapting their sense of self-interest' (Klare and Thomas 1994: 3).

On security as elsewhere, globalization impinges not simply from the outside in, but also from the inside out. If globalization is a factor in changing security, it operates within both realms simultaneously—both re-creating the state and setting new agendas as part of a single political process. We should speak less about globalization *and* the security state and think more about the globalization *of* the security state.

THE NORMATIVE STATE

By some normative accounts, the idea of a globalized state (as a contemporary state form) would be considered a contradiction in terms. If the state is the institutional embodiment and protector of the distinctive values of a particular community, then by definition it encompasses an exclusive section of value-sharing humanity. How then can a concept that has its foundation in the particular be adjusted to cope with the implications of globalization? Does not the notion of normative globalization undermine the state from within by eroding the identity of the specific value-community that it is taken to represent? It is precisely such a perspective that gives rise to the assertion that 'Globalization appears to be the first great historical process the modern state has not succeeded in objectifying, which means we cannot dissociate the crisis of the state from the crisis of meaning' (Laidi 1998: 7). How well does this claim stand up?

As with the case of security, theorists of globalization have paid comparatively little attention to the normative state. They are less impressed by the state's underproduction of values than by its underproduction of such 'goods' as sovereignty and economic management. And yet, the state's success as a producer of values hinges on its aggregate performance elsewhere. Its capacity to deliver a range of public goods is an integral element of its popular legitimacy and, in turn, provides a rationale for the obligations owed to, and the sacrifices made for, the state by its citizens. Ultimately, it is impossible wholly to disassociate the 'value' of a community from the ends that it seeks. Even the staunchest communitarian is hard-pressed to maintain that the community is a self-sufficient end, the only purpose of which is to reproduce itself indefinitely. However, transformation in the normative ends of the state is a prime symptom of globalization. What we must endeavour to do is to understand why this is happening.

In this chapter, we move to an exploration of the impact of globalization on the state as a source of values. Initially, and in conformity with preceding chapters, the issue will be presented in terms of the erosion of the normative capacity of the state in conditions of globalization. The mobility of the factors of normative production, it will be suggested, is constraining the state to adopt new forms of moral behaviour. Indeed, according to its critics, the state can no longer stay in this particular line of business, and is already seeking to privatize its normative industry. Any attempt to address these issues will require an assessment of the evidence in support of a less territorially based system of world values. In order to judge the significance of this, the discussion will need to be placed in the context of general normative theories, as traditionally deployed in International Relations, in order to ascertain what difference, if any, globalization makes. As the chapter unfolds, it will turn to an exploration of the nature of political community, and suggest that the most fruitful way of addressing normative change is through the linkage between conceptions of community and a restructuring of state functions. In short, the presence of globalization can be addressed in the normative sphere within the same framework of analysis as employed elsewhere in this volume.

The mobility of the factors of normative production

What does globalization mean for understanding both the source and the substance of values? Does it betoken an integrative and homogenizing process so that greater proportions of humanity converge on shared value systems? Alternatively, does globalization inject a powerful new source of division into world affairs in the context of which the espousal of particularistic values becomes an essential part of the cultural defence against the intrusions of globalization itself? This polarized choice is rejected in what follows, on the grounds that there is no single trend but rather a complex, and often seemingly contradictory, pluralization in the sources of value—a process of normative deconstruction in general and of state 'privatization' of values in particular. We might then accept one representative verdict that 'the general processes of globalization are contributing towards the development of global ethics in the plural' (Dower 1998: 111).

If this poses the issues somewhat abstractly, more tangible and pressing policy imperatives lurk underneath this formulation. These have been well expressed elsewhere:

Globalization and fragmentation raise crucial moral questions about how, for example, the world community should help minority groups whose rights are violated by sovereign authorities, about the responsibility of the world community for preventing further disorder and for rebuilding order in failed states and about when an argument for sovereignty deserves respect . . . and when it should attract suspicion. (Linklater and Macmillan 1995: 13–14)

At the same time, while recognizing that globalization does give rise to a novel ethical agenda of this kind, it is wise not to assume at the outset that it necessarily generates a universalist response to them. This is not intended as a snub to those cosmopolitanist arguments that will be set out below, but rather as a way of signalling the multi-faceted nature of globalization itself. We may thus admit the argument that this multidimensionality cautions against assuming a 'single logic' in globalization generally and, more specifically, thereby 'sensitizes us to similar complexities in normative debates' (Holton 1998: 197).

That said, it is possible to delineate two broad positions emerging from the literature. The first is persuaded that if globalization is a real social presence, then it is measurable in terms of normative consolidation and universalization. Globalization would be meaningless without some degree of normative convergence, although there can be legitimate differences over its extent. Unless this were the case, the whole notion would be deemed much less persuasive and certainly less interesting for the theorist of international relations. The second position regards its normative impacts as negative, and for the reason that globalization is inherently inegalitarian and divisive: it generates new areas of disharmony and ensures that social values become a major site of contestation. The two positions can be summarized in outline, as they provide a broad indication of the supposed connections between globalization and normative change.

There are first of all the optimists who generally depict globalization as symptomatic of progress, and of increasingly higher levels of value integration. They project an image of moral liberation at the heart of globalization:

New images of world order speak of the emergence of the global citizen and a global civil society, stimulated once again by the corrosive effect of migration and global communications on nationalism and parochialism. Underlying all these manifestations of globalization is the key idea of one single world or human society. (Holton 1998: 2)

The evidence which is appealed to, in order to substantiate such claims, falls under the generic heading of emerging forms of humane governance, itself a universalistic form both reflective of, and necessary for, heightened levels of normative convergence. As specific examples, most commentators draw attention to the development of doctrines of human rights since 1945: their consolidation in various declarations and conventions is testimony to the growth that has taken place in this area. Progress does not lie in the validation, as such, of a theory of human rights, as the 'existence of human rights predates processes of globalization and is unaffected by whatever processes are taking place' (Dower 1998: 114). That is to say that globalization makes no difference to human rights as claims. Those who base human rights on universalist assumptions (Booth forthcoming) are not suggesting that human rights claims provide evidence of recent normative integration, since these claims are timeless: to the extent that the doctrine has validity, such has always been the case. But it may make a difference to their realization. 'Globalization makes a difference to what obligations in respect to human rights we have in practice, but not in principle' (Dower 1998: 119). It is, therefore, in the implementation of human rights, rather than in the substantiation of their claims, that progress is deemed to have taken place.

Additionally, some prefer to see changes in the corpus of international law as indicative of broad normative integration. In a discussion of *ius cogens*, one authority argues its significance to be that 'for the first time, the international community has decided to recognise certain *values* (the dignity of the human person, self-determination of peoples, peace) that must *prevail* over any other form of national interest' (Cassese 1990: 168). The supposition must be that this realm of international law itself specifies core values that are shared globally.

Others are much more critical of such claims, even when appealing to the same body of evidence. While the emergence of an unprecedented transnational human rights dialogue in recent decades is undeniable, the significance that should be attached to this development remains debatable (Dower 1998: 120). A wide range of commentators strikes a note of scepticism, even when writing from different perspectives. One author (C. Brown forthcoming) reiterates an essentially communitarian position that 'rights have no separate ontological status', and issues the consequent injunction that to 'overemphasise rights in isolation from their social context is counterproductive'. This implicitly rejects any trend towards a de-contextualized universalization of rights. This is the case not least because of deep-seated disagreements about the substance of these rights in the first place (Held 1995a: 95). This, it has been asserted, 'throws into doubt the emergence of some kind of universalistic human rights framework within global politics' (Holton 1998: 117). Even one of the foremost optimists on this subject has acknowledged that, in the aftermath of the cold war, much the same impediments to effective human rights implementation still remain—to which have been added new threats from the nationalist agenda (Donnelly 1993: 138, 152). Chris Brown is led to state categorically that 'nothing in the recent history of human rights protection gives reason for believing that a meaningful consensus on human rights . . . actually exists' (1995b: 192).

In any case, the mechanisms through which human rights are actually administered fall far short of any model of globalization. Even those who subscribe to a 'progressive' view of human rights implementation often do so with due recognition of the essentially statist framework within which this has occurred. This alone must represent a major qualification to any supraterritorial account of its development. Whatever the role of non-governmental bodies in drawing attention to human rights abuses, we are enjoined to recall that 'Internationally recognized human rights, although held equally by all human beings, are held with respect to, and exercised against, the sovereign territorial state' (Donnelly forthcoming). The state remains the central institution for implementation of human rights, even when there are increasingly external constraints upon its freedom of action. To this extent it may be regarded as an ironic instance of the poacher turned gamekeeper. Despite his relatively optimistic standpoint, Donnelly candidly admits that 'state-centric conceptions of human rights obligations are likely to persist', in the absence of the development of a cosmopolitan moral community. He sees no evidence of this taking place (Donnelly forthcoming). Human rights, in practice, do not correspond to globalization, in theory.

The superficial solidarism of human rights discourse thus not only conceals the reality of normative dissension, but also becomes a means of prosecuting such differences. Huntington notoriously predicates his assessment of future world order on revived civilizational differences. 'To the extent that non-Westerners see the world as one', he writes, 'they see it as a threat' (1996: 66). In no small measure, this is because globalization itself has encouraged the re-emergence of particularist identities (Scholte 1996b: 53). At the same time, 'globalisation creates new forms of hegemonic power which threaten cultural differences' (Linklater 1998: 4). Others insist, in similar vein, that 'basing human rights claims upon processes of globalization runs the risk of substituting cultural conflict over rights for the ideological conflict of the Cold War' (Evans 1997: 137). Yet others question any implied association between globalization and a universalization of values, for the reason that the former remains inextricably intertwined with the propagation of inequalities (Hurrell and Woods 1995: 447), and thus negates in practice what universalism demands in theory. In all such arguments, it is evident that the relationship between globalization and human rights is far from straightforward.

A further fact that might be cited as evidence of the limits to normative globalization is that of state controls upon human migration. The worldwide flow of refugees has risen markedly in recent decades. It was estimated to stand at about 1.5 million in 1951 but to have reached some 13 million by 1997 (Chalk 1998: 149). The treatment of these refugees remains wholly at the discretion of state administrations, acting within international conventions, and there is little evidence that humanitarian compassion overrides pragmatic state interests. In general, the movement of people is increasingly restrictively regulated, and this stands in sharp contrast to the deregulation of non-human capital. One philosopher asks wistfully, 'what makes the inflow of people so very different from the inflow of finance capital?' (Goodin 1992: 6). Presumably the answer is, in part, that human beings, unlike financial flows, arrive encumbered by rights that states often find inconvenient.

But if there is still no overwhelming evidence in support of normative solidarism, at the same time moral values seem less clearly anchored in nation-state communities. It is in this sense that the argument for the underproduction of values by the state has been made. Its supercession by universal values may indeed be far from complete, but the challenge from 'without' seems clear enough. Simultaneously, the disintegration of consensus—consequent upon new and often multiple identities—questions the viability of the normative order 'within'. Just as in other areas of globalization, the state seems exposed to the pincer movement that weakens it on both fronts. However, as in those other areas, it remains more accurate to understand these movements as part of a single process, taking place both 'inside' and 'outside', and as a result of which the state itself comes to be repositioned in the field of social forces. This portrayal differs from that of the state in normative retreat, in so far as it gives equal emphasis to the reconfiguration of the state as a formative element within globalization, and not simply as a fortuitous outcome of it.

To the extent that any generalization can be made, the safest is that deeply ambivalent changes are afoot, and they point in no uniform direction. This is so on at least two separate levels. First, it is frequently pointed out that what is happening within the developed democratic world is not necessarily an accurate representation of what is happening elsewhere. The common image appealed to is of two distinct world orders, one of relative peace and wealth, and the other of turmoil (Singer and Wildavsky 1993). States in the latter find it harder to adapt to new global circumstances, and some of them 'are already falling to pieces' as a result (Buzan, Held, and McGrew 1998: 397). If this is intended as an account of the experiential conditions faced by many of the world's inhabitants, it also has a normative correlation. Thus the essential ambivalence of the world's moral experience is that the 'deepening sense of community in the advanced industrial world seems to be accompanied by an increasingly "system" oriented set of relationships between this emerging community and the rest of the world' (C. Brown 1995*b*: 196). Normative integration and disintegration are both occurring at the same time.

Secondly, what makes the ambiguity abundantly clear is that if the state has lost some normative power, this has not been yielded up to a cosmopolitan ethos. There is no zero-sum accounting visible in the unsettling normative transitions that are taking place. Thus, Linklater seems to confirm the above voices of scepticism about the universalization of human rights. While himself fully persuaded of the virtues and attainability of the cosmopolitan project, he laments the fact that 'the impact of cosmopolitan ideas on Western social and political theory has declined . . . in inverse proportion to the globalisation of social and economic relations' (1998: 62–3). Thus if the state has suffered an acute haemorrhage of its normative lifeblood, this has not been transfused into a global moral order. At the same time, diminished state normative consensus, and the erosion of its moral monopoly, is also noted by many analysts. Linklater for one attributes this to the process of pacification at the industrial core of the international system, itself both cause and effect of further globalization. The consequence of the diminished threat of hot war in those sectors of the globe is, he argues, that the 'elements of national coherence are more difficult to preserve' (1998: 8, 31), since war has historically functioned as a source of normative cohesion within societies. The trend is also hinted at in the widespread notion of 'disjuncture between state and civil society' and between 'cultural identification and social cohesion' (Felice 1996: 183). Further evidence of the loss of state moral monopoly comes from the field of international intervention, where state governments are no longer, it is claimed, the sole subjects and objects of intervention. The significance of this is that 'governments once were solely responsible for the common good; now they share this responsibility . . . with other institutions operating within and across state frontiers' (Onuf 1995: 44). This is the complex reality of moral globalization—geographically uneven, contested, and deeply ambivalent—and is a measure of the increasing mobility of moral identity. It remains to formulate a theoretical framework that can adequately apprehend these transformations.

Ethical systems, International Relations, and globalization

It should not be imagined that the ambiguities referred to above all result from conditions of globalization. Indeed, many are endemic to any normative theorizing about international relations. In order to carry forward this discussion about the normative impact of globalization, and hence to isolate its distinctive effects, it is first necessary to review the frameworks within which these issues have traditionally been debated, and to assess whether they remain adequate to the present task.

The first point to clarify is that globalization has by no means created complexity in a once-settled area of consensus. Normative theorists writing about international relations have all along been divided amongst themselves as to the frameworks within which they should operate, so much so that it has been possible to discern a round dozen such 'traditions' of ethical reflection (Nardin and Mapel 1992). Communication across such distinct traditions has often been a babel, and certainly unproductive. Above all, there is little agreement on moral categories or moral subjects. Is the moral 'person' the individual, the community, or the state? Should our moral referents include other collectivities, such as international society or humankind? In order to answer such questions, we need to 'identify' the moral subject since, as has been suggested, moral claims raise questions about identity: issues about what should be done finally come down to 'Who am I?' (C. Brown 1995*a*: 97).

Ethical analysis of international affairs has conventionally proceeded by way of various sets of dichotomies. These are, as outlined in Chapter 1: a morality of people versus a morality of states; cosmopolitanism versus communitarianism (and the cognate political theory divide between liberalism and communitarianism); and the more recent appeal to moralities both thick and thin. These are helpful categories as initial points of departure. However, they rely upon manifestations of the Great Divide and, as reiterated throughout this book, this renders them deeply problematic as normative tools for understanding the effects of globalization. We might then conceive of the moral processes that erode the Divide as operating in two directions—the accretion of shared values within the global community, or the diminution of distinctive values within the national community. The first is where the elements of cosmopolitan society become so invigorated as to begin to develop into a genuine, if embryonic, community. Alternatively, the separation might be progressively elided by the loss, on the part of the national community, of its distinctive cohesion and 'particular' set of values. Standard accounts of the moral consequences of globalization tend to suggest that it is the former that induces the latter. Once more, this is misleadingly one-sided. It is better that we imagine normative globalization as the interaction of both sets of processes, and recognize that transformation in the nature of the normative state is a key element within it.

There is no need to repeat the full details concerning the substance of these standard sets of normative categories. They contain, in distilled form, the contrasting claims associated with the particular and the universal. According to the former, and as embodied in realism, there is a focus 'on the interests of a given community, not on what it is right to do', in some abstract sense (Nardin 1992: 271). As against this, there is the liberal ethic that 'subordinates the principle of state sovereignty to the recognition and respect of human rights' (M. Smith 1998: 76). These two positions have been subsumed under what have been termed the 'internal' and the 'external' accounts of moral obligation, respectively. The former proceeds on the basis that since 'no contract is made with humanity in general, citizens owe no political or moral obligation to those outside their own specific association' (Chalk 1998: 150). In contrast, the latter 'is distinguished by the conviction that there is a universal moral framework which extends beyond the one surrounding insiders, so necessitating ethical as opposed to merely pragmatic orientations towards relations with outsiders' (Chalk 1998: 151). The latter position is defined by the three elements of individualism, universality, and generality (Pogge 1992: 48), as against the collectivism, particularity, and specificity of the former.

Translating these debates into the language of 'internal' and 'external' helps draw attention to the inappropriateness of such schemes in providing a coherent normative account of globalization. That separation fails to enlighten us, for the very reason that it is the one that globalization does most to overthrow. Indeed, the moral significance of that dichotomy is in any case under pressure from the emergence of 'pluralist' and 'multicultural' societies 'within' individual communities. As Thompson remarks, the essence of the communitarian position is that 'what counts is how tightly individuals are bound together in relations of identity'. On that basis, communitarianism already has difficulty in providing a coherent account of 'how justice is possible in a pluralist modern society' (Thompson 1998: 187–8). It might be added that this complaint questions the validity of the normative divide more generally, since it is this very lack of 'identity' that communitarians take to be the flaw in the cosmopolitan account.

Nonetheless, the previous discussion of communitarian and liberal positions (Chapter 1) is important for understanding the basis of moral community, extant or otherwise. As will be seen, it is precisely the question of whether an incipient global moral community might be thought to be emerging—or whether this matters at all—that lies at the heart of the disagreements about normative experience in a globalizing world order. Cosmopolitanists tend to adhere to an 'evolutionist' view of community as something that grows, develops, and transforms. Communitarians tend instead towards a 'creationist' view of community, as something which 'is', rather than something which 'becomes'. The critical issue remains, however, the normative status of the community under discussion. For many communitarians, there is a qualitative threshold that cannot be passed, no matter how materially and ideationally integrated societies become. If some pre-existing 'idea of the good is required for true community', this is not something which can develop. For this reason, there will always be a normative gap between true communities and mere communities of interdependence, and hence 'general principles of right should not prevail over a community's idea of the good' (Thompson 1998: 188).

Sensitive appraisals of the basis of moral community are essential to the ongoing analysis of the implications of globalization. They cut across superficial comments about whether or not globalization amounts to moral homogenization, and counsel us to be more discriminating in our assessments. A case in point is Walzer's (1994) analysis of thick (specific community) and thin (abstract universal) moral codes. Were we to allow his argument, it would follow that universality does not mean sameness, and that globalization is not inconsistent with high levels of normative heterogeneity. As against this, his analysis creates a potential difficulty for some versions of moral globalism. If the sequence is as outlined by

Walzer, thickness is not a *post hoc* accretion on the thin, but co-exists with it, and is the only 'free-standing' moral code. If that is the case, how might globalization unsettle it from the outside? The short answer, to reiterate the theme of the book, is that globalization does its work not only from the outside, but also as an 'inside job'. Normative globalization is then not about the extent to which the globalizing thin can pull the thick into line. It is rather about the extent to which transformation within the community gives rise to new versions of the thick, and which may also be reflected in the thin. Again we can see how complex is the business of locating normative discourses about international relations within a globalization context. Not only are we bemused by the provenance of moral values, but we also need to distinguish between different categories of community, some possibly more moral than others. We need, perhaps, to discriminate between moral communities and communities of interdependence. We need to address subtle distinctions between communities of the right and communities of the good. Above all, we need to be mindful of the mechanisms of moral change. What purchase can these complex sets of categories offer on the subject of globalization?

These dichotomies are useful for an initial consideration of globalization, as they problematize what often tends otherwise to receive superficial discussion. But there is also a negative side, since the foregoing dualities tend to reinstate versions of the Great Divide, against which the present discussion is directed. Asked in a discussion whether, in an age of globalization, 'the separation of the domestic and external spheres no longer seems sacrosanct', Held readily acknowledged that ' "the division" is certainly called into question' (Buzan, Held, and McGrew 1998: 388). Why is this so?

In Chapter 1, the discussion focused upon the Great Divide represented in Kenneth Waltz's version of structural realism. How is this relevant to an analysis of normative issues? Isn't Waltz's argument simply a methodological one about analytical categories? Unfortunately, matters are not so clear-cut. Although ostensibly couched in the language of positivism, there can be no question that a profound moral analysis is at work in the scheme Waltz deploys. Underpinned as it is by assumptions about economic rationalism, abstract definitions of the interests of states, and categorical differences between domestic and international domains, neo-realism is replete with coded normative messages. These have been powerfully unpacked in a language that is highly suggestive for the present discussion:

The externalization of the public realm is the institutionalization of selfishness. The public realm within a given society socializes the self-interest of human beings by universalizing the possibilities of their good life. The public realm externalized as the *state* institutionalizes the self-interest of a society. The external state is the negation of the universality of society through the affirmation of each society's individuality. The external anti-sociality of the so-called state is a necessary part of its internal sociality. (Allott 1997: 352)

What Allott and others are reaffirming is that the reductionist/systemic analytical divide is not simply about the separate political domains of hierarchy and anarchy, but is also an argument about the moral limits of the international. However, while neo-realists proclaim that selfish behaviour is a function of structural constraints from the outside that press against co-operation, the more profound reality is that their image of anarchy is itself an inside-out normative construct, masquerading as a set of 'externalized' assumptions. Any such logic, if always suspect, now becomes completely untenable when placed in the context of globalization. What this makes clear is that the above dualities—morality of people versus morality of states, cosmopolitanism versus communitarianism, or thinness versus thickness—militate against the very kind of analytic approach that globalization demands. If globalization means what its proponents take it to mean, normative discussion in International Relations cannot proceed by way of fixed and unchanging categories, constructed around an increasingly artificial separation between what is inside, and what is outside, the state or community. We need to view such moral categories, not as exclusive, but as shifting, overlapping, and mutually transforming.

Thus there have been any number of clarion calls to move beyond the Great Divide, issued from a distinct concern with normative questions. Not all explicitly invoke the dynamic effects of globalization, but its presence is implicit in the analyses of many. What they centre on is a series of explorations about the unsettling conditions of identity and the potential reshaping of community, themes that are prominent in a multitude of recent writings. Gutmann, for example, complains of the constraining effect of these dichotomies, since they force us to see 'the moral universe in dualistic terms' (1992: 130). Similarly, others express their dissatisfaction that 'debates in ethical theory have been marked by a logic of the mutual exclusiveness of particularity and universality' (Hutchings 1996: 129). Others again detect the basic problem in the tendency for the very idea of 'legitimacy' to have become fragmented in accordance with the 'domestic-international divide' (J. Williams 1996: 40–1).

What unifies these expressions of disquiet is the widespread perception of the changing terms of identity and community that define the presence of globalization. To describe these processes as merely the erosion of state capacity, in this instance of the normative kind, is to remain within the confines of the Great Divide. Accordingly, we must discover more appropriate language and frameworks to depict the changes that are taking place. The shadowy presence of globalization thus runs through the following account, which points to a number of the present concerns:

In our public life, we are more entangled, but less attached, than ever before. It is as though the unencumbered self presupposed by the liberal ethic had begun to come true . . . As the scale of social and political organization has become more comprehensive, the terms of our collective identity have become more fragmented, and the forms of political life have outrun the common purpose needed to sustain them. (Sandel 1992: 28)

This both eloquently depicts the problem and, at the same time, demonstrates how existing categories are inadequate to capture its essence. Sandel's point translates precisely into a denial of the Great Divide for purposes of ethical analysis. If the claim was once to moral autonomy within the community but mere encumbrance without, this no longer holds true. Globalization subverts previous forms of moral experience in both domains.

The retreat of the normative state?

The depiction of the normative consequences of globalization as yet another version of the 'retreat of the state' is common enough, and follows naturally from the proclaimed logic of globalization: this must be the effect because that is what globalization both is and does. 'The mobile forces of capital, labour, technology, and information', one theorist summarizes, 'are presented as moving relentlessly to and fro across political and cultural boundaries, threatening the integrity of the nation-state and of national cultures as they go' (Holton 1998: 108). At the same time, and seemingly paradoxically, the legislative state has become empowered to intrude yet further into what was once fenced off as the private/family/moral sphere (Mann 1997: 491–2). What then are the consequences of the mobility of the factors of normative production? Are they, or are they not, inducing a retreat of the normative state?

This question is often answered in the affirmative, and the crisis of the contemporary state depicted as being as much about values as about policy autonomy: 'globalisation casts considerable doubt', Linklater roundly declaims, 'on the supposition that the nation-state is the only significant moral community' (1998: 216). What are the manifestations of this erosion? They are said to be both a loss of the singularity of domestic definitions of citizenship and, relatedly, a decline in the freedom of the state to pursue its own conception of the 'good life'. Sassen neatly summarizes the former. 'For scholars who see in the new international human rights regime a major political development', she contends, 'the erosion in the distinction between citizen and alien also devalues the institution of citizenship' (1996a: 96–7). The more rights come to be codified internationally, and to be protected beyond the confines of the individual state, the less are the benefits of particular citizenship: they become a form of international public good and, in that sense, invite free riding in their enjoyment. Nonetheless, this tendency may be regarded as a form of *positive* erosion: benefits do not cease to be enjoyed, but are no longer exclusively provided by any one state in particular.

But there is also a more *negative* account of globalization that stipulates a decline in entitlements as a consequence of the erosion of state autonomy. This view asserts that the state's project for a particular good is now unsustainable in the face of the constraints operating from the outside. The limits of the good life are set externally by the structure of globalization, and normative life is thereby also reduced to the realm of necessity. Ironically, if valid, this would represent the final sublimation of Martin Wight's (1966) classical distinction between political theory and international thought. 'The globalization of production', Donnelly (forthcoming) eagerly attests, 'is weakening state-centric schemes for implementing economic, social, and cultural rights'. This is the image of the globalized onslaught on welfarism, whereby 'national forms of redistributive politics according to social need are undermined by market-driven capital accumulation imperatives' (Holton 1998: 92).

For all the reasons set out hitherto, this is an inadequate account of the situation. The focus on state disempowerment is ahistoric, and relies too much on a static conception of what the state is, and of what it can best perform. It is also predicated on some abstracted relationship between the state and 'its' community when, in fact, the terms of that engagement are constantly shifting, and globalization is best understood as denoting the most recent set of shifts. This entails less the circumvention of the state than its re-creation, failing which globalization itself would become unsustainable. The development of this line of argument requires a re-examination of contemporary forms, and conceptions, of community. In particular, it needs some understanding of how communities come to be, and what common goals they must be thought to share.

Within the theory of international relations, the state and the community are regularly, if problematically, used as interchangeable terms. Communitarianism, thus transcribed, refers to the state as the bounded realm of moral affiliation and, because of this association, is deemed to be a fixed entity. It is, as it were, pinned down on territory and it shifts, if at all, only in accordance with the movement of state borders. Even in the case of diasporic communities—which might be thought to belie any such claim—the community is grounded in aspiration, if not in fact. This conflation of state and community is never intended quite literally, and yet is constantly reiterated in the notion, seemingly derived from Hobbes, that moral life is possible only under the sway of sovereign authority. At the extreme, where realism meets communitarianism, moral community and territorially defined coercive authority come to be identified with each other. However, the tendency within the globalization literature is to break this linkage, and to liberate community from its spatial definition. Once this is done, it becomes possible to think of communities as 'being constantly remade', rather than as complete (Linklater 1998: 2).

There is no necessary contradiction between this claim that communities are being remade on a non-national basis, and the seemingly recent revival of nationalist politics since the end of the cold war. Indeed, the two might be causally related. 'The steady decline in political participation at the nation-state level by individuals', Albrow suggests, 'coupled with value commitments which are defined outside national politics' can itself contribute to defensive strategies of renationalization because of the 'symbolic appeal of national identity' (1996: 181). Restatement of nationalist norms may, in this way, signify the scale of the threat from alternative sources of value.

But if, as argued earlier, it is not a cosmopolitan morality that is usurping the normative state, how can we best describe what is happening? This leads back to the earlier discussion of the basis of community, since the kind of moral community that might be thought to be emerging, or to exist already, depends on how it is understood. Is community a 'given'—historically speaking—or does it 'grow'?

This is central to those attempts to distinguish between material interdependence as a developing condition, and any normative implications that might be thought to attach to it. For example, Seyom Brown, echoing the argument originally set out by Beitz (1979), subscribes to the position that material globalization does create something more, such as a community of identity. He holds that 'the increasing mobility of economic goods and services . . . is creating more than societies of material interdependence . . . it is also creating . . . transnational, transborder community identities and political loyalties' (S. Brown 1992: 126).

In contrast, Chris Brown insists upon a sharp distinction between material trends towards 'one world', and the formation of community. 'Something further is needed', he avers, 'if an essentially *empirical* account of an increasingly unified world is to be accompanied by an essentially *normative* account of the emergence of a world community' (C. Brown 1995*a*: 94). The former may be a necessary precondition, but it is not by itself sufficient to create the latter. Indeed, he expresses some scepticism about any causal relationship between them: the economic inequalities of globalization call into question whether 'a trend towards a complexly interdependent world will, of its own accord, create community' (C. Brown 1995*a*: 93). Elsewhere, he has written that community additionally 'implies the idea of common interests and at least an emerging common identity' (C. Brown 1995*b*: 185). His argument attests that interdependence may not engender—indeed may impede—such an evolution.

But such notions are notoriously difficult to pin down, either within or beyond national communities. It is precisely because national identities do not literally create communities, in the material sense, that appeal has been made to the 'imagined community' (Anderson 1983) and the same notion can potentially be extended globally. This has been done in elaboration of Robertson's (1992) work. The claim is that the idea of the 'imagined community' seems 'equally applicable to globalization' since both involve 'images of a community composed of people most of whom will never meet face to face but who nonetheless possess a shared sense of common bonds' (Holton 1998: 33–4). Obviously at issue here is the complex interplay between material and ideational factors. Can there be 'really existing community' in the relative absence of a supporting material basis? What are the permissible limits of the moral 'imagination'? Appeals to interests, bonds, and identities—necessary as they are—do little to resolve these teasing problems.

Let us take the example of one strand of globalization theory, that relating to a postulated systemic environmental threat. Is the averting of global environmental disaster a shared interest that constitutes a community out of us all? Does humanity have an identity in relationship to it? The answers are as nuanced as they are ultimately inconclusive, even if they tend overall towards scepticism. Three will be reviewed at this point for illustrative purposes. The first comes from Chris Brown himself. He boldly pronounces that this is a 'global force which is incontrovertibly based in common interests, and provides a common identity'. However, he substantially qualifies the import of this when he adds that the identity it promotes is essentially 'biological' and does not translate well into cultural, social, or political terms (C. Brown 1995*a*: 100). We might presumably be at liberty to add 'moral' to his list. Linklater, secondly, makes appeal to a community of fate in the face of common threats, such as from the environment. In elaboration of this notion, he specifies that, in these situations, people may 'not share common sentiments', but see the wisdom of hanging together 'in the face of adversity'. Thus viewed, he reminds us of the distinction between an association and a community and, in Hegelian terms, describes people confronting environmental danger as belonging to a 'civil society' rather than being citizens 'of an ethical state' (Linklater 1998: 1). Thirdly, we have the reflections of Andrew Hurrell, who has contributed extensively to our understanding of the environment and its implications for international relations. He provides the intriguing thought that 'a political theory of the environment is concerned not simply with the ideas of the "good life", but also with the means to ensure human survival best' (Hurrell 1995b: 130). This again collapses Wight's distinction between international and political theory, but in an unexpected direction. It does not so much put the 'good life' into international environmental relations, but instead puts survival into domestic environmental policy.

What can we conclude from these thoughtful and well-informed observations? Are they saying the same thing in different ways, or giving expression to fundamentally incompatible views? Arguably, although the differences are there, the most striking thing to emerge is that all three arguments, in common, seem to push toward a reduction, if not elimination, of the force of the argument that environmental crisis generates moral community. For Brown, it creates shared interests and identities but, on closer examination, these do not extend beyond the realm of biological necessity. For Linklater, it creates a 'second best' association, rather than moral community. And likewise, in the case of Hurrell, his argument, if taken to extremes, would remove the whole issue out of the normative debate by reducing it to the realm of necessity, rather than of free moral choice. On these testimonies, it would seem that we are unable to reach global moral community via environmental emergency.

Globalization and the constituted normative community

But perhaps, for the combined reasons given above, this was the wrong direction from which to approach in any case. Much depends on the type of community for which we are searching. Returning to some of the distinctions reviewed earlier, we are still confronted with unresolved issues about the relative standings of cooperative association versus community, and the unencumbered individual versus the constitutive community. These, and similar ideas, relate to the distinction originally formulated by Oakshott (1975) between a civil and an enterprise association, and subsequently reworked by others. For example, Oakshott's idea was refined and elaborated by Nardin (1983), yielding his categorization into practical and purposive associations. We can also argue that there have been genealogical connections between such categories, and those incorporated into theories of international society, where they reappear transmuted as 'pluralist' and 'solidarist' prototypes (Bull 1966; Dunne and Wheeler 1996). Some of these appear to be based on a distinction between society and community, whereas others seem to distinguish between different forms of community itself. If the latter is the pertinent consideration, what kind of community suffices to validate the argument that normative globalization might be taking place?

The question can be clarified by addressing cognate issues about the nature of international society, the manner of its development, and its relationship to a wider world society. It has been convincingly demonstrated that for 'English School' theorists, international society is not some preordained structure within which states are compelled to behave, but is itself a social construct: it is shaped by, but also reinforces, state practice (Dunne 1995). International society, in Dunne's adaptation of Wendt, is thus 'what states make of it' (Dunne 1995: 384). Implicit in this argument is the potential for the evolution of both state practice and international society, however strong might be the constraints for social reproduction.

At the same time, other theorists have discerned a dynamic—and positive—relationship between international and world society:

There is therefore a plausible case that world society and international society can only develop hand-in-hand. An international society cannot develop past a fairly primitive level without being supported by the development of elements of 'world' culture . . . Conversely, a world society cannot emerge unless it is supported by a stable political framework, and the state system remains the only candidate for this. (Buzan 1993: 340)

In this way, the connection to globalization can be made. International society is itself adaptable and can change to further the emergence of a world-culture-based 'human'—as opposed to inter-state— society. States, international society, and world society are by these means seen to co-constitute each other in a complex dynamic. Bearing this thought in mind, we might then explore the implications for international society, and for a potential global community, of the reconfiguration of normative functions within states.

As against the notion of state normative redundancy, it might be that the moral basis of the state itself is undergoing transformation. This, in turn, can be described in various ways. Might it be that, in the context of globalization, the state is undergoing transformation from a constitutive to a co-operative community (in Sandel's terms), but a community nonetheless? Such a conception recognizes the great amount of 'entangling' that still occurs within the state, while allowing also for the entanglements stretching beyond. At the same time, such a framework is comfortable with the problematic notion of identity, both within and across states, since this is a function of the redefinition of the state, rather than a consequence of some directionless globalization impacting from the outside. It is not that states have lost their moral character, but that they are in process of changing it. Globalization is as much an effect, as a cause, of what is happening to states.

Employing Linklater's argument, we can see that states have constantly redefined their community bases by new terms of incorporation and exclusion. Just as they previously became 'genuinely national' in order to soften class antagonisms by submergence in the national whole, they have more recently fragmented from the inside along a series of social axes (Albrow 1996: 169–70). We should be careful, however, not to confuse the demise of the old forms of state corporatism (and the normative appeals evoked in support of it) with the final abandonment of the state's moral claims as a whole. Viewed historically, we can see that the age of state moral monopoly, bound up with notions of the exclusive national community, and more recently brokered through corporatist deals and welfarism, was very much the exception rather than the rule.

In any event, the argument for state normative retreat accepts too readily the preordained course of history in the face of globalization, and does not sufficiently recognize the political reality of contestation, within which the redefined state may yet re-emerge as the major protagonist (Mann 1997: 491–2). This is simply to acknowledge the clear evidence of interplay between the 'domestic' and the 'international'. Linklater demonstrates how a reconstitution of the state previously had negative effects upon international relations, such as during the first half of this century. 'Increased rivalry between more exclusionary sovereign states', he suggests, 'was one result of the development of more inclusive national communities', since the extension of citizens' rights intensified national loyalties to the exclusion of all others (1998: 189). If we can discern this process in one historical period, we might assume its presence more generally, although not always operating in the same direction. Neo-realism has been berated for its 'failure to recognise that the international system can be transformed by reconstituting exclusionary political communities' (Linklater 1998: 14). This is certainly the case, but it should be added in refinement of this critique that, at the same time, reconstitution of the international can exercise its own transformational effect upon individual political communities, not least upon their own self-perception. Sassen tilts the balance too far in the opposite direction, but makes a telling observation nonetheless: 'As the global economy creates new conditions', she remarks, 'the institution of citizenship may evolve yet again' (1996a: xiii). Both observations are correct, but one-sided. The reality is that the two domains are mutually transformational and, in so far as this is the case, the state still matters, in the normative sphere as much as in any other.

This emerges clearly in some of the discussions of counter-globalization, a position that explicitly takes globalization as an unacceptable normative tendency that must be resisted. Much of this literature focuses upon the role of new social movements and is, by its very nature, extremely distrustful of state power. Indeed, the function of many of these movements is deemed precisely to be one of mobilizing direct citizen activism, rather than operating through state instrumentalities. Typically, the role of states and the role of the new social movements are viewed as zero-sum:

The recent era has seen the global emergence of strong subgroups and social movements which have struggled to define a new normative framework from a global perspective.

Given the authority crisis confronting the nation-state system, the importance of these subgroups and social movements will continue to grow. As current economic and political systems weaken, individuals will look not only to nation-states for their identity and support, but also to local and international groups of all sorts. (Felice 1996: 103–4)

For all this, the role of the state in counter-globalization should not be dismissed lightly (Falk 1994: 138), and through it a redefined normative project may be retained. This is accepted in a number of contexts. Some regard it as of particular importance in a North–South context, considering the state to be the only effective barrier to the negative features of globalization. This sentiment can be found in the rather extreme proposition that 'conserving the "bad" of corrupt, brutal and repressive regimes in some places, may be the price to be paid for conserving and promoting the "good" of cultural diversity' (J. Williams 1996: 61).

More generally, and embracing other contexts, it has equally been suggested that the state has a role to play. Noting the widespread tendency of social movements to be 'anti-statist', some regard the confrontation with globalization to be a possible exception. 'But where the problem of globalization is concerned', it has been pointedly remarked, 'the stance vis-à-vis the state . . . is thrown into question . . . a return to the state is in all probability necessary to meet the dislocations and poverty generated by the latest round of globalization' (Lynch 1998: 163–4). Again this is seductive, but misses one critical point. Its implication is that the state might be a solution to the problem of globalization 'out there'. The state, we need to remind ourselves once more, is already part of this problem.

The normative state we are in

During the long period of the predominance of realism within IR theory, normative issues struggled to find a secure place on the disciplinary agenda. Nonetheless, they have enjoyed a long period of revival, reaching back long before the discussion of globalization became fashionable. Debates about the ethics of war, human rights, distributive justice, and, more recently, humanitarian intervention have ensured that normative concerns received some kind of hearing, however uncongenial their reception within much mainstream IR (S. Smith 1992). That revival is now set to be further stimulated by the analysis of globalization, but possibly for the wrong reasons.

The encouragement that globalization lends to normative reflection comes from a perception that it further breaks down those very intellectual barriers that have traditionally held it at bay. While IR theory has, of course, been prepared to countenance the idea of 'duties beyond borders' (Hoffmann 1981), it was always coy about doing so and realized that this entailed, in the very act, a step across a still significant moral boundary. To the extent that globalization enjoins us to be less preoccupied with territory and borders, it creates a more hospitable intellectual atmosphere within which to advance the normative project. Unhappily, it does so by simplification. According to the conventional logic, globalization progresses in so far as the state recedes. This is as much the case with normative concerns as with other spheres. In short, we can now engage in ethical theory unencumbered by the inconveniences of the special moral status to which the state has hitherto laid claim. Globalization facilitates normative theory, so the argument runs, precisely because it takes the state out.

This is superficial at best and seriously misleading. The thrust of the present discussion is that we should 'not anticipate the demise of the state but envisage its reconstitution' (Linklater 1998: 44). If this is the case in the policy areas earlier considered, it remains equally convincing as an account of the normative state as well. The state is without question losing some of the moral stature that it enjoyed during the recent historical period. That it should so do is fully intelligible, as this is reflective of the reformulated bargain that is in the process of being struck between state and citizen. The state delivers less in some policy areas than previously, and delivers less in the way of rights that are distinctive to any one community in particular. By the same token, it makes fewer demands on its citizens in some fields, such as national security.

It might then not be misleading to portray this, in the language encountered above, as some kind of drift away from a fully constituted moral community to a more instrumental co-operative, or practical, type of association. There is, in Laidi's words (1998: 62–3), an imbalance between the demand for identity and its supply, and the nation-state is unable to make good the shortfall. If this move is allowed, then we might also be permitted to envisage the transnational society becoming, in parts, more solidarist—at the same time as the individual states become more pluralist. But these changes need to be viewed as shifts by degrees and in the relative balance between them, rather than as some absolute change in kind. However, to repeat again, it is misleading to consider what is happening to the state as simply the by-product of change from outside: the pluralization of the once purposive national society, and the solidarization of the once practical international society, are both fundamentally interrelated. In this sense, one apologia for realism misses the point. Buzan sympathetically attributes the seeming shortcomings of realism to the fact that 'realist theory focuses on the state, and all these other things are happening, as it were, elsewhere' (Buzan, Held, and McGrew 1998: 390). This is precisely the most serious mistake of realism. It assigns these developments 'elsewhere', when the changes entailed by globalization are, in fact, happening as much within states as outside of them.

We should also beware of any rash presumption that moral leakage from the state seeps into a reified and reinvigorated cosmopolitanism. There are too many alternative communities in between, and if there is any one characteristic that seems to be emerging at the moment, it is surely the plurality of identities and of potential moral communities. Much of this is associated with globalization, and suggests a rebalancing between the state as moral actor and the wider system of which it forms a part. We are witnessing a period of renewed, and likely intense, moral encounter and realignment. As in other areas, this is not painless or cost-free and, for the moment, most of the dislocation is being experienced within the nation-state community, which is most under pressure. But this is unlikely to be the end of history and the state may yet again stake a normative claim to be the principal instrument of social protection against globalization. Within the currently volatile conditions of identity and community, it would be presumptuous on our part to deny that the moral balance may yet begin to tilt back again in the opposite direction. The state's resilience in morally reinventing itself should not be underestimated.

What does this brief excursion into normative theory entail for the place of globalization in IR theory? In summary, it is a salutary reminder that many of the established categories through which IR has traditionally pursued its reflection on the subject are no longer fully suited to the task. Much moral and political theorizing remains highly pertinent to the examination of globalization, as it asks penetrating questions about the nature of moral community and about its potential for development. It guards against vapid generalizations that identify global technology and infrastructures with a global moral order. As against this, the conventional systems of IR normative analysis are deficient, since they tend to reinforce clear separations no longer tenable in conditions of globalization. Above all, when projected on top of such dualistic schemes, globalization has to be accommodated to them. This results in one or other of two distorted styles of argument. The first is that globalization has little or no significance for IR normative theory because the community is the community, and as such is immune to all unsettling conditions around it. The other, and possibly predominant, position is that globalization is contributing to the moral hollowing out of the state. Both assessments depend upon a reified dichotomy between state (and community) and globalization. In the normative sphere, as elsewhere, these contentions are superficial. They ignore the profound—and more complex—reality that the state is not the passive victim of normative globalization, but is itself one of its progenitors. At the same time, global community is by no means the uncontested heir to the state's former patrimony, but is itself, however embryonic its present condition, a measure of the renegotiation of normative compacts already under way within states.

That the literature on globalization should provoke a new wave of normative theory in IR is much to be welcomed. However, the enterprise must not be allowed to proceed on a false basis. Normative explorations of new forms of community, including those of transborder and potentially global import, should not be predicated upon assumptions of the state's moral redundancy, but need to incorporate revamped moral theories of the state at their intellectual core. To do otherwise is to fail to see what it is that is interesting about globalization in the first place.

THE DEMOCRATIC STATE

In general, IR theory has not been much exercised by concerns with democracy. Only very occasionally have the two interacted, as, for example, in Wilsonianism. This essentially espoused the view that foreign policy had not been democratized in the same way as had other aspects of policy, and that this presented itself as the next great challenge for liberal politics. Those aspects of international life which Woodrow Wilson so often denounced—secret diplomacy, alliances, balances of power, and arms races—were little more than manifestations of the incompleteness of the democratic process. Pervading this worldview was a striking faith in public opinion and in its benign and restraining effects on national policy. It was but a small step from such an analysis to the adoption of an institution, such as the League of Nations, that would function as the court of world public opinion. However, for the League to be effective in exercising restraint against its individual members, they must themselves be truly democratic. Hence the League was to be a League of democratic states—but one which might need to resort to collective military action against any delinquent, just in case such moral pressure should prove inadequate.

Wilsonianism apart, IR theory's neglect of democracy lingers on in certain core assumptions. Those who might not mourn the demise of the state in general must nonetheless be concerned about what globalization is doing to it, we are told, because 'of its role as a territorial anchor for modern democratic politics' (Low 1997: 242). The reason for this is that, traditionally, political theory has made a profound connection between democracy and the nation-state as polity. In terms of the Great Divide, democracy is properly a domestic business. This association has also been echoed within IR theory. It has had the effect, as Holden neatly points out, that democracy seems to apply only 'to the actions *of*... not the interactions *amongst* states' (1996b: 137–8). As long as this is thought to be the case, International Relations might consider itself entitled to pay scant regard to democracy except inasmuch as, as an attribute of some actors, it has an effect on international outcomes: it is not, by itself, the stuff of the subject. In the same way, and for similar reasons, international law 'has left the implications of globalization for democratic theory and practice largely unaddressed' (Crawford and Marks 1998: 82–3).

Does democracy matter?

More recently, however, democracy and IR theory have touched each other at three principal junctures, all of which also fall under the shadow of globalization. The first is an argument about the increasing spread of democratization and the global forces that have encouraged this process. This took on the note of triumphalism early in the 1990s, when the benign proliferation of democratic states both marked out the progress, and embodied the promise, of the more euphoric visions of globalization. While still omnipresent, that argument is more subdued these days.

The second is the thesis that the state now underproduces democracy. Just as in other functional areas, globalization is deemed to have eroded state democratic capacity: the institutions of accountability and responsibility are no longer coextensive with the affairs over which they have oversight, and democratic deficits are now set to be the global norm. The course of globalization can thus be followed by looking at the trail of damaged states left in its wake, even if this occasionally fosters illusions about a past 'golden age' of democracy. It tends to be a hazard of the globalization literature that 'national forms of democracy are credited . . . with powers in retrospect which it is unclear they had in the first place' (Low 1997: 245).

The third is the voluminous literature on the liberal or democratic peace that links democratic forms with the avoidance of military resolutions between liberal states. The extension of its logic is the expectation that—under the impetus of globalization, as above—liberal democracy will extend its reach, and thereby the prospects for an expanding liberal peace will be greatly enhanced. These sets of claims are interlinked, but also suffer from internal contradictions, and it is difficult to see how all three might be valid at the same time.

The interrelationships are striking enough, if sometimes paradoxical, and yet are not commonly brought into focus in the literature on democracy. Some do detect an element of irony in the fact that 'democracy and the national state have come to define the norm in politics even as they have come to mean rather less' (Cronin 1996: 280–1; see also Held and McGrew 1993: 261). Others point to the 'central paradoxes of globalization' in that it simultaneously 'provides the conditions for thinking beyond our own immediate community' but also 'weakens the effectiveness of the traditional institutions of liberal democracy' (T. Evans 1997: 145–6). At a purely semantic level, there are deep-seated ambiguities about what is entailed by the globalization of democracy. Does it mean the emergence of a genuinely transnational or cosmopolitan structure of democracy, operating at global and regional levels, as well as at the national and local (Held 1998: 24)? Does it require a focus on non-territorial actors, such as transnational social movements, regarded as 'well-springs of global governance' (Rosenau 1998: 42)? Or does it simply mean democratization within larger numbers of, but still separate, national settings? Or can it mean some combination of all these things?

On even closer investigation, there are tensions between some of these bodies of argument, and more than a hint that the reasoning may be circular. It is easy enough to see the connection between the 'democratic peace' theory and the momentum to encourage democratization as a matter of policy, even if cautionary notes have been struck about the instabilities associated with the transitional phases to democracy (Mansfield and Snyder 1995: 5, 38). Typically, one exponent of the theory observes that 'understanding that democracies rarely fight each other . . . should encourage peaceful efforts to assist the emergence and consolidation of democracy' (Russett 1993: 135), a claim which even critics of the theory are happy to acknowledge (Cohen 1994: 223).

But, from the perspective of IR theory, there must assuredly be important implications for the democratic peace arguments, flowing from the simultaneous spread and weakening of democracy brought in the wake of globalization. What hold does democracy have on future peaceful inter-state relations if it 'means less', even if there happens also to be more of it around? If the democratic 'structuralists' are correct to claim that national democracy has been hollowed out, then there is every reason to expect that democracy—whatever its role in sustaining peace in the past—will no longer have the same pacific effects in the future. On the other hand, if democracy *does* continue to be a force for peace, this perhaps suggests that democracy is more robust than some of its detractors would have us believe.

In any case, if, as previously argued, the state as security actor is undergoing transformation in globalized conditions, it would seem to follow that the capacity of any state—democratic or otherwise—to produce 'peace' will be substantially different, even if not necessarily less. Turning the argument on its head, to what extent also is further democratization itself parasitic upon the already established liberal peace? If this is appreciably the case, how can we escape the empty tautology that the prospects for democracy are dependent upon the prospects for democracy, or the prospects for peace upon the prospects for peace? These are some of the perplexing issues that lie at the core of the present chapter.

They connect directly to the previous discussion about the nature of community and its potentiality for change. In the context of the normative state, it was suggested that communitarians tend to view community as a given, whereas cosmopolitans regard all extant communities as merely embryonic expressions of the grand community of all humankind. The former believe that only real communities can implement the good, and that they are thereby exempt from any demands of the right that the international community might seek to impose upon them. This debate is echoed in the sharply contrasting communitarian and cosmopolitan views of the functions of democracy. For the former, democracy is already an end, giving expression to the community and its collectively constructed values (Bellamy and Castiglione 1998: 160). Cosmopolitans, in contrast, tend to regard democracy 'as a means of constructing a community identity' (Thompson 1998: 193). In short, the debate is about whether democracy requires a pre-existing community to sustain it, or whether democracy itself can be the instrument whereby new communities are created. The implications of the normative state are thus replicated in a scrutiny of the present condition of the democratic state.

These implications are fundamental to the ongoing concerns of this book. They include, for example, the analytical separation between reductionist and systemic theory, and related manifestations of the Great Divide. Within the specific context of the democratic peace literature, the relevance is straightforward. Acceptance of the idea that democratic forms of government issue in an international effect, namely peace, represents a frontal challenge to structural realist theory, as is commonly recognized: 'it apparently refutes', states Cohen, 'the realist view that systemic factors, not domestic traits, mould international politics' (1994: 207). This is presumably the reason why neo-realists have, in turn, been so scathing about this theoretical claim (Layne 1994). But while it is simple enough to see that the democratic peace adopts reductionist, in preference to systemic, theory, that is not the argument to be presented here. Globalization once again calls this dichotomy into question. The point then is not to privilege reductionism, but to enquire what real meaning can attach to reductionism in conditions of globalization. If democratization is itself dependent upon external, and possibly systemic, factors, what is the point in attributing 'external' behaviour to allegedly 'domestic' conditions of this kind?

We can then broaden the point under discussion. The issue of reductionism arises not only in the specific context of the democratic peace, but more generally in terms of an understanding of the democratic state itself. There is a sense in which much theory about the liberal democratic state has been reductionist, in so far as it is a condition believed to have been self-generated from within. However, the point made by a number of writers, and none more forcefully than David Held, is that such an understanding is now wholly inadequate. Liberal democracy is as much constituted from without as from within, and its future viability depends, in fact, on overcoming precisely these lines of separation. Within a context of globalization, the self-contained liberal democratic state is an illusion:

Simply stated, there cannot be an account of the liberal democratic state any longer without an examination of the global system and there cannot be an examination of the global system without an account of the liberal democratic state. The way forward is to transcend the endogenous and exogenous frameworks of, respectively, the theory of the state and international relations. (Held and McGrew 1993: 282)

If this is the case, it enjoins us once more to abandon the imagery of the democratic state, engulfed from without and in process of enforced retreat. The reason for this rejection is that what is occurring 'without' is as much a reflection of the internal restructuring of the state as vice versa. It is not that globalization is causing the end of the democratic state: rather, the transformation in the nature of the democratic state is part and parcel of what is driving globalization. What many of the cosmopolitan-democracy school seem to argue is that current democratic practice falls short only inasmuch as its reach is not extensive enough, confined as it is within the state. But if the argument is allowed that globalization is, in part, a measure of the failings of democracy closer to home, the analysis becomes yet gloomier still.

Nonetheless, the presence of the Great Divide makes itself felt in virtually all discussions of democracy and international relations. It is the inescapable starting point for any enquiry into a relationship that has been labelled an 'awkward and distinctly unfriendly' encounter (Walker 1993: 150), so much so that some theorists of democracy remain unreceptive to hosting any such meeting at all (Birch 1993). And yet some are willing to see that the 'international diffusion of liberal democracy' is a key manifestation of globalization in practice and, hence, is one of the prime movers in attempts to cut across 'the disciplinary boundaries of political theory and international relations' (McGrew 1997c: 231–2).

What would such a 'cutting across' look like? Its principal exponent, David Held, has sketched it in the following broad terms. 'Democratic institutions and practices have to be articulated', he writes, 'with the complex arena of national and international politics, and the mutual interpenetration of the national and the international must be mapped' (1992b: 11–12). The meaning and force of this claim will be considered in the remainder of this chapter. But to repeat, at face value this represents a significant problem for the current version of democratic peace theory. In so far as that theory postulates an 'international' effect as resulting from 'national' conditions, it is not clear how adaptable it is to Held's idea of interpenetration without at the same time sliding into the circularity of reasoning depicted above.

No democratization without globalization

This section serves to make and elaborate the twin claims that democratization is prime evidence of the march of globalization, and also that globalization is a major source of the spread of democratization. Where the literature makes any link at all between the two, it is usually in one or other of these forms. However, while the former is largely unproblematic, the latter needs to be refined. Its implication is that democratization is simply a contingent by-product of globalization, whereas, more accurately, there is a much more fundamental relationship. If globalization fosters democratization, it is not because of what it *does*, but because of what it *is*.

There has been some kind of sea change in the understanding of democratization. It was once largely regarded as an indigenous development, promoted or held back by characteristics peculiar to the individual political system and its setting and, indeed, some continue to adhere to such a viewpoint (Ray 1995: 81). As against this, writers such as Huntington (1991) have tended to draw attention to external factors. In particular, the post-cold war situation seemed to exemplify a 'wave' of democratization and this encouraged the idea that more general, or systemic, factors must be at work (Mannin 1996: 232–3; Archibugi 1998).

It is not difficult to generate a shopping list of the most likely contributory factors operating from the 'outside'. These need not be detailed at any length, but would include the following, in no particular order of priority. The process is unquestionably associated with the globalization of human rights values that place a higher premium on political procedures respectful of the autonomy of the individual. Where this has not occurred, as it were, as a natural development, it has been fostered from the outside by activist policies of conditionality, linked to such goods as aid and loans. It might further be argued that, in an age of global communications, and the global activities of INGOs such as Amnesty International, it is that much easier to monitor and publicize instances of abuse. Global audiences can be kept informed of the political iniquities of a Marcos, a Ceausescu, or a Suharto. The fundamentally non-democratic nature of the former South African regime was kept daily before world public attention for two decades before it crumbled.

More specific external influences are associated with the end of the cold war. Obviously, there was some domino effect in the collapse of the old authoritarian order throughout central and eastern Europe, the failure of one beleaguered dictatorial system undercutting the ability of others to stand against the tide. Some commentators also draw attention to the 'liberation from the West' as well as to the 'liberation from the East', highlighting the significance of changes in Western policy. From this perspective, after the cold war there was no longer the same strategic imperative for the Western powers to bolster unscrupulous regimes simply in return for *Realpolitik* benefits. In this context, liberation was often taken to mean embarking on the road to economic development and success, and in their eagerness, academic pundits as much as political practitioners were often tempted to conflate democracy and capitalism. Whatever the particular spur, there was unquestionably a degree of international socialization, a pressure to emulate and to seek the rewards for doing so. Finally, there is the argument that the need to conform is itself an integral part of the neo-liberal project that has characterized the recent phase of economic globalization. With regard to the South, the realization that 'opting out, in short, is out' (Strange 1995: 299) handed over to the North immense influence in setting the political terms of the new re-engagement. If the South were to be a beneficiary of the global economy—and what country could afford not to?—then democratization was the price of admission.

All these arguments might suggest that this range of global external factors, loosely associated with globalization, has inevitably pressed in the direction of greater democratization. This is certainly not the case. Commentators have equally drawn attention to the large number of obstacles to democratization and these, in turn, can also be related to aspects of globalization. For example, it has been said that the prospects for global democracy are held back by a combination of the following: uneven economic development; diverging political traditions; cultural and ethnic identities; and solidarities that are primarily local or national in character (Resnick 1998: 129). From previous arguments, it can readily be seen that many of these characteristics are either attributes of, or at least aggravated by, globalization. And so the relationship between globalization and democratization is not straightforwardly positive: 'there is nothing about McWorld that automatically entails or supports democracy', is one summary judgement (Barber 1996: 153).

However, the main critique has tended to be centred less on the detailed accounting of the positive and negative balances of democratization, and more on the *form* taken by any democracy encouraged by globalization. Applied to the South, this analysis normally develops a version of the theme of 'low intensity democracy' (Gills and Rocamora 1992), itself conducive to the interests of international capital. In short, the question is not whether globalization does or does not promote democracy but, if so, of what kind. The common verdict returned is that 'While the nature of the ongoing liberalization, or globalization processes, constitutes a stimulus to the extension of *formal* democratic practices', the very structure of the world economy also impedes the development of '*substantive* democratization' (Gills 1997a: 60–1). Citizens in the South are, by the spurious forms of democracy foisted upon them, to be 'excluded from the compromise of "embedded liberalism" ' (Cammack 1996: 47), and thereby denied substantial measures of social protection.

Beyond such structural arguments, there is the more general critique based on cultural relativism, which nonetheless shares some concerns in common with those above. A good example is provided by Parekh, who maintains that 'liberal democracy is a historically specific form of democracy', in that it emphasizes the autonomy of the individual and starts from the assumption that the individual is 'conceptually and ontologically prior to society' (1992: 160–1). To the extent that globalization has promoted democracy, it has been its liberal version that has been encouraged. Thus the democratization project at the heart of globalization is taken to be a culturally specific variant, best designed to erode the capacity of both state and civil society in the South to resist its economic logic.

It is then possible to draw a number of possible connections between globalization and democratization. Without engaging in the specifics of this debate, it might be concluded that globalization, in general, has raised the pressures for further democratization while, at the same time, it has itself been responsible for placing impediments in its way. Above all, however, it is associated with democratization of a certain kind. To the extent that this is so, globalization encourages democratization not as some incidental side-effect, but as an essential expression of globalization itself. The two cannot be radically dissociated from each other. This becomes of considerable importance when trends towards democracy in the South and East are set against the current experience with democracy in the North.

No globalization without representation

Whatever the complexities in the relationship between globalization and democratization in the South and East, its impact on democratic practice in the North is taken to be universally negative. Moreover, it is within this context that the stylized notion of democratic 'underproduction' (Cerny 1996c 97) enjoys its widest appeal. This section will cover the following: the evidence for the problems that globalization presents to democracy; the diagnoses as to why these problems arise; and finally the proffered solutions to them. It will end with some wider reflections on the significance of these issues.

Given the close identity between the state and the democratic polity, it is scarcely surprising that premonitions of the retreat of the state should also have become coupled with laments for the demise of democracy. Typically, and as an echo of the fate of the state itself, it has been pronounced that 'democracy is being hollowed out' (Gamble 1996: 126–7). Cox makes much the same claim. 'A consequence of economic globalization', he complains, 'has been to transform politics at the national level into *management*' (R. Cox 1997: 63). If governments do not dispose, but only manage, the need and scope for democratic accountability are that much the less.

Recognition of this problem is little more than a reiteration of the supposed home truth about globalization, namely that it makes the nation-state both too small and too big for effective government. If this is true in general, then it is also true of the democratic capacities of the state in particular: democracy is powerless in the face of global forces, and yet is still too remote from local concerns (Resnick 1998: 127–8). It fails the 'glocalization' test on both counts. Alternatively conceived, democracy deals with the less important aspects of peoples' lives but has 'little purchase' on the great forces that shape their circumstances (Albrow 1996: 181–2).

For some this is simply an incidental effect of globalization, one of the many casualties of the social and political restructuring that it has entailed. Democracy within the nation-state has, so far, been unable to adapt quickly enough to the radically different circumstances in which it now finds itself. It has become detached from prevailing historical conditions (McGrew 1997b: 13). In the words of one analyst, 'this "nesting" of democracy within the nation-state has become problematic' (Axtmann 1998b: 10). Others have spoken of 'accelerated globalization' leading to a widened gap between 'the capacity to govern and the demand for governance' (Zurn 1995: 150). What these claims assert, in sum, is a developing fracture between the forces that shape peoples' lives, and the instruments for political control over them. The former has become increasingly global, while the latter remains substantially national. In these circumstances, there is an impending crisis: no more globalization without representation.

However, this notion that globalization is associated with an incidental challenge to democracy is rejected by those who see a more insidious design at work. Just as in the case of the South, there is the argument that the erosion of democracy is not an accidental spin-off of globalization but part of its inner workings. Neo-liberal globalization is predicated on the explicit belief that the market knows best, and is entitled to its own legitimacy. The realm of political intervention should, indeed, be circumscribed in recognition of this. Accordingly, the placing of limits upon the provenance of democracy is precisely what globalization is about, and this should be made to apply internationally, as well as nationally. Thus, according to one critic, the 'solidarities, communities, civic traditions, and national sovereignties which sustained democratic politics had to be made compatible with the more fundamental reality of the market order' (Gamble 1996: 127–8). The hollowing out of democracy is thus a core feature of globalization, rather than some fortuitous by-product of it.

What, in greater detail, are the diagnoses of this situation? Why should democracy be presented as a victim of globalization? Three key elements can be discerned that, although often overlapping in practice, individually are thought to be responsible for the globalized democratic deficit. These are as follows: the problem of the democratic 'fit'; policy leakage; and the non-democratic nature of international governance.

The first of these is relatively straightforward. It relates back to the idea of a separation between policy flows and their political management, and to the fact that the former often 'stretch' beyond the latter (Held 1992*b*: 22). Held elaborates that this lack of fit has profound implications for a number of aspects of democracy, such as consent, legitimacy, constituency, representation, and participation. All are thrown out of alignment by the processes of globalization.

Secondly, the lack of fit is itself a measure of the degree of policy leakage. This refers, of course, to the previously encountered arguments about the erosion of the state's capacity to manage its own economy. Thus a motley collection of writers refer to states 'losing their monopoly over who governs in their territories' (Hirst 1996: 98), or suggest that 'the very process of governance can escape the reach of the nation-state' (Held 1992*b*: 21). If, by its nature, the policy agenda is replete with issues that are inherently global in nature, then 'the institutions of national democracy alone cannot be expected to provide a framework for the people to participate in seeking solutions' (T. Evans 1997: 123). The obverse side of this situation, unhappily, is that it offers national politicians a convenient pretext for disclaiming all responsibility. This is what is so deeply subversive of the essence of democracy. 'Might there be a limit', it has been asked, 'to how far electorates are prepared to accept the sight of their representatives wringing their hands and attributing domestic economic problems to world-wide difficulties over which they claim to have no control?' (Parry 1994*b*: 8). The image of democratic impotence is, to this extent, given substance by those practitioners who hide behind its logic.

Thirdly, there is the discernible problem of the environment into which the policy leakage takes place—the realm of international governance. This is, in conventional usage, the domain of the non-democratic, since democracy is traditionally contained only within individual state political systems. There is clearly a problem in bringing 'external' agencies under democratic control. Thus Held locates the problem in the nature of the international order, which is 'structured by agencies, organizations, associations and companies over which citizens have minimum, if any, control' (1995*a*: 135). In so far as international governance is conducted through the medium of international regimes, and they in turn become to a degree independent of the governments which first created them, there is the extra danger of the emergence of an 'international "quangocracy" ' (Cerny 1996*b*: 133). Democratic states, by themselves, do not create 'democratic multilateralism' (Scholte 1997*a*: 451). This is compounded by the negative impact of globalization: 'in theory democracy means accountability to the governed', notes one observer, while 'in practice leaders are accountable to market forces' (Mittelman 1996*b*: 9).

If these are the diagnoses of the problem, what is the solution to them? There is by now an extensive literature that, although differing in its details, shares certain fundamentals in common. Above all, these are the assumptions that the fit must be restored, the leakage repaired, and international governance in some way brought to account. In short, the solution appears to be the same in all cases. 'If there are events, processes and problems that transcend states and that require popular control,' it has been deduced, 'then there must be means of popular control that transcend states' (Holden 1996*b*: 144). This is the heart of the project for cosmopolitan democracy. It demands a vision of 'democracy beyond borders' (McGrew 1997*c*: 241). It falls short of appeals for world government (Parry 1994*b*: 11), but requires that democracy 'become a transnational affair if it is to be possible both within a restricted geographic domain and within the wider international community' (Held 1992*b*: 33).

Here lies the nub of the argument. Transnational democracy is not to be conceived as an alternative to national democracy but in part as its salvation as well. To work at one level, it must work at several. And here also is the rub. As policy is thought to have run beyond the bounds of any one state's effective control, so democratic procedures must chase beyond the boundaries of the state in an attempt to catch up. What can no longer be democratized within the state must now be democratized in the realms beyond. But doesn't this rely on a possibly misleading diagnosis? It would appear from such accounts that the problem of democratic accountability is occurring 'out there', and the domestic malaise is no more than a symptom of this external condition. If the transnational problem can be fixed, the democratic state will be set to rights as well. The danger here is that there is at work a deep-seated replication of the logic of globalization itself: the management of democracy is no longer possible within the national state and salvation must be found in the realm beyond. Just as globalization has led to the death of the national economy, it now entails the death of national forms of democracy, except in so far as the latter are restructured as part of a global system. While the proponents of cosmopolitan democracy would without exception be fierce critics of the 'neo-liberal project', might it not be a fine irony that, in their proposed solution, they have themselves succumbed to its logic?

A different appreciation of the situation is that the solution to the problem lies much closer to home. Rather than regard the problem as one pressing from outside, and requiring some transnational reconfiguration of democracy, might it not be that, in part, the problem has been projected outside by those unwilling to grasp domestic nettles? Thus viewed, the alternative plea can be entered that it is as much the failures of 'domestic' democracy that are sustaining globalization as that globalization is the source of the erosion of democracy. To pretend otherwise is to be seduced by the fallacy that globalization occurs independently of states, which in turn become its unwitting victims.

The suggested approach, then, is not to imagine the state's loss of functional control over such things as economy, communications, and security as *causes* of the failings of democracy. Instead, they are little more than symptoms of these failings. Democratic deficiency and globalization both depend upon each other, and the one cannot be addressed in isolation from the other. In so far as this is the case, there is no compelling logic to the priority attached to cosmopolitan means in the rectification of the shortcomings of democracy. This admission is similar to Panitch's invocation, albeit made from a different starting point. 'Those who want to install a transnational democracy in the wake of the nation-state allegedly having been bypassed by globalization', Panitch comments scathingly, 'simply misunderstand what the internationalization of the state really is all about' (1996: 109). It is his conclusion that we must 'reorient strategic discussions toward the democratic transformation of the state rather than toward the transcendence of the state' (1996: 109). Others have called for recognition of the central role of the state in transitions to, and the sustainability of, democracy (Przeworski 1995: 11–12).

So which way round is it? Does the (un)democratic state generate globalization? Or must we step beyond the bounds of the individual state to salvage domestic forms of democracy? Perhaps this choice is as artificial as the premises upon which it is based. We will return to this issue below. In the first instance, we must now consider the third of the encounters between democracy and International Relations, namely the implications of globalization for the democratic peace.

Globalization and the democratic peace

In general, the claim made within the democratic peace literature is not that democracies are inherently more peaceable against all opponents, but that they tend not to fight amongst themselves (Doyle 1983, 1986; Russett 1993; Ray 1995). Elements of that argument have been adapted from what is reported to be Kant's discussion of the virtues of the republican state:

In sum, there are three elements behind Kant's claim that democracy leads to peace. The first is the mere existence of democracies, with their culture of peaceful conflict resolution. Second, the democracies hold common moral values and the bonds they forge because of these values lead to the formation of a pacific union. Finally, the pacific union is strengthened through economic co-operation and interdependence. (Sorensen 1993: 94)

This is not the place to rehearse the substance of the vexed arguments that have raged over the definition of democracy, the statistical base, and the historical accuracy of the claims made on the theory's behalf. For purposes of the present discussion, the objective is simply to enquire how well the standard arguments hold up when placed in the context of globalization. Is democracy the force for peace that it is claimed to be, in the light of the above problems of democracy associated with globalization?

In order to answer this question, we need to look more closely at the reasons why the proponents of the liberal peace think that it works. What is it, in particular, about democracies that might explain their relative peacefulness towards each other? Here it is common to distinguish between the role of democratic norms and that of democratic structures (Russett 1993: 30). In terms of the former, avoidance of war with other liberal states derives from norms 'favoring the peaceful resolution of disputes', or which at any rate express the popular reluctance to 'pay the price of war in blood and money' (Russett 1993: 30). In the latter, the focus is upon institutional factors, such as the obstacles which democracy places in the path of war initiation. 'Democracies are constrained in going to war', it is claimed, 'by the need to ensure broad popular support, manifested in various institutions of government' (Russett 1993: 38).

There is no consensus on how convincing or compelling these arguments might be. However, a moment's reflection suggests that the claims emerging from the globalization literature must be deeply problematic for any and all of these assertions. As has been discussed above, globalization questions some essential aspects of the state's pursuit of national security as traditionally conceived. If this is so, it presumably extends also to the state's warmaking capacity. Beyond this, and more generally, globalization is thought to erode state policy capacity in a range of functional areas. It is also claimed to destabilize the entire operational concept of democracy. If there is no longer a fit between policy process and democratic community, and if all states suffer from policy leakage, how is the democratic process to serve as the constraint on going to war that the liberal theorists assume? And finally, if the terms of democracy are being set from the 'outside', as the critics of neo-liberalism imply, how can national attributes be the source of international outcomes?—the whole idea of the internationalization or transnationalization of democracy seems to point in the opposite direction. According to the cosmopolitan democrats, the extension of democracy into the international sphere is now necessary for the rescue of the democratic state and yet, at the same time, we are being asked to look to the democratic state as the saviour of the international order. Deep, and multiple, confusions appear to be at work here.

There may be a way of clarifying these matters. One of the issues contested within the democratic peace debate is whether, and to what extent, there might not be a deeper level of causation and explanation at work, namely that democracy is itself correlated with some other factor(s). For example, some have questioned the association between democracy and peaceful outcomes: 'the correlation may be spurious altogether in that a common cultural preference for the peaceful resolution of conflict may have preceded both the appearance of democracy and the emergence of a pacific union' (Cohen 1994: 222). Others adamantly reject this approach and insist that the liberal peace is 'a result of some features of democracy rather than being caused exclusively by economic or geopolitical characteristics correlated with democracy' (Russett 1993: 11). How might we break into this circle and what is its potential significance for the present discussion?

The parallel is that, just as the 'correlates of democracy'—rather than democracy as such—may be the source of peace, so it might be 'the correlates of globalized democracy' that need to be subjected to scrutiny in this context. A reflexive process is evidently at work that might be depicted as follows. The faith of the liberal peace theorist is powerfully illustrated in Russett's argument:

But if enough states become stably democratic in the 1990s, then there emerges a chance to reconstruct the norms and rules of the international order . . . A system created by autocracies centuries ago might now be created by a critical mass of democratic states. (1993: 138)

The assumption that pervades this analysis, as befits a champion of the liberal peace, is that the international order is malleable from the inside out. However, there are two problems with this suggestion. First, its notion of the democratic state is itself 'timeless' and 'static', as if the only transition that matters is from autocracy to democracy. This fails to recognize any potential for major restructuring of the democratic state itself. Secondly, and possibly more problematically, it divorces the process of democratization from its wider context by seeming not to allow that it may itself be an element within the international order, rather than something which stands—domestically—apart from it. Russett's imagery is based on a clear separation between the democratic state and the achievement of peace within the international order, in the sense that their distinctiveness allows the one to be causally related to the other. There is no scope within such a scheme for the idea that the (changing) democratic state and the international order are, in fact, necessary parts of each other. It is this unity that the idea of globalization attempts to capture. Neither is this to say that globalization independently causes the present condition of democracy, or establishes the prospects for peace. It is simply a reminder that globalization describes the integral relationship between all three. In that sense, there is no other 'underlying' force with which all are 'correlated', beyond their synchronic relationship with each other.

In the same way that globalization is best understood as a transcription of a certain kind of state, so the construction of certain forms of state is a transcription of the 'international order' within which they are to be found. Democratic states are not exogenous social actors that can reconstitute an externalized international order along non-authoritarian lines; nor, for that matter, can they build a liberal peace. If a liberal peace exists, they are already part of it, just as the order is part of them. And if globalization is unsettling democracy, it does not do so from the outside but is instead a manifestation of the changing form of the democratic state itself.

Constructing democracy and peace

In the narrower—economic—sense of the term, globalization developed out of the core of democratic states during the post-1945 generation. There were compelling strategic reasons for this to occur, and the process was mediated through the corporatist-welfare state, which set protective limits upon the extent of the economic globalization that could take place. By the 1970s, a new phase of economic globalization began to set in which itself reflected domestic moves away from the key assumptions of mid-century corporatism and welfarism. The present-day ills of democracy, as outlined above, are not a consequence of these changes, but a description of them. To the extent that the democratic peace has endured this transition, this must be an expression of the degree to which it is a part of both the 'embedded liberal' and the 'neo-liberal' state. Is this surprising, and what does it tell us that is of a more general theoretical interest?

Perhaps there is no reason to be surprised at this outcome. The embedded liberal state balanced domestic against international needs in such a way that domestic stability would in fact become a constitutive element of a stable international order. By undercutting the excesses of national assertiveness of the interwar period, the compromise nested the socially protected state within the expanding network of international relationships that developed around it. In the past two decades, this bargain has steadily unravelled, and the balance has shifted ever more in favour of assigning priority to international needs over domestic harmony. This is to say that globalization has been privileged over social protection, and the state reconstituted on this basis. It is within such a framework that the development of the liberal peace is best to be understood: it reflects the degree of state transformation but is not, as it were, something caused by an exogenous rush to democracy. Democracy and peace participate in an international order that is constitutive of them in turn. It is thus simplistic to break into the relationship and pronounce that it is democracy that determines everything else.

Once this is recognized, it establishes an important framework both for the discussion of the democratic peace literature and also, and more generally, for the 'solutions' to the problems of the democratic state. These can be reviewed in sequence, before the chapter turns finally to some wider issues of IR theory.

As set out above, discussions of democratic practice in a globalized setting do appear to present some formidable difficulties for the standard arguments of the liberal peace theorists. These proceed on the basis that peace between liberal states is preserved by the operation of democratic norms or structures, either separately or in some combination. Both of these now appear a much more questionable basis on which to sustain a convincing theory. Let us take first the case predicated upon democratic norms. The assumption must be that these represent a universal facet of democracy in all conditions. But plainly the matter is not so straightforward. In a telling argument, one author has challenged the notion that liberalism is operative only between democratic states—that it is in some sense mobilized only interactively. As against this, his counter-claim is that its impact is

more wide-ranging and resides 'in the nature of the liberal political project itself'
(Macmillan 1996: 299). He thus argues, contra Doyle and Russett, that the liberal
peace cannot be a *separate* peace. If the norm operates, 'its restraining potential is
not relational in nature', as it is independent of the 'political character of the
adversary'. The conclusion is then that such liberal norms are 'constitutive rather
than interactive' (Macmillan 1996: 287). The point is well made and has considerable merit in context. But it also has the wider implication that democratic
norms, if constitutive, must in effect be changeable rather than given by nature.
Is it then safe to assume that democratic norms, as presently constituted, remain
the same as in earlier periods? In any case, how does any such notion deal with the
potential diversity of democratic norms? If, as suggested above, the democratic
ideal favoured by the West is one inescapably rooted in liberal individualism, is
this a necessary part of all democratic norms? It is this kind of objection that
informs the view that it is 'difficult to envisage a common democratic space at the
global level in the absence of reasonably common democratic traditions at the
national one' (Resnick 1998: 132). In short, we are faced with the problem of
drawing consistent conclusions about the impact of a set of norms that may well
be changeable across time, as well as diverse at any one point in time. Are the
norms of low-intensity democracy the same as those within a fully democratized
culture of civil society? Are democratic norms the same in the neo-liberal state as
within states wedded to forms of social democracy?

Secondly, if not by common norms, does democracy keep the peace by its
enduring structures and institutions? This raises a series of further questions.
How well do democratic institutions function within the problematic setting of
globalized disjuncture? Given the lack of fit between polity and social flows, and
the policy leakage that characterizes this situation, how effectively can democracy
exercise restraint? If the efficacy of democracy in general is questionable—it having been 'hollowed out'—it would be a remarkable coincidence indeed if the one
remaining area in which it was thought to be still influential was in the preserva-
tion of peace. Can democracy be said to have lost control of interest rates, but still
have world peace firmly in its grasp? The notion, once thus articulated, beggars
belief. Either the suggestion of democratic incapacity must be flawed, or the
premises of the democratic peace theory become themselves highly suspect.

This turns the discussion around to the projected solutions to the democratic
deficit. At their core is the recommendation that domestic underproduction can
now be remedied only by a globalization of the production of democracy itself. It
has already been pointed out that this falls much too conveniently into the mainstream of neo-liberal globalization—national democracies have 'no choice' but to
restructure themselves in order to compete more effectively in the global market
for democracy. But the argument also rests on an artificial separation between
the internalized democratic order, at the state level, and the externalized international order that is presumed to exist apart from it—even at the same moment
as it seeks to forge a relationship between the two. Moreover, the separation is further confirmed when the latter is held out as the potential saviour of the former.
Such an image of separation and salvation is more than implied in some of the

expressions used by the cosmopolitan democrats. This, in turn, depends on the presumption that they are independent entities that need to be *brought* into conjunction with each other. 'The establishment of a cosmopolitan model of democracy', Held maintains, 'is a way of seeking to strengthen democracy "within" communities and civil associations by elaborating and reinforcing democracy from "outside" through a network of regional and international agencies' (1995*a*: 237). What this fails to address is how it might be that a collective of democracies, deemed to be failing from within, should then have the capacity to construct viable democratic structures beyond themselves. One might be forgiven for pointing out that the diagnosis of the problem somewhat contradicts the proposed solution. One might then also suggest that Held's argument is substantially correct, but for the wrong reasons. The fate of the democratic state is attached to the international order, not in the sense that the latter can now rectify the problems of the former, but because the former is already and indistinguishably a part of the latter.

If this is the case, the democratic state and the international order must be considered to be entering a phase of renewed mutual constitution. What does this mean in practice? It means, at the very least, the commencement of a testing, and likely costly, process of political adjustment. While the recent period of neoliberal globalization has privileged the international at the expense of the domestic, the main dislocations have shown up domestically and this is the reason for the apparent crisis of democracy. However, the notion that this is some kind of 'isolated' domestic crisis is wholly illusory, since the globalized democratic state works this way as part of a wider order. For the same reason, the problem cannot be solved by simple extensions of democratic practice into the realm beyond, as if this is itself divorced from the shortcomings showing up within the state. The crisis of democracy, if that is what it is, is symptomatic of that rebalancing of domestic and international forces currently under way, and which occurs through the medium of states.

This returns the discussion to issues considered in the previous chapter about the normative basis of the state and reconfigurations of community. It is assuredly here that the major transitions are taking place. If there is some validity in the notions set out in that chapter, they are equally germane in the present context. It was previously suggested that the nature of the national community might be changing, possibly from a constitutive to a co-operative association. At the same time, and as a matter of degree, it was hypothesized that there might be some evidence for the state, as normative structure, developing a more pluralist nature. These arguments were based on the actualities of state practice in that a diminished production of services evoked fewer obligations in return. Perhaps the account of democratic transition needs to be located within the same general framework: the state which delivers less—underproduces—has less need to be accountable to its citizens, who in turn are content to receive a smaller democratic dividend. The erosion of democracy can thus be seen, not as the consequence of some exogenous force working from the outside, but as a symptom of changing state–society relations at the heart of the democratic state itself.

In their quest for a solution, the cosmopolitan democrats pay too much attention to one side of the equation. If what is going wrong is the dislocation created between global communities of practical interdependence and national systems of democratic governance—because, as Held says, they no longer seem 'symmetrical' or 'congruent'—then the solution, according to the cosmopolitan democrats, must be to chase off in pursuit of the democratization of those affairs that have leaked out from the territorial state into the international order. But thought needs to be given to addressing the problem from the other end as well—at the source of this leakage, and its causes. In large measure, it is this reconstitution of the state that supports the global processes under way, and all the cosmopolitan democracy in the world will not do much, on its own, to impede their progress. Democracy needs to be brought home before it can be exported abroad, and not simply the other way around. In the words of one commentator, 'democracy can be deepened only if it is globalized, and it can be globalized only if it is deepened' (Sakamoto 1991: 122).

Democracy and IR theory

Democracy thus seems to assert its presence in IR theory in two respects. The first is its potential for modifying the condition of anarchy between democratic states. The second, by extension, is the analysis of the factors conducive to the spread of democracy. These, respectively, have been called the Kantian and the Hegelian dimensions of the issue (Ray 1995: 6).

It was suggested at the outset that the engagement with democracy has traditionally been peripheral to IR theory's main concerns. Such a divorce occurred because the 'Westphalian approach to sovereignty allowed democratic and IR theorists to ignore each other' (Wendt 1996: 61). This is no longer the case, largely because the perceived robustness of the Hegelian dimension at the end of the cold war lent added value to the study of the Kantian claim. On this basis, the plea was entered that 'analysts of international politics ought to pay more attention to a topic left until recently . . . mostly to area specialists and analysts of comparative politics' (Ray 1995: 204). But we can add that IR theory needs to be interested not only in the international aspects of democratization, and in the liberal peace, but also in democratic efficacy in conditions of globalization. This last aspect brings an important, and neglected, perspective to bear on the other two.

If it is true that theories of the state have now been brought back in to the heartland of enquiry, then it can be said in addition that theorizing the democratic state is now a core concern of the subject. The chapter will conclude with a number of propositions, drawn from the above analysis, which serve to establish this claim.

The first refers directly to the discussion of globalization, democratization, and the liberal peace. In crude summation of the points made above, it might be said that globalization serves to unravel the teasing, and often contradictory, claims made under these headings. This is best accessed through the specific projections that were made in the early 1990s—optimistic and pessimistic—about the likely state of international relations in the post-cold war world. For the pessimists, the end of the cold war was taken to represent the termination of that peculiar geopolitical constellation that had given rise to high levels of international integration. The gloomy expectation was of a succeeding phase that would be marked by disintegration, renewed conflict, and a return to unilateralism. As against this, the optimists argued that those very forces of integration, which had been promoted by the cold war, had served finally to bring it to an end. This would ensure a basic continuity in these trends. This was the argument that Jervis articulated so powerfully:

These dramatic breaks from the past and the general peacefulness of the West are to be explained by increases in the costs of war, decreases in its benefits and, linked to this, changes in domestic regimes and values . . . these changes in the developed world are so deep, powerful, and interlocked that they cannot readily be reversed by any foreseeable event. (1991/2: 47)

The peaceful nature of the ending of the cold war was also adduced as compelling evidence of the deep-seated transformations that had taken place. Had it been otherwise, we might have expected a global conflagration to mark its passing. Jervis's point is not narrowly an example of the democratic peace theory but it bears at least a strong family resemblance to that theory. And it is against this view of radical transformation that the post-cold war pessimists have set out their alternative stall (Mearsheimer 1990, 1994/5). By the mid-1990s, pessimism had also affected Hegelian expectations about the spread of democracy. 'In short, the "third wave" toward democratization of the globe', Ray remarked, 'seems at present to be receding' (1995: 49).

It is this debate about the fundamental nature of the post-cold war order that continues to be deeply embroiled in the issues of globalization and democratization. As already indicated, the linkages are perplexing and often circular. This can be briefly illustrated. Whereas some arguments give predominance in their explanation of the peace to the democratic nature of the states involved, others argue that peace is a product of the interlocking of their relationships in such a way that war cannot be fought without unacceptable cost. It would then follow that globalization, rather than democratic norms and structures, has wrought the transformation in international politics. A second spin on these themes is the view that the greater incidence of peace makes it easier for regimes to be democratic, and so it is the peace that creates democracy and not the other way round. States more likely to be involved in wars, Layne asserted, were more likely to adopt autocratic forms (1994: 45). A third variant is that democracies were peaceful towards each other only during the cold war period, thus suggesting that 'common interests' rather than 'common polities' were at work (Farber and Gowa 1995: 124). But what is the role of globalization in this? As already discussed, is the spread of democratization to be viewed as only an accidental accompaniment to globalization, or is it in some sense an essential and integral part of it? In these various, and unresolved, debates we can see the extent to which democracy now occupies a central position in theories of international relations.

The impact that it has depends on technical debates within the democratic peace literature, as previously encountered. The anomaly identified by some critics is that the peace is claimed to derive from some essential quality of democracy, and yet it is operative only within the relational context of other democracies (Layne 1994: 8). The significance of this in a discussion of globalization relates back to the question of which aspect of democracy produces the peaceful constraint—the institutional or the normative, or, in an alternative formulation, the structural or the cultural (Ray 1995: 30). If globalization undercuts democracy, which set of constraints is weakened as a result? Intuitively, and following the cosmopolitan democracy analysis recounted above, it would appear that it is the institutional or structural constraints that are most at risk, since there is nothing in the nature of globalization that, by itself, would erode democratic norms or culture. It is the effectiveness of their institutional implementation that is rendered vulnerable.

Whether this then matters depends, in turn, upon which of the dimensions of democracy is deemed the more constraining in its effects. Some analysts have challenged the institutional explanations within the democratic peace on the grounds that, if they work, they should work in all cases, regardless of the political complexion of the opponent. 'If citizens and policymakers of a democracy were especially sensitive to the human and material costs of war,' Layne insists, 'that sensitivity should be evident whenever their state is on the verge of war' (1994: 12). The institutional argument is for similar reasons questioned by Siverson (1995: 486). If it is the institutional part of the democratic peace argument that is damaged by globalization—but this is the less convincing half of the argument in any case—the theory may retain validity on the basis of its cultural or normative leg alone. In this case, the globalization of democracy, if it is to be a source of peace, must be interpreted as a strengthening of democratic norms: it means a penetration of democracy into civil society and the emergence of a transnational civil society as a result (Sakamoto 1991: 122).

Secondly, International Relations theory is much preoccupied these days with the topic of 'identity' (Krause and Renwick 1996a; Lapid and Kratochwil 1996). We have already encountered this in the context of both the security state and the normative state. As far as the present chapter is concerned, this reminds us that any apparent failings of democracy are not to be understood simply as inadequacies generated by external circumstances. We previously noted Chris Brown's admonition, in terms of moral theory, that questions about what I should do are translatable into the question 'Who am I?' If this is the case in normative theory, it has considerable applicability to democratic theory as well. The unsettled condition of national democracies as much reflects puzzling developments about identity emerging from 'within', as it is imposed from 'without'. What the identity of the democratic state is at any given point in time is a composite of what it wishes to be, set in the context of the wider order of which it is a part: change in either has repercussions for both. Indeed, it might be best to think of political globalization as a manifestation of this kind of transformation. In that sense, globalization as such is not the 'cause' of anything: it is simply a way of speaking about these problems of identity, and its volatile quality at the moment. For this reason, the study of contemporary democratic forms is inescapably a way of addressing issues of identity that are paramount for any satisfactory theory of International Relations.

Finally, it is also clear from the pervasive discussion throughout this chapter that understanding the role of democracy in contemporary international relations is a convenient demonstration of a constructivist approach. In the various explorations that have taken place, this has been the underlying theoretical theme. The point can be further demonstrated in a specific, and in a more general, sense.

The particular example relates back to the arguments about the democratic peace. A recent exponent of constructivism claims that it is 'perfectly suited to the task of testing and fundamentally revising the democratic peace' (Hopf 1998: 192). The reason for this, it is suggested, is that 'if democracies do not fight each other, then it must be because of the way they understand each other'. This repeats the argument previously set out by Risse-Kappen. 'I claim that democracies to a large degree create their enemies and their friends', he maintains, 'by inferring either aggressive or defensive motives from the domestic structures of their counterparts' (1995*b*: 492). It is also compatible with the suggestion that democratic norms and institutions are both rooted in liberal ideas that become the cause of the differing behaviour toward democratic, and non-democratic, states. It is those same liberal ideas, in this account, which 'cause liberal democracies to tend away from war with one another', at the same time as they 'prod these states into war with illiberal states' (Owen 1994: 88). What constructs peaceableness in the one context is precisely what induces bellicosity in the other.

But the claim of this chapter is broader than any such specific application would seem to imply. The suggestion here is that those difficulties with which the contemporary democratic state is apparently beset are symptomatic of the way in which state transformation and the international order are reshaping each other. There is no denying that the democratic potential of the state is circumscribed by the wider order of which it is a part. But more than this needs to be said to make sense of the contemporary situation. In turn, the kind of order that we enjoy is itself a reflection of the forms of state that sustain it. In his early diagnosis of the problems of contemporary democracy, Held correctly delineated the effects of globalization on both the state and the relations among them (1991: 203). What he failed to make clear was the integral, and reflexive, nature of both sets of developments. The theme of globalization requires that we now do so.

This compels us to move beyond another version of the Great Divide. In its summary form, this maintains that the democratic shortcomings of the contemporary state have arisen because of the growth of globalized forces that disempower it from the outside. As a result, its democratic procedures barely conceal the nakedness within. If the situation is to be retrieved, the scope of democratic accountability must be extended beyond the state so that it matches the global reach of the influences that wash up on its shores. Such an analysis fails to take due account of the reciprocal manner in which democratic deficits on the inside have been the necessary accomplices of globalization. This alternative perspective helps make sense of those puzzling circularities—in the relationship between democracy, peace, and globalization—explored throughout this chapter. It is futile to seek for any causal primacy amongst them, since they are substantially embodiments of each other.

CONCLUSION

It has been the goal of this book to encourage a dialogue between globalization and IR theory in order to enrich thinking about both. The volume has adopted a particular perspective on globalization that emphasizes its occurrence within a single field of political forces in which both domestic and international constituents engage each other. The state is the principal arena within which this engagement takes place, and it is from the resulting transformations that the main points of theoretical interest emerge. By reviewing these, the book has sought to contribute to the current debates about IR theory but will hopefully also have enhanced our understanding of the political dynamics of globalization itself.

The task has been anything but straightforward, given the uncertainties associated with the concept of globalization. It is impossible to present a consensus position on this contested term, as there is no single dimension of life that can be presented as the 'real' embodiment of globalization, nor can a neutral definition be arrived at that avoids all normative judgements. Nonetheless, despite the dissension surrounding the term, it does depict a range of significant developments across a wide social field. The precise degree to which these have taken hold remains a matter of debate, but at the very least we should accept that they have the potential to destabilize our existing analytical frameworks. It is the task of theory to make as much sense of this as it can.

As has been seen, there are commentators who would dismiss globalization as no more than a fashionable myth and who dispute the evidence for its occurrence (Ascherson 1997; Miles 1997). When they do so, however, they invariably argue from within a narrow—usually economic—perspective. But economic data alone can no more dismiss the case for globalization in all its other manifestations—especially in the sphere of cognitive change—than a positive case why IR theory should take globalization theory seriously can be mounted on any such slender base. In these pages, globalization has been treated as a multi-dimensional process, even if more discernible in some areas than in others. This book has followed a fine line, confirming neither the excessively hyperglobalist, nor the curtly dismissive 'globaloney', schools of thought. It has taken globalization seriously enough to warrant a systematic review of its theoretical implications for International Relations, but remains agnostic about its more alarmist or millenarian appeals. This agnosticism is rooted in a historically informed political sensitivity that is deeply suspicious of claims about inexorable trends in either direction. The remainder of this concluding chapter will support that position by drawing together three stages of the unfolding argument: first, the claims that have been made about the nature of globalization; secondly, what these tell us about the capacities of states to engage in various dimensions of international relations; and thirdly, the wider significance of all this for theories of international relations.

Globalization

As previously detailed, much of the debate about globalization is dominated by arguments about its supposedly malign or benign effects. This is abundantly clear in the reviews generated by Gray's (1998) book, many of which took exception to the dismally one-sided portrayal contained in its pages (see, typically, Desai 1998; Krugman 1998). Other similarly dystopic books (Greider 1997; Martin and Schumann 1997) have been responded to in the same spirit: whatever the vices of the current global economy, it *does* also have its bright, and progressive, side (Taylor 1997). This book has not joined directly in the substance of these debates. However, its central themes focus on the form in which these respective arguments have been presented. Both the pessimists and the optimists share a set of untenable assumptions about what it is that is driving globalization and how states relate to this process. Whether they regard the impacts of globalization as benign or malign, they are united in the belief that globalization is a causal force that restructures state behaviour from the outside. Once this assumption is challenged, the certainties on either side begin to crumble.

One of the few areas of minimal agreement concerns the polarization that globalization seems to entail. Economically, globalization creates winners and losers. But the polarities extend well beyond those who simply profit or lose by their position in the global market. They incorporate also ideas about access to global networks, lifestyles, and the security of cultural identities: 'rather than homogenizing the human condition, the technological annulment of temporal/spatial distances tends to polarize it', is one such verdict (Bauman 1998: 18). Another kindred assessment speaks of the 'incorporation into globalization of an increased polarization of society, both globally and locally' (Sjolander 1996: 609).

To be sure, even when such polarities are recognized, the political prescriptions attached to them still tend to diverge. As previously recounted, the globalization pessimists see polarization in terms of regressive immiseration, pauperization, and disempowerment for the losers. The optimists, on the other hand, continue to believe in globalization as the last best hope for narrowing the gulf in material conditions, for spreading the freedom of consumerism—'the sovereignty of consumers' is one disparaging reference to this position (Barber 1998)—and for liberation from parochial cultural oppression.

This basic agreement on the existence of polarity, however, is significant. At the very least, it draws attention to an absence of equilibrium. The polarization that has accompanied globalization occurs at multiple levels, cutting across states, regions, and the globe as a whole. The pervasive notion of 'glocalization' makes simultaneous appeal to the homogeneity of the globalizing forces, and to the heterogeneity of their expressions and effects. To this extent, the polarity of experience is itself readily accommodated within most formulations of globalization theory. The lack of equilibrium to which this gives rise reinforces the validity of the model of political dynamism set out in these pages. States both act to mitigate the effects of globalization and, at the same time, if unevenly, reconstitute themselves to accord with the new world that they have helped to bring into being. Globalization is what states have made of it, but they also pay the price. Such a political dynamic, with its potential for retreat and reversal, is highly unpredictable in its future outcomes. This is as true of the likely volatility within individual states as it is within groups of states, such as the perceived 'losers' in the South.

The same diagnosis emerges clearly from investigations into the degree of 'order' entailed by globalization. The point has been made that globalization is not a distinctive social order, but simply one which depends upon the globalization of power relations (Saurin 1997: 109). The implication is that globalization as social substance can be heterogeneous, so long as it is understood within the context of the universalization of power relations. This interpretation echoes other sociological appraisals that highlight the degree of disorder due to the absence of overall control associated with globalization. The general claim is that 'no one seems now to be in control' (Bauman 1998: 58). ' "Globalization" is not about what we all . . . wish or hope *to do*', it has been said; 'It is about *what is happening to us all*' (Bauman 1998: 60). From this point of view, globalized life imitates International Relations art, since there is a unified field of power politics but no sovereignty over the domain of the international (global) as a whole.

That analogy serves as a salutary reminder that images of globalized 'disorder', and of a world 'out of control', may be overstated. Certainly, there is no single guiding intelligence (sovereign) that can shape globalization in a uniform direction. But the progress of globalization remains susceptible to the processes of politics, in the same way that International Relations has traditionally discerned order as possible within a structure of anarchy. Just as international relations may lack centralized government without descending into chaos, so globalization may have no single logic without being immune to all political action. The error lies in assuming that, since there is no single authority to control it, globalization has escaped all checks and balances. There is no reason to make this assumption, however imperfect these checks and balances might often be. Paradoxically, the 'out of control' theme is run in tandem with the proposition that 'globalization and territorialization are *mutually complementary processes*' (Bauman 1998: 69), without admitting of the implicit tension between the two claims. Territorialization remains a check on globalization because, politically speaking, that is where we are left to pick up the pieces. This does not mean that politics guarantees a 'solution' to globalization, only that the latter does not, in fact—and despite repeated claims to the contrary—enjoy a free run.

State capacity

Globalization mostly finds its way into the literature of IR theory in the form of claims about the loss of state capacity. Typically, we are informed that 'states today act in an environment so transformed by market forces that no institution . . . can master it. In this environment the most unmanageable forces spring from a torrent of technological innovations' (Gray 1998: 76). Globalization is thereby presented as an exogenous, technology-driven process that creates a new environment in which states must find their way. At best, they react uniformly in response; at worst, they can no longer be said to act at all. It is this type of understanding that needs to be dispelled.

The book has, indeed, surveyed various forms of state capacity in conditions of globalization. The reason for doing so was not to engage in substantive debates about the retreat of the state but to suggest, by way of alternative, that we should think about globalization and state adaptation as a single process, not separately as active cause and passive effect. Whatever the particular strengths and weaknesses of states today in various policy domains, this situation has been brought about as much by reconfiguration from within as by imposition from without. There are winners and losers in both domains—domestic and international—and this lies at the heart of both state transformation and globalization. It is this that lends a restless quality to the present condition of globalization, and calls into question facile attempts to plot its future trajectory.

The argument from the state's incapacity to produce sovereignty is the most fundamental of all, since this is not merely a commodity to be traded, but the essential constituent of the international market itself. Change in sovereignty thus shows up in all other aspects of state performance. That said, much of the contemporary discussion of the 'end of sovereignty' is misplaced. Claims that 'all three legs of the "sovereignty tripod" have been broken beyond repair', since 'military, economic and cultural self-sufficiency' are no longer viable (Bauman 1998: 63–4), can be dismissed as tendentious. Sovereignty has never been static and, under its rubric, states have delegated and devolved a range of powers; they have also arrogated new ones, and continue to do so. The sovereignty game, to this extent, has always been fluid in its constitutive rules, and globalization encapsulates this latest phase. Globalization, however, cannot be construed as a force apart from the practice of sovereignty, reshaping it from the outside. Instead, the changing practices of sovereignty register in the development of globalization, and signal the transitions taking place. Sovereignty and globalization actively refashion each other, and should not be thought of as each other's negations.

The continuing vitality of state policy control seems most doubtful in the economic realm. It is here that the state is depicted as suffering the greatest damage from the buffeting storms of globalization. This conventional image does little to elucidate the import of globalization. It reiterates the diagnosis that the state is hollowed out on the inside, as a consequence of forces impacting from the outside. The play of globalization is, however, much more subtle. Changes in state power, in Weiss's words, 'have to do not with diminution but with reconstitution of power around the consolidation of domestic and international linkages' (1998: 209). In part, globalization itself is an emanation of these changing economic functions of state, and not their cause. Changes in state identity are most manifest in the economic sphere and the rearticulations of interest, and the modalities of economic management, reflect those changes. State transformation precedes and accompanies economic globalization, and is not some incidental and contingent effect that occurs in its aftermath.

The end of the territorial state is thought by many to herald the demise of the security state, since, historically, defence of territory is what the state did best. Does the new security agenda, and the potentially lower profile of military-territorial aspects within it, portend the state's progressive inability to produce security? As against this widespread interpretation, the book has argued that the state's performance in the security field cannot be understood within such an 'externalist' framework alone. The nature of, and the expectations about, security are not fixed points of state identity, but reflect the complex interactions between the domestic and international bargains of which they are a part. Arguably, as the state becomes less distinctively the producer of a range of economic, social, and human rights goods, domestic bargains are renegotiated as to what citizens are prepared to sacrifice for the state, and expect from it in return. This shows up in the type of security activities in which states are prepared to engage, and the extent to which they are willing to pursue them unilaterally. Globalized security agendas are as much a reflection of these new domestic accommodations as autonomous sources that have brought them into being.

The changing security characteristics of the state are, in this way, intimately bound up with its changing normative basis. What kind of value community is the state and for what purposes does it exist? There are few, if any, timeless answers to these questions. This is not to imply that the state can simply reinvent itself as it sees fit. These are not matters of state 'free will', as it were: to be sure, the range of choice in state moral identity is constrained from the outside as well. This is attested by the spread of human rights doctrines in recent decades, as well as by the need of states to emulate the normative successes of their peers—just as they once emulated the example set by their military-administrative practices.

But any sense that there is a crisis of the normative state must be placed in the context of this unbundling of domestic bargains. The state moves along the spectrum of normative cohesion—variably as between policy concerns—in simultaneous response to the counter-pressures arising from the demand pull from within, and the supply push from without. Commensurate movements also take place in the degree of moral solidarism expressed within the international system. There is the potential for more rapid change when, as argued above, the factors of normative production seem themselves to be highly mobile. However, the state is not made redundant by such mobility, nor is it merely the structural prisoner of their movement. It is a key player in the redefinition of community, within and beyond the state. The globalized normative order tells us much about what is happening at the state level, and is not merely the operative structure within which states are compelled to 'reidentify' themselves.

Much the same is true of the democratic state, and for much the same reasons. The preceding chapter has demonstrated that there are deep-seated confusions within the existing literature. It seems to hold that democracy is under erosion from global forces while simultaneously insisting that a peaceful international order remains the outcome of these selfsame 'second image' democratic practices. There are profound tensions at the heart of these competing positions. And yet these tensions accurately describe the complex reality uncovered in a more reflexive interpretation of the state acting through globalization, just as globalization acts through the state. The democratic state is no more hollowed out as a domestic institution by the marauding 'external' forces of globalization than the democratic peace is sustained by the purely 'domestic' qualities of democratic statehood. Both sets of arguments require precisely the artificial separation that it has been the endeavour of this volume to subvert.

The untenable dualism underpinning images of the state besieged by a globalizing environment needs to be rejected. In its stead, we can concur, albeit for different reasons, with the verdict that 'globalization is not necessarily best understood as an independent variable that "affects" the nation-state and its policy capabilities' (Axtmann 1998*b*: 18).

Theory of international relations

What is the significance of the foregoing argument for IR theory? Specific points have been addressed in the course of this work and need not be itemized at this stage. It suffices to conclude with a general summation. In the first instance, and as reiterated throughout, globalization offers a strategy for overcoming the Great Divide. Indeed, any intelligible analysis of globalization requires us to proceed in this fashion. We can, in summary, agree with the rejection of the distinction between the intranational and international domains, since globalization itself 'rests on the proposition that domestic and international politics have been inextricably intertwined from the start' (Cerny 1996*a*: 620–1).

But how is this intertwining to be theoretically described? It is best done, at a general theoretical level, by appeal to a form of constructivist analysis. This is not to suggest that constructivism is a theory which 'explains' globalization. It assuredly does not: to say that state and globalization are mutually constituted provides an insight into the character of their relationship but does not, by itself, provide any account of the substance of globalization, nor of why it should have moved in this historical direction in the first place. To do all these things, constructivism would need to import much from beyond its own intrinsic claims. It can provide the analytical outline, but needs other bodies of theory to help colour it in.

The more modest assertion of this book is that globalization conforms to, and requires, an analytical scheme that is fully compatible with the salient character-

istics of constructivism. This proceeds from the assumption that states do not
have given or fixed identities. For the same reason, the identity of the society
(international or global) in which states find themselves should not be regarded
as finally settled either, even if elements of it display considerable durability over
long periods of time. Each adapts to changes in the other, although the mutuality
need not in any way be symmetric: at different historical phases, the state or the
international system may respectively, so to speak, have the upper hand.

This is not to lapse into some kind of idealistic voluntarism, nor to claim that
it is only cognitive processes that matter. It has been said of constructivism that it
assumes the 'building blocks of international reality are ideational as well as material' (Ruggie 1998: 33). Such a view is endorsed in these pages because it reminds
us that there is a material context as well. In the case of globalization, this is
demonstrably the case, as aspects of it are indeed dependent upon technological
developments, such as in transport and communications, as enabling conditions.
What constructivism brings to the discussion is an important emphasis on the
ideational. Globalization is no mere material structure that constrains state
behaviour, but is itself reflective of movement in ideas about what states are, and
what roles they can best perform.

Constructivism problematizes the nature of state identity. It is tolerant of
'transformation as a normal feature of international politics' (Ruggie 1998: 27),
without necessarily requiring it. Critically, however, it brings state and system
into a relationship of mutual adjustment. In Wendt's formulation, 'state interests
are in important part constructed by systemic structures, not exogenous to them'
(1995: 72–3). All such claims are sympathetic to the foregoing account of globalization—as a description of the changing identity of states within the changing
identity of the social universe that surrounds, and suffuses, them.

It remains to bring to life this abstract and formulaic description by specific
application to globalization. What is the relevance of constructivism to its analysis and how do globalization and constructivism in unison improve on existing
theoretical schemes couched within the Great Divide? They do so by providing
integrative strategies that deny the dichotomy between globalization as external
cause and state transformation as internal effect. More specifically, they allow us
to overcome a number of associated, and theoretically troublesome, separations.
Two examples make the more general point.

First, the focus on globalization responds to a particular challenge that has
been issued to IR theory. It meets the complaint that the state system and transnational forces are parallel developments, rather than negations of each other. The
one presupposes the other and, it has been claimed, the recent resurgence of
transnationalism merely reveals 'the dynamic of the international system as it has
been operating for half a millennium' (Halliday 1995: 54). Such an integration of
state, state system, and transnational forces is precisely the kind of framework to
which the analysis of globalization aspires.

Secondly, it deals also with Halliday's rebuke that IR theory has conventionally
ignored capitalism as an institution (1995: 39). For the IR theorist, globalization
needs to be viewed as more than a theory of the capitalist system, but it is

nonetheless a theory that takes capitalism seriously. It recognizes that capitalism operates both through and beyond states and that in so doing is an important constituent of their (changing) identity. Globalization is precisely a set of claims about the most recent accommodation between state interest and capitalism, and accepts their intimate embrace. But the model of globalization advanced in these pages is distrustful of claims that the former is simply a creature of the latter. It also takes seriously their *mutuality*.

Finally, globalization offers a framework within which political change can be understood. Critics of constructivism have denounced it on the grounds that although 'it is deeply concerned with radically changing state behaviour, it says little about how change comes about' (Mearsheimer 1995: 91). Whatever its validity as a critique of constructivism in general, this charge is wide of the mark when applied to an account of globalization as set out in this book. Indeed, if globalization does anything, it makes possible a theory of change. When Rosenberg criticized realism for its neglect of change, he did so for the reason that it took state identity as a given, anterior to the structure in which it was then placed, and by which it was then constrained. He viewed this as ahistorical (1994: 28). Globalization offers the same kind of corrective. By providing an integrated and dynamic account, it takes for granted neither the identity of the state nor the identity of the system.

Above all, the analysis in this book is predicated upon a notion of political dynamism that is itself the source of change. Globalization causes polarization and seems to spiral out of control. The more it does so, the more it evokes counter-tendencies that express themselves at the state level, in the absence of effective alternative sites for doing so. The outcome at any one historical period is, to this extent, open-ended. We can then confirm an earlier finding, albeit reached by a different interpretative route: 'Interdependence and globalisation are . . . always changeable, as well as manipulable, conditions, and it is in the realm of the "political" that the immediate sources of such change or manipulation are to be found' (Barry Jones 1995: 15). This does not predetermine the course of change, but certainly locates it at the centre of theoretical investigation. Once we accept that globalization is not some end-state in the course of realization, but instead is an ongoing political struggle, IR theory can more readily accommodate it. Both may be enriched as a result.

BIBLIOGRAPHY

ADLER, E. (1997), 'Imagined (Security) Communities: Cognitive Regions in International Relations', *Millennium*, 26 (2).

ALBROW, M. (1996), *The Global Age: State and Society beyond Modernity* (Cambridge).

ALLOTT, P. (1997), 'Kant or Won't: Theory and Moral Responsibility', *Review of International Studies*, 23 (3).

ALTVATER, E. and MAHNKOPF, B. (1997), 'The World Market Unbound', in Scott (1997a).

AMIN, A. and THRIFT, N. (1994a) (eds.), *Globalization, Institutions, and Regional Development in Europe* (Oxford).

—— —— (1994b), 'Holding Down the Global', in Amin and Thrift (1994a).

—— —— (1994c), 'Living in the Global', in Amin and Thrift (1994a).

AMIN, S. (1996), 'The challenge of globalization', *Review of International Political Economy*, 3 (2).

AMOORE, L. *et al.* (1996), 'Overturning "Globalisation": Resisting the Teleological, Reclaiming the Political', paper presented to the 21st BISA Annual Conference, University of Durham, 16–18 Dec.

ANDERSON, B. (1983), *Imagined Communities: Reflections on the Origin and Spread of Nationalism* (London).

ANDREWS, D. M. (1994), 'Capital Mobility and State Autonomy: Toward a Structural Theory of International Monetary Relations', *International Studies Quarterly*, 38 (2).

ARCHIBUGI, D. (1998), 'Principles of Cosmopolitan Democracy', in Archibugi, Held, and Kohler (1998).

—— (1997), 'Technological Globalisation and National Systems of Innovation: An Introduction', in Archibugi and Michie (1997).

—— and HELD, D. (1995) (eds.), *Cosmopolitan Democracy: An Agenda for a New World Order* (Cambridge).

—— —— and KOHLER, M. (1998) (eds.), *Re-imagining Political Community: Studies in Cosmopolitan Democracy* (Cambridge).

—— and MICHIE, J. (1997) (eds.), *Technology, Globalisation and Economic Performance* (Cambridge).

ARMSTRONG, D. (1998), 'Globalization and the Social State', *Review of International Studies*, 24 (4).

ASCHERSON, N. (1997), 'Don't Be Fooled: Multinationals Do Not Rule the World', *Independent*, 12 Jan.

ASHLEY, R. K. (1988), 'Untying the Sovereign State: A Double Reading of the Anarchy Problematique', *Millennium*, 17 (2).

AVINERI, S. and DE-SHALIT, A. (1992a) (eds.), *Communitarianism and Individualism* (Oxford).

AVINERI, S. and DE-SHALIT, A. (1992b), 'Introduction', in Avineri and de-Shalit (1992a).

AXFORD, B. (1995), *The Global System: Economics, Politics and Culture* (Cambridge).

AXTMANN, R. (1998a) (ed.), *Globalization and Europe: Theoretical and Empirical Investigations* (London).

—— (1998b), 'Globalization, Europe and the State: Introductory Reflections', in Axtmann (1998a).

AYOOB, M. (1997), 'Defining Security: A Subaltern Realist Perspective', in Krause and Williams (1997).

BALDWIN, D. (1997), 'The Concept of Security', *Review of International Studies*, 23 (1).

—— (1993) (ed.), *Neorealism and Neoliberalism: The Contemporary Debate* (New York).

BANKS, M. and SHAW, M. (1991) (eds.), *State and Society in International Relations* (Hemel Hempstead).

BANURI, T. and SCHOR, J. B. (1992), *Financial Openness and National Autonomy* (Oxford).

BARBER, B. (1998), 'Disneyfication that Impoverishes Us All', *Independent*, 29 Aug.

—— (1996), 'Three Challenges to Reinventing Democracy', in Hirst and Khilnani (1996).

BARKIN, J. S. (1998), 'The Evolution of the Constitution of Sovereignty and the Emergence of Human Rights Norms', *Millennium*, 27 (2).

—— and CRONIN, B. (1994), 'The State and the Nation: Changing Norms and Rules of Sovereignty in International Relations', *International Organization*, 48 (1).

BARRY, B. and GOODIN, R. (1992) (eds.), *Free Movement: Ethical Issues in the Transnational Migration of People and Money* (University Park, Md.).

BARRY JONES, R. J. (1997), 'Globalisation versus Community', *New Political Economy*, 2 (1).

—— (1995), *Globalisation and Interdependence in the International Political Economy: Rhetoric and Reality* (London).

BAUMAN, Z. (1998), *Globalization: The Human Consequences* (Cambridge).

BAYLIS, J. and SMITH, S. (1997) (eds.), *The Globalization of World Politics: An Introduction to International Relations* (Oxford).

BEETHAM, D. (1998), 'Human Rights and Cosmopolitan Democracy', in Archibugi, Held, and Kohler (1998).

BEITZ, C. (1979), *Political Theory and International Relations* (Princeton).

BELL, D. V. J. (1993), 'Global Communications, Culture, and Values: Implications for Global Security', in Dewitt, Haglund, and Kirton (1993).

BELLAMY, R. and CASTIGLIONE, D. (1998), 'Between Cosmopolis and Community: Three Models of Rights and Democracy within the European Union', in Archibugi, Held, and Kohler (1998).

BERNARD, M. (1997), 'Ecology, Political Economy and the Counter-movement: Karl Polanyi and the Second Great Transformation', in Gill and Mittelman (1997).

BERRY, C. J. (1989), *The Idea of a Democratic Community* (Hemel Hempstead).

BEST, G. (1995), 'Justice, International Relations and "Human Rights"', *International Affairs*, 71 (4).

BETTS, R. K. (1992), 'Systems for Peace or Causes of War? Collective Security, Arms Control, and the New Europe', *International Security*, 17 (1).

BIDDISS, M. (1994), 'Global Interdependence and the Study of Modern World History', in Parry (1994).

BIERSTEKER, T. J. and WEBER, C. (1996a) (eds.), *State Sovereignty as Social Construct* (Cambridge).

—— —— (1996b), 'The Social Construction of State Sovereignty', in Biersteker and Weber (1996a).

BIRCH, A. H. (1993), *The Concepts and Theories of Modern Democracy* (London).

BOOTH, K. (forthcoming), 'Three Tyrannies', in Dunne and Wheeler (forthcoming).

—— (1998*a*) (ed.), *Statecraft and Security: The Cold War and Beyond* (Cambridge).

—— (1998*b*), 'Cold Wars of the Mind', in Booth (1998*a*).

—— (1998*c*), 'Conclusion: Security within Global Transformations', in Booth (1998*a*).

—— (1991), 'Security and Emancipation', *Review of International Studies*, 17 (4).

—— and SMITH, S. (1995) (eds.), *International Relations Theory Today* (Cambridge).

BOWKER, M. (1997), 'Nationalism and the Fall of the USSR', in Scott (1997*a*).

—— and BROWN, R. (1993) (eds.), *From Cold War to Collapse: Theory and World Politics in the 1980s* (Cambridge).

BOYER, R. (1996), 'State and Market: A New Engagement for the Twenty-first Century?', in Boyer and Drache (1996).

—— and DRACHE, D. (1996) (eds.), *States against Markets: The Limits of Globalization* (London).

BRACE, L. and HOFFMAN, J. (1997*a*), *Reclaiming Sovereignty* (London).

—— —— (1997*b*), 'Introduction: Reclaiming Sovereignty', in Brace and Hoffman (1997*a*).

BRETHERTON, C. and PONTON, G. (1996) (eds.), *Global Politics: An Introduction* (Oxford).

BRIERLY, J. L. (1963), *The Law of Nations*, 6th edn. (London).

BRODIE, J. (1996), 'New State Forms, New Political Spaces', in Boyer and Drache (1996).

BROWN, C. (forthcoming), 'Universal Human Rights: A Critique', in Dunne and Wheeler (forthcoming).

—— (1995*a*), 'International Political Theory and the Idea of World Community', in Booth and Smith (1995).

—— (1995*b*), 'International Theory and International Society: The Viability of the Middle Way?', *Review of International Studies*, 21 (2).

—— (1992), *International Relations Theory: New Normative Approaches* (Hemel Hempstead).

BROWN, P. (1994), *A New Europe? Economic Restructuring and Social Exclusion* (London).

BROWN, R. (1995), 'Globalization and the End of the National Project', in Macmillan and Linklater (1995).

BROWN, S. (1994), 'World Interests and the Changing Dimensions of Security', in Klare and Thomas (1994).

—— (1992), *International Relations in a Changing Global System: Toward a Theory of the World Polity* (Boulder, Colo.).

BULL, H. (1977), *The Anarchical Society: A Study of Order in World Politics* (London).

—— (1966), 'The Grotian Conception of International Society', in Butterfield and Wight (1966).

BUTTERFIELD, H. and WIGHT, M. (1966) (eds.), *Diplomatic Investigations* (London).

BUZAN, B. (1995), 'Security, the State, the "New World Order", and Beyond', in Lipschutz (1995*a*).

—— (1993), 'From International System to International Society: Structural Realism and Regime Theory Meet the English School', *International Organization*, 47 (3).

—— (1991), *People, States and Fear: An Agenda for International Security Studies in the Post-Cold War Era* (London).

—— HELD, D., and McGREW, A. (1998), 'Realism vs Cosmopolitanism: A Debate', *Review of International Studies*, 24 (3).

—— JONES, C., and LITTLE, R. (1993), *The Logic of Anarchy: Neorealism to Structural Realism* (New York).

BUZAN, B. and WAEVER, O. (1997), 'Slippery? Contradictory? Sociologically Untenable? The Copenhagen School Replies', *Review of International Studies*, 23 (2).

CABLE, V. (1995), 'What is International Economic Security?', *International Affairs*, 71 (2).

CAMILLERI, J. A. and FALK, J. (1992), *The End of Sovereignty? The Politics of a Shrinking and Fragmenting World* (Aldershot).

—— JARVIS, A. P., and PAOLINI, A. J. (1995a) (eds.), *The State in Transition: Reimagining Political Space* (Boulder, Colo.).

—— —— —— (1995b), 'State, Civil Society, and Economy', in Camilleri, Jarvis, and Paolini (1995a).

CAMMACK, P. (1996), 'Domestic and International Regimes for the Developing World: The Doctrine for Political Development', in Gummett (1996).

CAPORASO, J. (1997), 'Across the Great Divide: Integrating Comparative and International Politics', *International Studies Quarterly*, 41 (4).

CASSESE, A. (1990), *Human Rights in a Changing World* (Oxford).

CERNY, P. G. (1996a), 'Globalization and Other Stories: The Search for a New Paradigm for International Relations', *International Journal*, 51 (4).

—— (1996b), 'What Next for the State?', in Kofman and Youngs (1996).

—— (1996c), 'International Finance and the Erosion of State Policy Capacity', in Gummett (1996).

—— (1995), 'Globalization and the Changing Logic of Collective Action', *International Organization*, 49 (4).

—— (1994), 'The Infrastructure of the Infrastructure? Toward "Embedded Financial Orthodoxy" in the International Political Economy', in Palan and Gills (1994).

—— (1993a), 'Plurilateralism: Structural Differentiation and Functional Conflict in the Post-Cold War World Order', *Millennium*, 22 (1).

—— (1993b) (ed.), *Finance and World Politics: Markets, Regimes and States in the Post-hegemonic Era* (Aldershot).

—— (1993c), 'The Political Economy of International Finance', in Cerny (1993b).

—— (1993d), 'The Deregulation and Re-regulation of Financial Markets in a More Open World', in Cerny (1993b).

—— (1993e), 'American Decline and the Emergence of Embedded Financial Orthodoxy', in Cerny (1993b).

—— (1990), *The Changing Architecture of Politics: Structure, Agency and the Future of the State* (London).

CHALK, P. (1998), 'The International Ethics of Refugees: A Case of Internal and External Political Obligation', *Australian Journal of International Affairs*, 52 (2).

CHIPMAN, J. (1993), 'Managing the Politics of Parochialism', *Survival*, 35 (1).

CHURCHILL, R. P. (1994) (ed.), *The Ethics of Liberal Democracy: Morality and Democracy in Theory and Practice* (Oxford).

CLARK, I. (1998), 'Beyond the Great Divide: Globalization and the Theory of International Relations', *Review of International Studies*, 24 (4).

—— (1997), *Globalization and Fragmentation: International Relations in the Twentieth Century* (Oxford).

COCHRAN, M. (1996), 'The Liberal Ironist, Ethics and International Relations Theory', *Millennium*, 25 (1).

—— (1995), 'Cosmopolitanism and Communitarianism in a Post-Cold War World', in Macmillan and Linklater (1995).

COHEN, R. (1994), 'Pacific Unions: A Reappraisal of the Theory that "Democracies Do Not Go to War with Each Other" ', *Review of International Studies*, 20 (3).

Cox, K. R. (1997a) (ed.), *Spaces of Globalization: Reasserting the Power of the Local* (New York).

—— (1997b), 'Introduction: Globalization and its Politics in Question', in Cox (1997a).

—— (1997c), 'Globalization and the Politics of Distribution: A Critical Assessment', in Cox (1997a).

Cox, M. (1998), 'Rebels Without a Cause? Radical Theorists and the World System after the Cold War', *New Political Economy*, 3 (3).

Cox, R. W. (1997), 'Democracy in Hard Times: Economic Globalization and the Limits to Liberal Democracy', in McGrew (1997a).

—— (1996a), *Approaches to World Order* (Cambridge).

—— (1996b), 'A Perspective on Globalization', in Mittelman (1996a).

—— (1996c), 'Production and Security', in Cox (1996a).

—— (1987), *Production, Power, and World Order: Social Forces in the Making of History* (New York).

CRAWFORD, B. (1995), 'Hawks, Doves, But No Owls: International Economic Interdependence and Construction of the New Security Dilemma', in Lipschutz (1995a).

CRAWFORD, J. and MARKS, S. (1998), 'The Global Democracy Deficit', in Archibugi, Held, and Kohler (1998).

CRONIN, J. E. (1996), *The World the Cold War Made: Order, Chaos and the Return of History* (New York).

CZEMPIEL, E.-O. and ROSENAU, J. N. (1989) (eds.), *Global Changes and Theoretical Challenges: Approaches to World Politics for the 1990s* (Lexington, Mass.).

DANCHEV, A. (1995) (ed.), *Fin de Siècle: The Meaning of the Twentieth Century* (London).

DANIELS, P. W. and LEVER, W. F. (1996) (eds.), *The Global Economy in Transition* (London).

DAVIS, M. J. (1996) (ed.), *Security Issues in the Post-Cold War World* (Cheltenham).

DESAI, M. (1998), 'Doom's Silverish Lining', *The Times Higher Education Supplement*, 26 June.

DESSLER, D. (1989), 'What's at Stake in the Agent–Structure Debate?', *International Organization*, 43 (3).

DEUDNEY, D. (1995), 'Political Fission: State Structure, Civil Society, and Nuclear Security Politics in the United States', in Lipschutz (1995a).

—— and IKENBERRY, G. J. (1994), 'After the Long War', *Foreign Policy*, 94.

DEVETAK, R. (1995), 'Incomplete States: Theories and Practices of Statecraft', in Macmillan and Linklater (1995).

DEWITT, D. (1993), 'Introduction: The New Global Order and the Challenges of International Security', in Dewitt, Haglund, and Kirton (1993).

—— HAGLUND, D., and KIRTON, J. (1993) (eds.), *Building a New Global Order: Emerging Trends in International Security* (Toronto).

DICKEN, P. (1992), *Global Shift: The Internationalization of Economic Activity*, 2nd edn. (London).

—— FORSGREN, M., and MALMBERG, A. (1994), 'The Local Embeddedness of Transnational Corporations', in Amin and Thrift (1994a).

DONNELLY, J. (forthcoming), 'The Social Construction of International Human Rights', in Dunne and Wheeler (forthcoming).

—— (1993), *International Human Rights* (Boulder, Colo.).

DORAN, C. F. (1991), *Systems in Crisis: New Imperatives of High Politics at Century's End* (Cambridge).

DORE, R. (1994), 'World Markets and Institutional Uniformity', in Parry (1994*a*).

DOUGLAS, I. R. (1996), 'The Fatality of Globalization', paper presented to the 21st BISA Annual Conference, University of Durham, 16–18 Dec.

DOWER, N. (1998), 'Human Rights, Global Ethics and Globalization', in Axtmann (1998*a*).

DOYLE, M. (1986), 'Liberalism and World Politics', *American Political Science Review*, 80 (4).

—— (1983), 'Kant, Liberal Legacies and Foreign Affairs', *Philosophy and Public Affairs*, 12 (3 and 4).

—— and IKENBERRY, G. J. (1997) (eds.), *New Thinking in International Relations Theory* (Boulder, Colo.).

DUNN, J. (1995) (ed.), *Contemporary Crisis of the Nation State?* (Oxford).

DUNNE, T. (1998), *Inventing International Society: A History of the English School* (Houndmills).

—— (1995), 'The Social Construction of International Society', *European Journal of International Relations*, 1 (3).

—— and WHEELER, N. (forthcoming) (eds.), *Human Rights in Global Politics* (Cambridge).

—— —— (1996), 'Hedley Bull's Pluralism of the Intellect and Solidarism of the Will', *International Affairs*, 72 (1).

DUNNING, J. (1994), *The Globalization of Business* (London).

DYER, H. C. (1997), *Moral Order/World Order: The Role of Normative Theory in the Study of International Relations* (Houndmills).

EDEN, L. and POTTER, E. H. (1993) (eds.), *Multinationals in the Global Political Economy* (London).

ELIAS, R. and TURPIN, J. (1994) (eds.), *Rethinking Peace* (Boulder, Colo.).

EPSTEIN, G. A. and GINTIS, H. (1992), 'International Capital Markets and the Limits of National Economic Policy', in Banuri and Schor (1992).

EVANGELISTA, M. (1997), 'Domestic Structure and International Change', in Doyle and Ikenberry (1997).

EVANS, P. B. (1993), 'Building an Integrative Approach to International and Domestic Politics: Reflections and Projections', in Evans, Jacobson, and Putnam (1993).

—— JACOBSON, H. K., and PUTNAM, R. D. (1993) (eds.), *Double-edged Diplomacy* (Berkeley).

—— RUESCHEMEYER, D., and SKOCPOL, T. (1985) (eds.), *Bringing the State Back In* (Cambridge).

EVANS, T. (1997), 'Democratization and Human Rights', in McGrew (1997*a*).

FALK, R. (1997*a*), 'State of Siege: Will Globalization Win Out?', *International Affairs*, 73 (1).

—— (1997*b*), 'Resisting "Globalisation-from-Above" through "Globalisation-from-Below" ', *New Political Economy*, 2 (1).

—— (1995), 'Regionalism and World Order after the Cold War', *Australian Journal of International Affairs*, 49 (1).

—— (1994), 'The Making of Global Citizenship', in van Steenbergen (1994).

FALKNER, G. and TALOS, E. (1994), 'The Role of the State within Social Policy', in Muller and Wright (1994*a*).

FARBER, H. and GOWA, J. (1995), 'Polities and Peace', *International Security*, 20 (2).

FAWCETT, L. and HURRELL, A. (1995) (eds.), *Regionalism in World Politics: Regional Organization and International Order* (Oxford).

FEATHERSTONE, M. (1990) (ed.), *Global Culture: Nationalism, Globalisation and Modernity* (London).

FELICE, W. F. (1996), *Taking Suffering Seriously: The Importance of Collective Human Rights* (Albany, NY).

FERGUSON, Y. H. and MANSBACH, R. W. (1996), *Polities: Authority, Identities, and Change* (Columbia, SC).

FREEDMAN, L. (1998), *The Revolution in Strategic Affairs*, Adelphi Paper 318 (Oxford).

FREEMAN, C. (1997), 'The "National System of Innovation" in Historical Perspective', in Archibugi and Michie (1997).

FRIEDEN, J. A. (1991), 'Invested Interests: The Politics of National Economic Policies in a World of Global Finance', *International Organization*, 45 (4).

FUKUYAMA, F. (1992), *The End of History and the Last Man* (London).

GADDIS, J. L. (1992/3), 'International Relations Theory and the End of the Cold War', *International Security*, 17 (3).

—— (1992), *The United States and the End of the Cold War: Implications, Reconsiderations, Provocations* (New York).

GAMBLE, A. (1996), 'The Limits of Democracy', in Hirst and Khilnani (1996).

GERMAIN, R. D. (1997), *The International Organization of Credit: States and Global Finance in the World-Economy* (Cambridge).

GIDDENS, A. (1998), 'Affluence, Poverty and the Idea of a Post-scarcity Society', in Booth (1998a).

—— (1985), *The Nation-state and Violence* (Cambridge).

GILL, S. (1997a) (ed.), *Globalization, Democratization and Multilateralism: Multilateralism and the UN System* (London).

—— (1997b), 'Global Structural Change and Multilateralism', in Gill (1997a).

—— (1995), 'Globalisation, Market Civilisation, and Disciplinary Neoliberalism', *Millennium*, 24 (3).

—— (1993), 'Global Finance, Monetary Policy and Cooperation among the Group of Seven, 1944–92', in Cerny (1993a).

—— and MITTELMAN, J. H. (1997) (eds.), *Innovation and Transformation in International Studies* (Cambridge).

GILLS, B. (1997a), 'Whither Democracy? Globalization and the "New Hellenism" ', in Thomas and Wilkin (1997).

—— (1997b), 'Editorial: "Globalisation" and the "Politics of Resistance" ', *New Political Economy*, 2 (1).

—— and PALAN, R. P. (1996), 'Introduction: The Neostructuralist Agenda in International Relations', in Palan and Gills (1996).

—— and ROCAMORA, J. (1992), 'Low Intensity Democracy', *Third World Quarterly*, 13 (3).

GILPIN, R. (1987), *The Political Economy of International Relations* (Princeton).

—— (1971), 'The Politics of Transnational Economic Relations', in Keohane and Nye (1971).

GOLDBLATT, D., HELD, D., McGREW, A., and PERRATON, J. (1997), 'Economic Globalization and the Nation-state: Shifting Balances of Power', *Alternatives*, 22 (3).

GOODIN, R. (1992), 'If People were Money . . .', in Barry and Goodin (1992).

GOODMAN, J. (1997), 'The European Union: Reconstituting Democracy beyond the Nation-state', in McGrew (1997a)

GRAHAM, G. (1997), *Ethics and International Relations* (Oxford).

GRAY, J. (1998), *False Dawn: The Delusions of Global Capitalism* (London).

GREIDER, W. (1997), *One World, Ready or Not: The Manic Logic of Global Capitalism* (London).

GRIECO, J. M., (1997), 'Realist International Theory and the Study of World Politics', in Doyle and Ikenberry (1997).

GRIFFIN, K. (1996), *Studies in Globalization and Economic Transitions* (Houndmills).

GROOM, A. J. R. and LIGHT, M. (1994) (eds.), *Contemporary International Relations: A Guide to Theory* (London).

GUEHENNO, J.-M. (1998/9), 'The Impact of Globalisation on Strategy', *Survival*, 40 (4).

GUIBERNAU, M. (1996), *Nationalisms: The Nation-state and Nationalism in the Twentieth Century* (Cambridge).

GUMMETT, P. (1996) (ed.), *Globalization and Public Policy* (Cheltenham).

GUTMANN, A. (1992), 'Communitarian Critics of Liberalism', in Avineri and de-Shalit (1992*a*).

HALL, J. A. (1996), *International Orders* (Cambridge).

—— (1986) (ed.), *States in History* (Oxford).

HALLIDAY, F. (1995), 'The End of the Cold War and International Relations: Some Analytic and Theoretical Conclusions', in Booth and Smith (1995).

—— (1994), *Rethinking International Relations* (London).

HARKNETT, R. J. (1996), 'Territoriality in the Nuclear Era', in Kofman and Youngs (1996).

HASSNER, P. (1993), 'Beyond Nationalism and Internationalism', *Survival*, 35 (2).

HAY, C. (1996), *Re-stating Social and Political Change* (Buckingham).

HELD, D. (1998), 'Democracy and Globalization', in Archibugi, Held, and Kohler (1998).

—— (1995*a*), *Democracy and the Global Order: From the Modern State to Cosmopolitan Governance* (Cambridge).

—— (1995*b*), 'Democracy and the International Order', in Archibugi and Held (1995).

—— (1992*a*) (ed.), *Prospects for Democracy*, special issue of *Political Studies*.

—— (1992*b*), 'Democracy: From City-states to a Cosmopolitan Order?', in Held (1992*a*).

—— (1991), 'Democracy and Globalization', *Alternatives*, 16 (2).

—— and McGREW, A. (1993), 'Globalization and the Liberal Democratic State', *Government and Opposition*, 28 (2).

HELLEINER, E. (1997), 'Braudelian Reflections on Economic Globalisation: The Historian as Pioneer', in Gill and Mittelman (1997).

—— (1996), 'Post-globalization: Is the Financial Liberalization Trend Likely to be Reversed?', in Boyer and Drache (1996).

—— (1994*a*), *States and the Reemergence of Global Finance* (Ithaca, NY).

—— (1994*b*), 'From Bretton Woods to Global Finance: A World Turned Upside Down', in Stubbs and Underhill (1994).

HEROD, A. (1997), 'Labor as an Agent of Globalization and as a Global Agent', in K. R. Cox (1997*a*).

HERZ, J. (1973), *The Nation-state and the Crisis of World Politics* (New York).

HIGGOTT, R. (1996), 'Beyond Embedded Liberalism: Governing the International Trade Regime in an Era of Economic Nationalism', in Gummett (1996).

HINSLEY, F. H. (1986,), *Sovereignty*, 2nd edn. (Cambridge).

HIRST, P. (1997), 'The Global Economy—Myths and Realities', *International Affairs*, 73 (3).

—— (1996), 'Democracy and Civil Society', in Hirst and Khilnani (1996).

—— and KHILNANI, S. (1996) (eds.), *Reinventing Democracy*, special issue of *Political Quarterly*.

—— and THOMPSON, G. (1996), *Globalization in Question: The International Economy and the Possibilities of Governance* (Cambridge).

HOBSON, J. M. (1997), *The Wealth of States: A Comparative Study of International Economic and Political Change* (Cambridge).

HOFFMAN, J. (1997), 'Is it Time to Detach Sovereignty from the State?', in Brace and Hoffman (1997*a*).

HOFFMANN, S. (1995/6), 'The Politics and Ethics of Military Intervention', *Survival*, 37 (4).

—— (1995), 'The Crisis of Liberal Internationalism', *Foreign Policy*, 95.

—— (1981), *Duties Beyond Borders: On the Limits and Possibilities of Ethical International Politics* (Syracuse, NY).

HOGAN, M. J. (1992) (ed.), *The End of the Cold War: Its Meaning and Implications* (Cambridge).

HOLDEN, B. (1996*a*) (ed.), *The Ethical Dimensions of Global Change* (London).

—— (1996*b*), 'Democratic Theory and Global Warming', in Holden (1996*a*).

HOLLIS, M. and SMITH, S. (1991), *Explaining and Understanding International Relations* (Oxford).

HOLM, H.-H. and SORENSEN, G. (1995) (eds.), *Whose World Order? Uneven Globalization and the End of the Cold War* (Boulder, Colo.).

HOLSTI, K. J. (1996), *The State, War, and the State of War* (Cambridge).

HOLTON, R. J. (1998), *Globalization and the Nation-state* (Houndmills).

HOOGVELT, A. (1997), *Globalisation and the Postcolonial World: The New Political Economy of Development* (Houndmills).

HOPF, T. (1998), 'The Promise of Constructivism in International Relations Theory', *International Security*, 23 (1).

HOWE, H. M. (1998), 'Global Order and the Privatization of Security', *Fletcher Forum of World Affairs*, 22 (2).

HUNTINGTON, S. P. (1996), *The Clash of Civilizations and the Remaking of World Order* (New York).

—— (1991), *The Third Wave: Democratization in the Late Twentieth Century* (Norman, Okla.).

HURRELL, A. (1995*a*), 'Explaining the Resurgence of Regionalism in World Politics', *Review of International Studies*, 21 (4).

—— (1995*b*), 'International Political Theory and the Global Environment', in Booth and Smith (1995).

—— and WOODS, N. (1995), 'Globalisation and Inequality', *Millennium*, 24 (3).

HUTCHINGS, K. (1996), 'The Idea of International Citizenship', in Holden (1996*a*).

IKENBERRY, G. J. (1996), 'The Myth of Post-Cold War Chaos', *Foreign Affairs*, 75 (3).

—— (1995), 'Funk de Siècle: Impasses of Western Industrial Society at Century's End', *Millennium*, 24 (1).

—— (1986), 'The State and Strategies of International Adjustment', *World Politics*, 39 (1).

INAYATULLAH, N. and BLANEY, D. (1995), 'Realizing Sovereignty', *Review of International Studies*, 21 (1).

JACKSON, R. H. (1996), 'Is there a Classical International Theory?', in Smith, Booth, and Zalewski (1996).

—— (1995), 'The Political Theory of International Society', in Booth and Smith (1995).

—— (1993), 'Continuity and Change in the States System', in Jackson and James (1993*a*).

JACKSON, R. H. (1990*a*), *Quasi-states: Sovereignty, International Relations and the Third World* (Cambridge).

—— (1990*b*), 'Martin Wight, International Theory and the Good Life', *Millennium*, 19 (2).

—— and JAMES, A. (1993*a*) (eds.), *States in a Changing World: A Contemporary Analysis* (Oxford).

—— —— (1993*b*), 'The Character of Independent Statehood', in Jackson and James (1993*a*).

JAMES, A. (1986), *Sovereign Statehood: The Basis of International Society* (London).

JARVIS, A. P. and PAOLINI, A. J. (1995), 'Locating the State', in Camilleri, Jarvis, and Paolini (1995*a*).

JERVIS, R. (1991/2), 'The Future of World Politics: Will it Resemble the Past?', *International Security*, 16 (3).

JESSOP, B. (1990), *State Theory: Putting Capitalist States in their Place* (Cambridge).

JOHNSON, H. J. (1991), *Dispelling the Myth of Globalization: The Case for Regionalization* (New York).

KALDOR, M. (1998), 'Reconceptualizing Organized Violence', in Archibugi, Held, and Kohler (1998).

KAPSTEIN, E. B. (1996), 'Workers and the World Economy', *Foreign Affairs*, 75 (3).

—— (1994), *Governing the Global Economy: International Finance and the State* (Cambridge, Mass.).

KELLAS, J. G. (1991), *The Politics of Nationalism and Ethnicity* (London).

KELLNER, D. (1998), 'Globalization and the Postmodern Turn', in Axtmann (1998*a*).

KEOHANE, R. O. (1986) (ed.), *Neorealism and its Critics* (New York).

—— and MILNER, H. V. (1996) (eds.), *Internationalization and Domestic Politics* (Cambridge).

—— and NYE, J. S. (1977), *Power and Interdependence: World Politics in Transition* (Boston).

KILMINSTER, R. (1997), 'Globalization as an Emergent Concept', in Scott (1997*a*).

KLARE, M. T. and THOMAS, D. C. (1994), *World Security: Challenges for a New Century*, 2nd edn. (New York).

KOFMAN, E. and YOUNGS, G. (1996) (eds.), *Globalization: Theory and Practice* (London).

KOTHARI, R. (1997), 'Globalization: A World Adrift', *Alternatives*, 22 (2).

KRASNER, S. D. (1993), 'Economic Interdependence and Independent Statehood', in Jackson and James (1993*a*).

KRATOCHWIL, F. V. (1989), *Rules, Norms and Decisions* (Cambridge).

KRAUSE, J. and RENWICK, N. (1996*a*) (eds.), *Identities in International Relations* (Houndmills).

—— —— (1996*b*), 'Introduction', in Krause and Renwick (1996*a*).

KRAUSE, K. and WILLIAMS, M. C. (1997) (eds.), *Critical Security Studies: Concepts and Cases* (London).

KRITSIOTIS, D. (1998), 'Mercenaries and the Privatization of Warfare', *Fletcher Forum of World Affairs*, 22 (2).

KRUGMAN, P. (1998), 'Just an Old-fashioned Boy', *New Statesman*, 8 May.

LAIDI, Z. (1998), *A World without Meaning: The Crisis of Meaning in International Politics* (London).

LAPID, Y. (1996), 'Culture's Ship: Returns and Departures in International Relations Theory', in Lapid and Kratochwil (1996).

—— and KRATOCHWIL, F. V. (1996) (eds.), *The Return of Culture and Identity in IR Theory* (Boulder, Colo.).

LATHAM, R. (1997a), *The Liberal Moment: Modernity, Security, and the Making of Postwar International Order* (New York).

—— (1997b), 'Globalisation and Democratic Provisionism: Re-reading Polanyi', *New Political Economy*, 2 (1).

—— (1996), 'Getting Out from Under: Rethinking Security beyond Liberalism and the Levels-of-Analysis Problem', *Millennium*, 25 (1).

LAWLER, P. (1995), 'The Core Assumptions and Presumptions of "Cooperative Security" ', in Lawson (1995).

LAWSON, S. (1995) (ed.), *The New Agenda for Global Security: Cooperating for Peace and Beyond* (St Leonards).

LAYNE, C. (1994), 'Kant or Cant: The Myth of the Democratic Peace', *International Security*, 19 (2).

—— (1993), 'The Unipolar Illusion: Why New Great Powers Will Rise', *International Security*, 17 (4).

LEBOW, R. N. and RISSE-KAPPEN, T. (1995) (eds.), *International Relations Theory and the End of the Cold War* (New York).

LEYSHON, A. (1996), 'Dissolving Difference? Money, Disembedding and the Creation of "Global Financial Space" ', in Daniels and Lever (1996).

LIGHT, M. and GROOM, A. J. R. (1985) (eds.), *International Relations: A Handbook of Current Theory* (London).

LINKLATER, A. (1998), *The Transformation of Political Community* (Cambridge).

—— (1995), 'Community', in Danchev (1995).

—— (1982), *Men and Citizens in the Theory of International Relations* (London).

—— and MACMILLAN, J. (1995), 'Introduction: Boundaries in Question', in Macmillan and Linklater (1995).

LIPSCHUTZ, R. D. (1995a) (ed.), *On Security* (New York).

—— (1995b), 'On Security', in Lipschutz (1995a).

—— (1992), 'Reconstructing World Politics: The Emergence of Global Civil Society', *Millennium*, 21 (3).

LITTLE, R. (1994), 'International Relations and Large-scale Historical Change', in Groom and Light (1994).

—— (1985), 'Structuralism and Neo-realism', in Light and Groom (1985).

—— and SMITH, M. (1991) (eds.), *Perspectives on World Politics*, 2nd edn. (London).

LOW, M. (1997), 'Representation Unbound: Globalization and Democracy', in K. R. Cox (1997a).

LUARD, E. (1990), *The Globalization of Politics: The Changed Focus of Political Action in the Modern World* (Basingstoke).

LYNCH, C. (1998), 'Social Movements and the Problem of Globalization', *Alternatives*, 23 (2).

LYONS, G. M. and MASTANDUNO, M. (1995) (eds.), *Beyond Westphalia? State Sovereignty and International Intervention* (Baltimore).

McCARTHY, P. and JONES, E. (1995a) (eds.), *Disintegration or Transformation: The Crisis of the State in Advanced Industrial Societies* (London).

—— —— (1995b), 'The Crisis of the State in Advanced Industrial Countries', in McCarthy and Jones (1995a).

McGREW, A. (1997a) (ed.), *The Transformation of Democracy?* (Cambridge and Milton Keynes).

—— (1997b), 'Introduction', in McGrew (1997a).

—— (1997c), 'Conclusion', in McGrew (1997a).

McGREW, A. and LEWIS, P. (1992), *Global Politics* (Cambridge).

MACMILLAN, J. (1996), 'Democracies Don't Fight: A Case of the Wrong Research Agenda?', *Review of International Studies*, 22 (3).

—— and LINKLATER, A. (1995) (eds.), *Boundaries in Question: New Directions in International Relations* (London).

MAGNUSSON, W. (1990), 'The Reification of Political Community', in Walker and Mendlovitz (1990).

MAIR, A. (1997), 'Strategic Localization: The Myth of the Postnational Enterprise', in K. R. Cox (1997a).

MAJONE, G. (1994), 'The Rise of the Regulation State in Europe', in Muller and Wright (1994a).

MANN, M. (1997), 'Has Globalization Ended the Rise and Rise of the Nation-state?', *Review of International Political Economy*, 4 (3).

—— (1993), *The Sources of Social Power. Vol. II: The Rise of Classes and Nation-states, 1760–1914* (Cambridge).

—— (1986), *The Sources of Social Power. Vol. I: A History of Power from the Beginning to A.D. 1760* (Cambridge).

MANNIN, M. (1996), 'Global Issues and the Challenge to Democratic Politics', in Bretherton and Ponton (1996).

MANNING, C. (1998), 'Does Globalisation Undermine Labour Standards? Lessons for East Asia', *Australian Journal of International Affairs*, 52 (2).

MANSFIELD, E. and SNYDER, J. (1995), 'Democratization and the Danger of War', *International Security*, 20 (1).

MARSHALL, D. D. (1996), 'Understanding Late-twentieth-century Capitalism: Reassessing the Globalization Theme', *Government and Opposition*, 31 (2).

MARTIN, A. (1994), 'Labour, the Keynesian Welfare State, and the Changing International Political Economy', in Stubbs and Underhill (1994).

MARTIN, H.-P. and SCHUMANN, H. (1997), *The Global Trap* (London).

MASTANDUNO, M., LAKE, D. A., and IKENBERRY, G. J. (1989), 'Toward a Realist Theory of State Action', *International Studies Quarterly*, 33 (4).

MATHEWS, J. T. (1994), 'The Environment and International Security', in Klare and Thomas (1994).

MEARSHEIMER, J. (1995), 'A Realist Reply', *International Security*, 20 (1).

—— (1994/5), 'The False Promise of International Institutions', *International Security*, 19 (3).

—— (1990), 'Back to the Future: Instability in Europe after the Cold War', *International Security*, 15 (1).

MILES, D. (1997), 'Globalisation: The Facts behind the Myth', *Independent*, 22 Dec.

MILLER, J. D. B. (1981), *The World of States* (London).

MILNER, H. V. (1991), 'The Assumption of Anarchy in International Relations Theory: A Critique', *Review of International Studies*, 17 (1).

—— and KEOHANE, R. O. (1996a), 'Internationalization and Domestic Politics: An Introduction', in Keohane and Milner (1996).

—— —— (1996b), 'Internationalization and Domestic Politics: A Conclusion', in Keohane and Milner (1996).

MISHRA, R. (1996), 'The Welfare of Nations', in Boyer and Drache (1996).

MITTELMAN, J. H. (1997), 'Restructuring the Global Division of Labour: Old Theories and New Realities', in Gill (1997a).

—— (1996a) (ed.), *Globalization: Critical Reflections* (Boulder, Colo.).

—— (1996b), 'How does Globalization Really Work?', in Mittelman (1996a).

—— (1996c), 'The Dynamics of Globalization', in Mittelman (1996a).

MORAN, M. (1994), 'The State and the Financial Services Revolution: A Comparative Analysis', in Muller and Wright (1994a).

MORAVCSIK, A. (1993), 'Introduction: Integrating International and Domestic Theories of International Bargaining', in Evans, Jacobsen, and Putnam (1993).

MULLER, W. and WRIGHT, V. (1994a), *The State in Western Europe: Retreat or Redefinition?* (London).

—— —— (1994b), 'Reshaping the State in Western Europe: The Limits to Retreat', in Muller and Wright (1994a).

NARDIN, T. (1992), 'Alternative Ethical Perspectives on Transnational Migration', in Barry and Goodin (1992).

—— (1983), *Law, Morality and the Relations of States* (Princeton).

—— and MAPEL, D. R. (1992) (eds.), *Traditions of International Ethics* (Cambridge).

NAVARI, C. (1991a) (ed.), *The Condition of States* (Milton Keynes).

—— (1991b), 'Introduction: The State as a Contested Concept in International Relations', in Navari (1991a).

NETTL, J. P. (1968), 'The State as Conceptual Variable', *World Politics*, 20 (4).

NOTERMANS, T. (1997), 'Social Democracy and External Constraints', in K. R. Cox (1997a).

NYE, J. S. (1990), *Bound to Lead: The Changing Nature of American Power* (New York).

OAKSHOTT, M. (1975), *On Human Conduct* (Oxford).

OHMAE, K. (1995), *The End of the Nation State: The Rise of Regional Economies* (London).

ONUF, N. (1998), *The Republican Legacy in International Thought* (Cambridge).

—— (1995), 'Intervention for the Common Good', in Lyons and Mastanduno (1995).

—— (1991), 'Sovereignty: Outline of a Conceptual History', *Alternatives*, 16 (4).

—— (1989), *World of our Making: Rules and Rule in Social Theory and International Relations* (Columbia, SC).

OVERBEEK, H. (1993) (ed.), *Restructuring Hegemony in the Global Political Economy: The Rise of Transnational Neoliberalism in the 1980s* (London).

OWEN, J. M. (1994), 'How Liberalism Produces Democratic Peace', *International Security*, 19 (2).

PALAN, R. P. (1994), 'State and Society in International Relations', in Palan and Gills (1994).

—— and GILLS, B. (1994) (eds.), *Transcending the State–Global Divide: A Neostructuralist Agenda in International Relations* (Boulder, Colo.).

PANITCH, L. (1996), 'Rethinking the Role of the State', in Mittelman (1996a).

—— (1994), 'Globalisation and the State', in R. Miliband and L. Panitch (eds.), *Socialist Register: Between Globalism and Nationalism* (London).

PAREKH, B. (1992), 'The Cultural Particularity of Liberal Democracy', in Held (1992a).

PARKER, G. (1996), 'Globalization and Geopolitical World Orders', in Kofman and Youngs (1996).

PARRY, G. (1994a) (ed.), *Politics in an Interdependent World: Essays Presented to Ghita Ionescu* (Aldershot).

—— (1994b), 'Political Life in an Interdependent World', in Parry (1994a).

PELLERIN, H. (1996), 'Global Restructuring and International Migration: Consequences for the Globalization of Politics', in Kofman and Youngs (1996).

PERRATON, J., GOLDBLATT, D., HELD, D., and McGREW, A. (1997), 'The Globalisation of Economic Activity', *New Political Economy*, 2 (2).

PETRELLA, R. (1996), 'Globalization and Internationalization: The Dynamics of the Emerging World Order', in Boyer and Drache (1996).

POGGE, T. (1992), 'Cosmopolitanism and Sovereignty', *Ethics*, 103 (1).

—— (1989), *Realising Rawls* (Ithaca, NY).

POGGI, G. (1990), *The State: Its Nature, Development and Prospects* (Cambridge).

POLANYI, K. (1944), *The Great Transformation* (Boston).

POPPI, C. (1997), 'Wider Horizons with Larger Details: Subjectivity, Ethnicity and Globalization', in Scott (1997a).

PRINGLE, R. (1992), 'Financial Markets versus Governments', in Banuri and Schor (1992).

PRZEWORSKI, A. (1995), *Sustainable Democracy* (Cambridge).

RAWLS, J. (1972), *A Theory of Justice* (Oxford).

RAY, J. L. (1995), *Democracy and International Conflict: An Evaluation of the Democratic Peace Proposition* (Columbia, SC).

REICH, R. (1991), *The Work of Nations* (New York).

RENGGER, N. J. (1992), 'A City which Sustains All Things? Communitarianism and International Society', *Millennium*, 21 (3).

RESNICK, P. (1998), 'Global Democracy: Ideals and Reality', in Axtmann (1998a).

RICHARDSON, J. L. (1995), 'Problematic Paradigm: Liberalism and the Global Order', in Camilleri, Jarvis, and Paolini (1995a).

RISSE-KAPPEN, T. (1995a) (ed.), *Bringing Transnational Relations Back In: Non-state Actors, Domestic Structures and International Institutions* (Cambridge).

—— (1995b), 'Democratic Peace—Warlike Democracies? A Social Constructivist Interpretation of the Liberal Argument', *European Journal of International Relations*, 1 (4).

ROBERTSON, R. (1992), *Globalization: Social Theory and Global Culture* (London).

ROSENAU, J. N. (1998), 'Governance and Democracy in a Globalizing World', in Archibugi, Held, and Kohler (1998).

—— (1997a), *Along the Domestic–Foreign Frontier: Exploring Governance in a Turbulent World* (Cambridge).

—— (1997b), 'Imposing Global Orders: A Synthesised Ontology for a Turbulent Era', in Gill and Mittelman (1997).

—— (1990), *Turbulence in World Politics: A Theory of Change and Continuity* (London).

—— and CZEMPIEL, E.-O. (1992) (eds.), *Governance without Government: Order and Change in World Politics* (Cambridge).

ROSENBERG, J. (1994), *The Empire of Civil Society: A Critique of the Realist Theory of International Relations* (London).

RUGGIE, J. G. (1998), *Constructing the World Polity: Essays on International Institutionalization* (London).

—— (1995), 'At Home Abroad, Abroad at Home: International Liberalisation and Domestic Stability in the New World Economy', *Millennium*, 24 (3).

—— (1982), 'International Regimes, Transactions, and Change: Embedded Liberalism in the Postwar Economic Order', *International Organization*, 36 (2).

RUIGROK, W. and VAN TULDER, R. (1995), *The Logic of International Restructuring* (London).

RUMMELL, R. J. (1995), 'Democracies ARE Less Warlike than Other Regimes', *European Journal of International Relations*, 1 (4).

RUSSETT, B. (1993), *Grasping the Democratic Peace: Principles for a Post-Cold War World* (Princeton).

SAKAMOTO, Y. (1991), 'Introduction: The Global Context of Democratization', *Alternatives*, 16 (2).

SANDEL, M. (1992), 'The Procedural Republic and the Unencumbered Self', in Avineri and de-Shalit (1992a).

SASSEN, S. (1996a), *Losing Control? Sovereignty in an Age of Globalization* (New York).

—— (1996b), 'The Spatial Organization of Information Industries: Implications for the Role of the State', in Mittelman (1996a).

SAURIN, J. (1997), 'Organizing Hunger: The Global Organization of Famines and Feasts', in Thomas and Wilkin (1997).

—— (1995), 'The End of International Relations? The State and International Theory in the Age of Globalization', in Macmillan and Linklater (1995).

SCHAEFFER, R. K. (1997), *Understanding Globalization: The Social Consequences of Political, Economic, and Environmental Change* (Lanham, Md.).

SCHOLTE, J. A. (1997a), 'Global Capitalism and the State', *International Affairs*, 73 (3).

—— (1997b), 'The Globalization of World Politics', in Baylis and Smith (1997).

—— (1996a), 'Beyond the Buzzword: Towards a Critical Theory of Globalization', in Kofman and Youngs (1996).

—— (1996b), 'Globalisation and Collective Identities', in Krause and Renwick (1996a).

—— (1993), 'From Power Politics to Social Change: An Alternative Focus for International Studies', *Review of International Studies*, 19 (1).

SCHOR, J. B. (1992), 'Introduction', in Banuri and Schor (1992).

SCOTT, A. (1997a) (ed.), *The Limits of Globalization* (London).

—— (1997b), 'Introduction—Globalization: Social Process or Political Rhetoric?', in Scott (1997a).

SHAW, M. (1997a),'Globalization and Post-military Democracy', in McGrew (1997a).

—— (1997b), 'The State of Globalization: Towards a Theory of State Transformation', *Review of International Political Economy*, 4 (3).

—— (1994a), *Global Society and International Relations* (Oxford).

—— (1994b), 'Civil Society and Global Politics: Beyond a Social Movements Approach', *Millennium*, 23 (3).

SHAW, T. and QUADIR, F. (1997), 'Democratic Development in the South in the Next Millennium: What Prospects for Avoiding Anarchy and Authoritarianism?', in Thomas and Wilkin (1997).

SHEARER, D. (1998), *Private Armies and Military Intervention*, Adelphi Paper 316 (Oxford).

SINGER, M. and WILDAVSKY, A. (1993), *The Real World Order: Zones of Peace/Zones of Turmoil* (Chatham, NJ).

SIVERSON, R. M. (1995), 'Democracies and War Participation: In Defence of the Institutional Constraints Argument', *European Journal of International Relations*, 1 (4).

SJOLANDER, C. T. (1996), 'The Rhetoric of Globalization: What's in a Wor(l)d?', *International Journal*, 51 (4).

SKOCPOL, T. (1985), 'Bringing the State Back In: Strategies of Analysis in Current Research', in Evans, Rueschemeyer, and Skocpol (1985).

SLATER, D. (1996), 'Other Contexts of the Global: A Critical Geopolitics of North–South Relations', in Kofman and Youngs (1996).

SMITH, M. J. (1998), 'Humanitarian Intervention: An Overview of the Ethical Issues', *Ethics and International Affairs*, 12.

SMITH, S. (1992), 'The Forty Years' Detour: The Resurgence of Normative Theory in International Relations', *Millennium*, 21 (3).

—— BOOTH, K., and ZALEWSKI, M. (1996) (eds.), *International Theory: Positivism and Beyond* (Cambridge).

SORENSEN, G. (1997), 'An Analysis of Contemporary Statehood: Consequences for Conflict and Cooperation', *Review of International Studies*, 23 (3).

—— (1993), *Democracy and Democratization* (Boulder, Colo.).

SPIRO, D. E. (1994), 'The Insignificance of the Liberal Peace', *International Security*, 19 (2).

SPYBEY, T. (1996), *Globalization and World Society* (Cambridge).

STORPER, M. (1997), 'Territories, Flows, and Hierarchies in the Global Economy', in K. R. Cox (1997a).

STRANGE, S. (1997), 'The Problem or the Solution? Capitalism and the State System', in Gill and Mittelman (1997).

—— (1996), *The Retreat of the State: The Diffusion of Power in the World Economy* (Cambridge).

—— (1995), 'The Limits of Politics', *Government and Opposition*, 30 (3).

—— (1994), 'Global Government and Global Opposition', in Parry (1994a).

—— (1988), *States and Markets* (London).

STUBBS, R. and UNDERHILL, G. R. D. (1994) (eds.), *Political Economy and the Changing Global Order* (London).

SUGANAMI, H. (1989), *The Domestic Analogy and World Order Proposals* (Cambridge).

TAYLOR, P. J. (1996), 'The Modern Multiplicity of States', in Kofman and Youngs (1996).

TAYLOR, R. (1997), 'Global Claptrap', *Prospect*, Dec.

TEEPLE, G. (1995), *Globalization and the Decline of Social Reform* (Toronto).

THOMAS, C. (1997), 'Globalization and the South', in Thomas and Wilkin (1997).

—— and WILKIN, P. (1997) (eds.), *Globalization and the South* (Houndmills).

THOMPSON, J. (1998), 'Community, Identity and World Citizenship', in Archibugi, Held, and Kohler (1998).

—— (1992), *Justice and World Order* (London).

THOMSON, J. E. (1995), 'State Sovereignty in International Relations: Bridging the Gap between Theory and Empirical Research', *International Studies Quarterly*, 39 (2).

—— and KRASNER, S. D. (1989), 'Global Transactions and the Consolidation of Sovereignty', in Czempiel and Rosenau (1989).

TILLY, C. (1985), 'War Making and State Making as Organized Crime', in Evans, Rueschemeyer, and Skocpol (1985).

—— (1975), *The Formation of National States in Western Europe* (Princeton).

VAN STEENBERGEN, B. (1994) (ed.), *The Condition of Citizenship* (London).

VINCENT, R. J. (1986), *Human Rights and International Relations* (Cambridge).

—— (1974), *Nonintervention and International Order* (Princeton).

WAEVER, O. (1995), 'Securitization and Desecuritization', in Lipschutz (1995a).

WALKER, R. B. J. (1995), 'From International Relations to World Politics', in Camilleri, Jarvis, and Paolini (1995a).

—— (1994), 'Social Movements/World Politics', *Millennium*, 23 (3).

—— (1993), *Inside/Outside: International Relations as Political Theory* (Cambridge).

—— (1990), 'Sovereignty, Identity, Community: Reflections on the Horizons of Contemporary Political Practice', in Walker and Mendlovitz (1990).

—— and MENDLOVITZ, S. H. (1990) (eds.), *Contending Sovereignties: Redefining Political Community* (Boulder, Colo.).

WALLERSTEIN, I. (1991), *Geopolitics and Geoculture: Essays on the Changing World-System* (Cambridge).

WALTZ, K. (1993), 'The Emerging Structure of International Politics', *International Security*, 18 (2).

—— (1979), *Theory of International Politics* (Reading, Mass.).

WALZER, M. (1994), *Thick and Thin: Moral Argument at Home and Abroad* (Notre Dame, Ind.).

—— (1977), *Just and Unjust Wars* (New York).

WATERS, M. (1995), *Globalization* (London).

WEBB, M. (1991), 'International Economic Structures, Government Interests, and International Coordination of Microeconomic Adjustment Policies', *International Organization*, 45 (3).

WEBER, C. (1995), *Simulating Sovereignty: Intervention, the State and Symbolic Exchange* (Cambridge).

WEISS, L. (1998), *The Myth of the Powerless State: Governing the Economy in a Global Era* (Cambridge).

WENDT, A. (1996), 'Identity and Structural Change in International Politics', in Lapid and Kratochwil (1996).

—— (1995), 'Constructing International Politics', *International Security*, 20 (1).

—— (1992), 'Anarchy is What States Make of It: The Social Construction of Power Politics', *International Organization*, 46 (2).

—— (1987), 'The Agent–Structure Problem in International Relations Theory', *International Organization*, 41 (3).

—— and FRIEDHEIM, D. (1996), 'Hierarchy under Anarchy: Informal Empire and the East German State', in Biersteker and Weber (1996).

WHEELER, N. J. (1992), 'Pluralist or Solidarist Conceptions of International Society: Bull and Vincent on Humanitarian Intervention', *Millennium*, 21 (3).

WIGHT, M. (1977), *Systems of States*, ed. H. Bull (Leicester).

—— (1966), 'Why Is There No International Theory?', in Butterfield and Wight (1966).

WILKIN, P. (1997), 'New Myths for the South: Globalization and the Conflict between Private Power and Freedom', in Thomas and Wilkin (1997).

WILLIAMS, H. (1996), *International Relations and the Limits of Political Theory* (London).

WILLIAMS, J. (1996), 'Nothing Succeeds like Success? Legitimacy and International Relations', in Holden (1996a).

WILLIAMS, M. (1996), 'Rethinking Sovereignty', in Kofman and Youngs (1996).

WYN JONES, R. (1996), ' "Travel without Maps": Thinking about Security after the Cold War', in Davis (1996).

YOUNGS, G. (1997), 'Political Economy, Sovereignty and Borders in Global Contexts', in Brace and Hoffman (1997a).

—— (1996), 'Beyond the "Inside/Outside" Divide', in Krause and Renwick (1996a).

ZURN, M. (1995), 'The Challenge of Globalization and Individualization: A View from Europe', in Holm and Sorensen (1995).

INDEX